A HOME FOR
THE HEART

HOME AS THE KEY TO HAPPINESS

by

Angela Neustatter

Other titles by Angela Neustatter

Losing a Loved One
Racism
My family
Depression
Relationships & Sex
Eating Disorders
Young Offender
Bullied
Runaway
Excluded
Refugee
Locked in – Locked Out
Look the Demon in the Eye
This is Our Time: Mid-Life
Hyenas in Petticoats
Mixed Feelings: The Experience of Abortion (with Gina Newson)
Parenthood: Warts and All (with Caroline Foley)

First edition published in the UK by

UK Tel: +44 (0)20 7096 1100
    Fax: +44 (0)20 7993 2214

US Tel: +1 646 216 9813
    Fax: +1 646 216 9488

Eire Tel: +353 (0)1 657 1057

        info@gibsonsquare.com
        www.gibsonsquare.com

        ISBN   9781906142797
        eISBN   9781908096333

CONTENTS

For Olly, Zek, Cato, Kimiko, Carolina, the enchanting Isana and Andrew, honorary member of the family. They are the heart of my home.

INTRODUCTION

This book grew from my own experience of learning how much home mattered when Olly, my husband and I, got to the point of discussing separating. The realization that we were contemplating selling up which would mean ditching the home we had done up from a wreck with sweat and tears if not blood, was a stark reality check. This was the place in which we had lived most of our children's lives with them, where we had had monumental rows and conversely some of our happiest and most formative moments. The realization of just what would be lost if we couldn't do better than all this destruction was a kind of epiphany. We needed to find a more constructive way of sorting out our troubles than upping sticks and abandoning our cherished home.

I was telling this to my publisher, explaining how it had set me thinking, exploring, the ways in which home is such a vital root in life, and yet how it has been so diminished in the last three years of pressurised consumerism, conspicuous consumption, the idea that individualism tops community, privacy is primary. I jested that home could be the new therapy and he ran with the idea, asking me to write this book.

I do not mean therapy in the clinical sense. I have aimed in the eleven chapters to look at what home means and why it matters for our psychological and physical well-being, happiness, authenticity, connectedness, because I believe understanding these may encourage us to think about the many ways home is so very significant.

Exploring this theme, I look at the ways we may pull away

from and damage the chance of home being a root in our lives.

Running through the book are my own reflections on how and why I have come to see home as of primary importance, yet a thing we too easily undervalue.

You will see a good deal of emphasis in *A Home for the Heart* on the important role home plays in supporting and enhancing family life, on how if we invest in it and appreciate it well enough, it may hold us steady through the difficult times, or offer opportunity for a shift in emphasis as it did for me and Olly. It may mean families can live to enjoy later life, and lived history, together in their home.

Yet I need to offer a caveat. I am not talking of 'the family' as the structure (mum, dad, two-point-something children) which some believe is the antidote to Broken Britain. I see solutions in the idea of 'Home' rather than in one type of family. While accepting that the traditional family has much to offer, my aim has been to explore through my own and others' experiences, prejudices and pleasures, the meaning of home in a broad sense for all of us who live together with one or more people. (After all, parents whose children have left the home, aren't suddenly a non-'family' or homeless because there are no children left!) I aim to bring a perspective that puts the home at a very central place in our lives in a way I have not found done elsewhere.

I begin with the story of how Olly and I chose 'Separate Togetherness' – the title of the first chapter – within our house. Alongside this are stories of other people I have interviewed, who have found ways to bring space into their relationships through their homes.

Among those who have talked of their experience of the meaning of home are the writer Allison Pearson, the entrepeneur Jonathan Self, the human rights lawyer Helena

Kennedy and her daughter Clio, the journalist and social commentator Lynsey Hanley, Dame Elisabeth Mudoch, the architect Christopher Day.

I consider what it means when long working hours demand the bulk of our most animated and energetic hours away from home, so that what we have to offer those we share home with is all too often a depleted self, the scrag end of ourselves. Is prioritizing home a solution or too great a sacrifice if it means curtailing an ambitiously pursued career?

What happens when our relationships go into hell and chaos mode and we become 'emotional terrorists' in the home? And how may involving ourselves more closely in the home be a healing process? These are the subjects of the chapter 'A Home to Be In'.

In our age of celebrity showman/womanship buying hugely priced homes is the name of the conspicuous consumption game. And with it the message is beamed out that somehow these celebrities can buy a greater quality of happiness than us less well off mortals. 'In Trading Up' I look at this phenomenon, the impact it has on our feelings about home, the myths embodied in the message

In the chapter 'Not Forsaking all Others' I observe the growing pressure for society to relax its attitude to infidelity and sexually broader arrangements than monogamy – polyamory and honestly open marriages. How do homes keep intact in these arrangements, when the strait-jacket of monogamy is undone?

'In the Best Interests' starts from the position that home is the place children are likely to experience the most significant part of their growing years. So how we organize and manage – or mismanage – their young lives at home, the place that, at best they trust they are lovingly cared for, is all important.

In 'A House Is Not a Home' I look at when a home breaks,

the affect on children and adults and the best and worst of how people manage to keep children in mind and a sense of home intact, during the fraught business of separation and divorce.

The last three chapters deal with the way homes are used in the 21st century. There are ever more people looking for ways to live that offer support and friendship but also autonomy, that will bring us back to a connectedness that seems to be diminishing.

In 'We Want to Be Together' I explore the growing, contemporary, co-housing movement, which I term the elder sibling of the earlier commune movement because it is about combining autonomy and privacy along with communality.

In 'Building Dreams' I talk to people about the meaning of creating a home for themselves built around an ideology, and how far this affects their personal relationships, the experience of their homes.

Finally there is my chapter 'Friendship Families'. By this I mean people who have committed to living together with friendship as the essence of the arrangement. So there are multi-generational families who have chosen to make common cause either under one roof or living so close they might as well be under.

There are single parents realizing that setting up a home with others can improve life dramatically; people who have chosen to buy or rent homes together because it is more environmentally friendly and comforting than living alone; couples who were once together, broke up but in later life have come back together as friends.

1

SEPARATE TOGETHERNESS

I was standing over Olly, seated in his favourite chair in front of the television screen. I had one hand on my hip; with the other I gesticulated angrily towards the pictures on screen. I had just arrived home from a demanding job of work, jaded and fraught. Why should I have to find myself competing with the television for my husband's attention? I was in small child mood and primed to be put out very easily.

The best thing I could have done would have been to take myself off to the bedroom to spend a bit of time, on my own, recuperating after the jagged business of travelling across London by public transport. Instead I went straight into our sitting room to find Olly watching TV. It infuriated me. I didn't like the idea of Olly sitting there watching the drivel that seems to fill most of the channels early evening.

I had not stopped to look for long enough to see that there was, in fact, an architecture programme playing which was of considerable interest to Olly. Of specific interest in fact as he has been the primary force in working out designs to create what we wished from the bare bones of the homes we have gone on to inhabit.

I felt the evening was out of control already. Had Olly made supper? Did he plan to jump up and offer me a glass of wine? Ask me about my day? Any or all of these might have happened if I hadn't expressed my aggravation in an immediate outburst, a releasing of tension by letting fury combust unchecked.

In one sharp movement Olly was on his feet, flicking the television off. The pictures of ornate brickwork, soaring glass and steel vanished into abrupt silence and darkness. He turned to face me eyes glimmering, seriously blue and furious.

'You really ought to live on your own!' was what he said.

The words came out unplanned, unintended. Olly hadn't been aware he might say such a thing, and I certainly hadn't expected to hear this spontaneous howl of frustration at how it felt to have a wife who did not even pause to consider that he might have every reason and right to be watching a programme he had chosen.

Whatever our intentions, the words were there as if an aeroplane had streamed them across the sitting room. Unlike aeroplane vapour the words did not fade and disappear.

What place had we reached?

Olly and I had been together more than 30 years. We had two children and we were living in the second family home we had taken on as a wreck and which Olly with a bit of input from me, had fashioned into a place that felt like the kind of home in which we wanted to live and be parents in. Places in which to mature our lives.

Could it be that this was more than just another 'domestic' to be given time and a bit of cooled-down common sense, so that we could get on as before?

Was it recognition that the effort to make two very diverse backgrounds and personalities work together, had finally hit the skids? That our polarities were not the stuff of a challenging but worthwhile life's journey, but rather a fundamental flaw line that could no longer be disguised?

Our relationship had long been tumultuous. Our differences are considerable: Olly is working class from Holland with memories of growing up in a poor, huddled together district of Amsterdam in the post-war years. He would accompany his mother when she went to work soon after dawn, lighting fires in the grates of Amsterdam's schools before the pupils arrived and before she went to her next job. He had a brother 20 years older – Olly is the first to agree he was entirely an accident, not even an afterthought – who had been traumatised as a war prisoner had escaped and arrived home his feet bleeding through makeshift bandages. In the 'Hungry Years' when the war ended went hunting for food for his wife, his son – Olly's nephew of the same age – and for Olly.

Their father was one of a family of 12, who worked in the docks for a meagre living, enjoyed camaraderie and drink during the hours afterwards, so he was not much at home. Olly talks of how little he knew him. But Olly's mother was a woman through whom kindness was stamped like the message in Brighton rock. The bright-eyed, jokey delight with which she regarded her second son made it plain that, accident or not, he was adored.

Olly went to sea as an able seaman at the age of 15 – it was one of the few sure ways of earning a living for boys like him from the impoverished, working class Wittenburg harbour district. The years into his twenties were spent journeying the world in cargo ships, a picaresque lifestyle in which he gained a great knowledge of geography the idiosyncratic behaviour of different harbour-side communities. In due course he had had enough and gave up the sea to live nomadically working in different jobs and travelling a good deal. It was a life on the hoof, and Olly had no thoughts of building a career or doing anything but experiencing the day as it came. Like a surfer his philosophy was to catch the best waves life threw up in the here and now.

My upbringing was a pretty good study in contrast. I had an aspirational home-counties upbringing although with parents whose liberal beliefs meant my brother and I had a delightfully free-range existence. I am the daughter of a forensic psychiatrist and a thoughtful mother who wrote a little. I recollect childhood as a time of growing up slowly and gently in a spacious suburban home with a long garden and dilapidated horse stables at the end, just perfect for ghostly adventures in the spider-webbed shadows.

My memories are of a gently unfolding time of growing. Accompanying my mother first thing in the morning when she pottered around the garden, her slippers damp with dew from the grass. She would be tending the old-fashioned roses of palest yellow splashed with pink, creamy whites and huge blooms of deepest crimson. They would shake their heads as we brushed past, filling the air with sudden perfume.

A Quiet Rhythm to Life

There were weekend days when I spotted my father at his vegetable bed tutting at the spinach and broccoli he had planted scatter-gun style, now running amok. Or he would erupt into a sudden 'hell and damnation!' as he saw the lacy cabbages that had provided meals for many a slug.

My father's wrath was only ever directed at his vegetables and he would greet me with a big soppy smile. On these occasions, leaning on his fork, looking down at me, he rarely failed to tell how he had never wanted children, then follow with a revelation that in other circumstances could have been devastating: 'But I am very glad indeed that your mother talked me into it'.

I was cocooned from the savagery of what the war had meant for so many. Not by money – we were not especially well off – but by the constancy of my parents; the domesticity of how we lived. True, when I was a baby, during the bombings, my mother had taken me down shelters, and coped with the fear alone, during the times my father was posted abroad. Once the war was over, however, my parents created a quiet rhythm to life, with our education, family holidays, friendships fostered and occasionally discouraged by my parents, at the centre. And the irony, as I now see it, is that my conventionally middle-class and, yes, a tad snobbish parents, would probably not have been thrilled at the idea of my ending up with a working class man who had left school and 15, and had no obvious prospects. Yet I also know that my mother would have adored Olly with his good heart, his generosity, his fierce determination to follow a trajectory that did not fit the conventions of my class, yet a commitment to his family which means that he has always done his share, and more than at times, of supporting us all. She would also have loved him for the care he showed my father after her death.

So what on earth led Olly and me to choose each other with an eye to making a future as a couple? The glib 'opposites attract' was a bit of it, but more I think we were easy together, I never felt unsure of myself or feared being judged by him. There were fundamental values articulated differently but that mattered to us both. We found it interesting to be forced to learn about each other's hinterland when we came up against disagreements and problems of non-communication. Olly got on with my friends and his different class seemed not to matter because he was from 'abroad'. Besides, he was good at finding common cause with people. But as important as anything it was he who persuaded me that my widowed, and fast-ageing father, should not be left alone in the family home, but should live with us.

At the same time those differences which brought us close, and appreciative of the novelty that infused our relationship, also brought us into head-on collision plenty. I railed against Olly's unwillingness to engage in psychological exploration of the underbelly of our annoyance with each other, and he challenged my inability to understand that, in his book, life was frequently less complicated, less prone to emotional disembowelling. If you accepted things as they appeared you didn't need to burrow beneath the surface and risk trying to mend something that wasn't broken.

Would we, indeed, have gone on thinking all this was worth it if we had not had children? I don't know. That remains an imponderable. When we met I had wanted children in an abstract way, but had no picture of how or when. Olly, who had brought up the two young children of a former girl-friend, for the four years he was living with her, wasn't at all sure. He had suffered a good deal parting from those kids, even though he kept in contact and still sees them regularly. So I count it extraordinarily fortunate that our son Zek insistently made his way into the world as a 'Freudian slip'. Cato was planned. Zek had shown us the pleasure of children and another was definitely wanted.

Children shape and dictate life in a way nothing else can, unless you are so cold-hearted, unremittingly narcissistic, or profoundly emotionally damaged as to remain totally cut off from them. They demand, too, that you grow up and become parents to them and that you create a suitable nest in which they can thrive.

There is the shell-shock that a first baby brings, the exhaustion that just about every parent recollects, the realisation that you will not get much in the way of space for yourself, or tranquillity for some long years. Home is an altered state, answerable to the desires, wills, needs of our young, while we as adults need to accustom ourselves to enjoying our home, finding respite in it, with this new invasion.

It is awesome stuff and no surprise that relationships may stagger on their feet, as partners struggle to get time to be the people they were before. To wonder what it takes to experience each other as something other than new parents; to suppress understandable jealousies when the new child seems to fill home life, getting all the time and attention that once you had. Relationships all too often split up within the first year of a first child.

Yet having Zek and later Cato, had the opposite effect on Olly and me and I have seen this in many other parents. I was enchanted by the way Olly fell so absolutely in love with both the boys as they were born. Exhausted as I was after my first birth lasting 13 hours, and with an aching episiotomy as souvenir, I watched Olly pick up Zek in the standard-issue blue honeycomb hospital blanket, and cradle him close, just looking at him with a kind of stunned amazement before he bent over to kiss the tiny, crumpled forehead.

He was impressed that, without his having planned any such thing, we had brought such sweet alteration into our life.

Olly set about home-making with a vengeance once Zek was born. With the kind of optimistic lunacy which guides us when young and looking forward, we bought a huge wreck of a Georgian house in North London. The dishevelled garden stretched far – the perfect playground for our children, we reckoned, not recognising how many hours' hard-labour would be involved in getting rid of the brambles knotted together wherever you looked. How many deeply rooted nettles and wilful spreads of convulvus would put up a mighty battle not to be removed.

When Olly was not occupied running a magazine distribution business and later working, as well, as a technician on films and pop promos, he was to be seen in his denim dungarees repairing walls, plastering and patching up.

He was up on the roof with our Burmese Irish builder who worried us somewhat when we discovered he kept a stash of Carlsberg Special Brew up there, replacing tiles, sorting out blocked gutters and broken drainpipes. At ground level there was a great deal of sawing of wood to replace rotten floorboards, patch up original shutters, build kitchen structures and so on... and on...

Home was a work in progress over many years, and tough wearisome work. But we shared the excitement at what we were creating, patching and painting up bedrooms for Zek and Cato, splashing rose pink emulsion over the sun-filled bedroom we had for ourselves. In a rugged, unsentimental way all this necessary homework brought us close much of the time.

Close enough and invested enough in home and family that, when the rows broke out we doggedly found a way to break our stand-offs. We both recognised, if inchoately, that this had to be done or all that we had invested in with our strength and souls would be lost.

Now, however, the words 'You really ought to live on your own!' were there like a barbed wire fence between us. Not easy to circumnavigate or demolish.

Likely to do us considerable harm if we let it.

The nostalgic era of creating our own first home for a family, was history. We were adults on our own, the boys flown from the nest, and we had reached this impasse. So we stood, facing each other, in the sitting-room of the building – an erstwhile pub we had converted into our family home after moving as our second real family home. The foundations of all we had created seemed in this moment fragile indeed.

Family history was in the bones of our home. The times we had negotiated life as a foursome, the happy memories but also those of learning to cope with the good, the bad and the ugly of the different life stages of our young, were all inscribed here. Olly's passion for design, his idiosyncratic ideas on what you can do with a building, so far from what I could ever have envisaged, were the hallmark of the place.

Yet now, as we stood on this revelatory evening, in a state of not-at-all disguised rank dislike of each other, it seemed that perhaps the meaning, the point of it all had gone.

And perhaps we had reached a point of reckoning. The past months had been a bad time during which we had bickered, criticised, been ever-tetchy with each other. Over the most banal things, too. It was only faintly comforting to have read a newspaper article telling how many couples find it is the washing-up, the clothes on the floor, one person's obsession with the toothpaste lid being on, etc. etc. etc. that were major sources of conflict. So we were in good company watching the fabric of our relationship pull apart over something that was so apparently mundane.

So it was that meal-times, walks along the canal or on Hampstead Heath, which had once been a sure-fire source of companionable pleasure, were no longer so. You could be sure that sooner or later one or other would find a subject that would spark irritation in the other. We would be sharp, reactive and ungenerous in finding middle ground or just not minding too much about things. The sum total of this behaviour, which became the fabric of daily life, was that we were both obstinately miserable and resentful as a more or less permanent state when we were together. I spent increasing time in my isolated office. Olly expressed his loneliness by accusing me of running away from him and being a workaholic. We didn't voice it then, but both of us wondered, what point there was in a life lived this way.

Looking back, I think this change in the dynamic of our relationship, was classic empty-nest stuff, the echoing depletion of home. The children had recently moved on – Cato to university, Zek into his own home with his girlfriend (now wife) Kimiko – and suddenly the whole meaning and form of life had altered. The routines and patterns that we frequently moaned about as an imposition, were perhaps the very thing that had kept life on the rails and vibrant. We felt the lack of activity keenly: the raucous music, voices on the stairs late at night, the regularity of someone foraging in the fridge, the evenings the boys stretched their absurdly long bodies over the sofa while we watched a DVD on the television (yes, I approved of that!), or the young with all their conviction of superiority ticking us off for our very existences.

Faced with the silence replacing all this we were like empty vessels, mourning the loss, and seeing nothing in each other to compensate. It was in this desolate state that we projected our sense of a life having ended without our consent, and with no picture of another that would satisfactorily replace it, onto each other. Oh yes, we had imagined the pleasure of having a free-form life many times when shackled with hefty domestic demands, but this was not what we had had in mind.

So was this the point at which there was nothing to do but separate? To say thanks, it was nice while it lasted, but who wants to settle for a life in which all we do is make each other miserable?

Not Just Bricks and Mortar

I found myself imagining the faces of our children when they learned what was happening. They may be young adults but, as much psychological research shows, our children, even as adults, frequently find the breaking up of the family home, antagonism replacing a loving core within their parents, surprisingly disturbing. There is the poignant observation of Adam Nicholson, son of Nigel and grandson of Harold Nicholson, talking of the time his mother left home, 'The warmth left Sissinghurst that day. The warmth left with her. The kitchen there never smelled good or right again. It became cold and inert.'

In that room, with the television so conspicuously dark and silent, we could not find a way forward. We went to separate bedrooms and woke next day, each grey and ragged as the other.

It wouldn't be easy to talk, we knew, but it was what had to be done. We needed to face the possibility that what Olly had blurted out was right. We were no longer capable of being 'at home' together.

Gingerly, uncharacteristically formal, we asked each other where we should go from here. There was a good deal of defensive gruffness, non-committal posturing, before we got to talking. Talking about how we didn't actually want to pull our lives apart with the finality that seemed to be threatened. The selling of the house, so that we could each have something of our own, a definitive step away from the joint life of our home.

It wasn't just bricks and mortar we were concerned with. Neither of us wanted to lose the good, the bad and the chaos of a family life we treasured, built up over years of routine, repetition, rituals. Bath and bedtime, when the boys would appear downstairs pink as blancmange and angelic beyond measure in their fluffy jumpsuit pyjamas. Meals around the long wooden table, through the stages of babies spitting out toast soldiers, screeching 'YUUUK' at the sight of some new culinary experiment offered to them, to Sunday lunches where their friends and ours gathered, when the day meandered sociably on until early evening. The evenings when we snuggled on the sofa watching videos, Olly flanked by the boys who periodically wanted to play fight. Choosing our 57 varieties black puppy who licked the kids into giggling fits, and snarled at anyone who looked at them in a bad way.

The tantrums after school, when one or other would lie on the floor and bellow with rage at some inexplicable thing. The occasions when 'helping' with homework was a dreaded stretch of cantankerous after-school time; the teenage years when realization dawned that our kids did not find us particularly interesting, let alone the kind of people with whom they wanted to spend their free-time. But the back-handed pleasure of that was that they filled the house with their mates and we were caught up in a maelstrom of noisy, farting, hi-jinks; a steady stream of unintelligible youthful patois, and then the heart-warming moment when friends had departed and a laddish voice would tell with the utmost insouciance, 'My friends think you are actually quite cool dudes for parents'.

Living apart Together

I am not sure, at the time of reckoning, who came up with the idea of what we have named 'separate togetherness'. Yet somehow we hit on the realisation that, since our children had moved out, we were in the fortunate position that it would be possible to re-configure the house and have a private floor each for ourselves. In fact, with bathrooms and kitchen on each floor – the young had lived on one of these, we on the other – lent itself to a great deal of privacy and autonomy.

It was a step back from the brink, a way of living on our own, as much or as little as we wished. We could choose to see each when and as we wanted. If we found time on our own easier, more agreeable, then we could have it. If on the other hand the idea of a bit of closeness seemed desirable, well we would come together because it was what we actively chose not just the way the house was organised.

It seemed worth trying.

Indeed we were startled at how eminently sensible and grown up our idea seemed. We both acknowledged that the phrase separate togetherness seemed to encapsulate what we hoped could come out of the arrangement. Enough separateness and autonomy to get beyond the petty, pathetic arguments, the deeply destructive sniper's pattern we were locked into and that had pushed out the erstwhile loving, co-operative stuff. At the same time leaving the possibility that we could enjoy and re-ignite the best of what life in the home had meant to us.

Why, then, did it feel so precarious, we so shaky? Not least it was because friends regarded what we had done with wonderment, while at the same time many murmured sotto voce, 'But isn't this really a way of breaking up?'

On the contrary, we responded heartily. Too heartily. We knew it was counter-intuitive to the romantic notion built into our psyches, that couples should yearn to be together 24/7. It is to scribble over the storyline, to hold up to the light an act of faith, and show its flaw lines.

In truth Olly and I didn't know if our separate togetherness would be destructive, or creative. The best case scenario was that it should give us the space and autonomy to be able to live as we wished, and to come together when we wanted to, be it making a mid-morning coffee in one or other of our kitchens, having friends round for a drink, sitting in front of Olly's cackling stove, or in my airy studio room. Or making love and spending the night together. Most of all that our home would be, as ever, a place that was familiar and where we would gather as we always had with our children, in a family unit.

The worst scenario was that we would draw further and further apart, choose to spend little or no time in each others' company and become 'just good friends.' But even that seemed preferable, in my view, to destroying the whole structure, a home that had grown, organically, with us.

So there we were deciding who would have each chair, the linen sofa. I took half the crockery and cutlery and within weeks I had had several walls painted new colours. Things were organised in the kitchen as I wished. I created a bedroom on my own floor, bolstering myself with girl-friend chats about the pleasure in doing things all my own way.

All the time wondering where it would lead.

I came across the term LATs (Living Apart Together situations) being used to describe the estimated thousands of couples who, for one reason or another, are sharing a home but with a much more absolute separation than we were reaching towards. These include people who have a fully-functioning happy partnership, but know they function best with the possibility of distance from each other. Those who cannot sell their house after a divorce so have to go on living together and construct rules for a separate lifestyle. Those who put the desire to separate entirely on the back burner in order to be able to have their children as part of daily life, and to share parenting, but acknowledging that their intimate relationship is history.

There are also people who see themselves as no longer a

committed couple but who choose to live under the same roof because it is the most economically viable option or because they are good enough friends to want to do so. Psychologist Dr Funke' Baffour sees the trend as part of the 21st century lifestyle where couples 'want relationships on their own terms' and are not prepared to shut up and put up in the way earlier generations appear to have done.

All the same I find the term LAT arid. It conjures the notion of a stoic practicality, which too often seems to be the *faute de mieux* solution rather than one of positive choice. Separate togetherness, on the other hand, implies optimism that it is possible for a relationship to be more separate in terms of physical space, yet to maintain personal closeness – indeed possibly enhance it.

As Olly and I struggled with our individual dilemma, I became curious to know how other couples who have wanted some apartness in their lives, had made this work.

Inevitably I came across the high-profile examples of couples. Actress Helena Bonham Carter and film director Tim Burton who have three houses in North London with connecting doorways. Their two young children flow between them. Yet Helena has refused to feed the media tribes forever hunting for cracks in showbiz relationships, giving a throwaway answer to the question 'why' when asked. Her line is that it's a necessary arrangement to prevent Tim and her bickering over interior design, 'His side is messier. My side is cutesy, like Beatrix Potter, which is fine for him to visit but there's no way he could live in it. He thinks his side is James Bond'. To the predictable question about what happens to their love life, she has let it be known that, although they each have their own bedrooms, Tim is a frequent visitor to hers.

Toyah Wilcox is said to spend just one month a year in the same house as her husband of more than a decade Robert

Fripp, which might sound a bit too economical on the togetherness side for a relationship to get adequate nourishment, but
Toyah explains that she loves the solitude of being alone.

I spent an afternoon with Clive James, writer, TV personality and gloriously witty raconteur. Towards the end of the time,
after I had completed an interview I was doing with him, we
had a drink together sitting at a Thames-side café, a couple of
minutes stroll from his London docklands apartment.

We had been discussing family life and how much he values
it – values it but needs distance from it too. So it is that he and
his wife the medievalist Prue Shaw, who both work in London
during the week, have their own apartments in the city, but do
not meet. He says simply, 'My wife and I both have demanding, quite independent lives.' It is only at the end of the week
that he returns to the house they share in Cambridge, and
where they have brought up their two daughters and to this he
is committed, as to his marriage of more than four decades,
insisting 'I fly from wherever I am in the world for that.'

Yet when, earlier, I had talked with his artist daughter
Claerwyn she acknowledged that children are very conscious of
their parents not fitting the norm. and this, inevitably, is one of
the things you must deal with when organising life in an
unorthodox way. She said: 'My parents have a strange relationship. They have separate flats and separate – and fulfilling –
lives in the week.'

Choosing separate togetherness is of course the polar
opposite to the mind set with which many people begin their
partnered home lives. At this time it is most commonly built on
the dream of a future *ad infinitum*, a home that will grow with
us, organically, the place for a life evolved from the singularity
of growing years. Perhaps we imagine dogs and cats, follies and
objects enthusiastically bought, as a couple. All this and much
more goes with the putting down of tentative roots. No

wonder it feels so tough when the picture like a Photoshoped image, seems to have been altered.

Psychologist Dr Janet Reibstein, who works with couples in conflict, and is author of a book on what makes relationships work over the long haul, *The Best Kept Secret* (Bloomsbury), understands this.

'Most of us see – or want to see – the home as a refuge, the place where you feel together and strong as a couple. But when you no longer feel home is offering this, it stops being com-fortable. At which point it is natural to want to retreat from home which has become a symbol of what you are not able to do as a couple any longer. Being able to talk about this and find a solution – and separate togetherness may be one – can help to bring back the sense of being united.'

The story of a couple, we shall call them, Liz and Sebastian illustrates how boldly some people simply recognize that too much closeness is the thing that harms their relationship. In their case, rather than harming the relationship by living in the traditional way expected of couples with children, they worked out their own style of separate togetherness.

Both had come out of long-term relationships when they met, and between them they had six children. For the first three years they lived apart, deciding this was easiest for the children they had had separately. However when their own three chil-dren were born they concluded that they should move in together.

The pair tried living in Sebastian's house but it felt too cramped with them all there. When they moved into Liz's house Malcolm missed his own place. The arguments during the time they shared a house brought them to the brink of breaking up.

So with the kind of honesty many people would find very difficult to express, they were able to discuss how they both wanted their own space, to run their own households their own way.

Out of this came the decision to keep both houses – a mile apart – and live separately. They evolved a pattern of seeing each other most days, and of spending nights together regularly, and found they were a great deal happier. So even after marrying they decided to stay with their separate togetherness and even though it caused many curious questions and raised eyebrows, it is how they plan to go on.

Others who do not have the opportunity to live with the kind of absolute separateness of Liz and Sebastian or Olly and I, have nevertheless seen the need to establish some place of privacy and aloneness.

Janine is one such person. She and Darren were able to buy a small terraced house in the north of England when they had their first child and as the baby grew up and went through school, the jobs they both had, and the demands of parenting did not leave time for asking questions about individual happiness or needs. But when their son went to university Janine took a course in renaissance art and went on to do another at degree level. She began to yearn for a place where she could read and write her work in solitude, and where she could spend uninterrupted time thinking her thoughts.

'It wasn't that Darren was especially disruptive or demanding of my attention, but there is something about being in the same room as the person you are married to that is not entirely peaceful. Our sitting room was also the kitchen and that detracted from its restfulness.'

At the top of their house there was a small box-room crammed with junk gathered over the years, and Janine found herself thinking it could be turned into the sanctuary she craved. 'I found it very difficult to tell Darren what I wanted. I was truly worried he would see it as my rejection of him, and it took me a long time to open my mouth.'

In fact Darren not only understood why Janine wanted this separateness but spent weekends clearing and preparing the room where she spends on average two evenings a week.

There are couples, deeply committed to each other, but who know themselves well enough to be wary of blending their lives too thoroughly, aware they need separateness to be able to retreat entirely from the presence, requirements, demands, delights, of a partner who is not less loved because of this. It may be, as was apparently the case with writers Margaret Drabble and Michael Holroyd, who for many years had separate houses close by, that the possibility of being apart with agreement actually enhances the time they choose to spend together.

The author Jenny Diski wrote about how she moved to Cambridge to be close to her new partner the poet Ian Patterson, but chose to live across the street from him. A few years on she decided to move in with him but only once the top part of the house had been converted to her private space with a study and bathroom. In an interview she remarked that given the urge and a few tins of beans, she would isolate herself up there.

If we can recognize the desire – need – to have separate togetherness, a different pattern and rhythm of life as we mature and grow in individual ways, then we may be able to maintain the home we have evolved.

A home in which we have experienced some of the most significant and defining times, where we have learned how to create a refuge that embodies us and our individual way of living. This idea is well expressed by the writer Will Self, 'The past decade has seen that most strange of things: the gradual accretion of memories, and sensations and memories of those sensations, that perfuse mere bricks and mortar and possessions, to end up, quite inevitably, creating a genuine sense of home.

A genuine sense of home is what most of us seem to want, in some way or other, so the question is how to obtain and maintain that sense of home. Separate togetherness is not a strategy or a lifeplan model, it is a notion that we may adapt to our own circumstances, desires and needs. It is just one of many ways we may find to create and maintain the centrality of home

As we embarked on our separateness, Olly and I had no idea how it would all pan out. Would the space we had put between ourselves bring greater togetherness or would it take us further away, and reduce our cherished home to a place that houses each of us in the most dedicatedly, chillingly separate way?

As we embarked on the re-organisation we could only wait and see what the answer would be.

2

A HOME FOR THE HEART

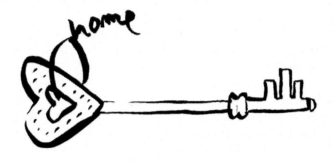

Dame Elisabeth Murdoch was planning her 100th birthday at her home Cruden Farm when Olly and I went to visit. She lives an hour out of Melbourne in a white clapperboard house, the interiors panelled with Tasmanian hard wood, walls hung with a spectacular array of paintings, and set in 135 acres of garden. The invitation to lunch came because Dame Elisabeth was patron of a recently formed society to commemorate my great aunt Henry Handel Richardson, who lived for years in Australia writing Victorian novels and became one of the country's most cherished writers. On the back of this she had agreed to do an interview for the *Guardian*, much of it about home life with her children, most notably the controversial Rupert.

Cruden Farm has been home to her since 42-year Keith, then Australia's most prominent newspaper baron, gifted it to 19-year-old Elisabeth as a marriage gift, celebrating their nuptials in 1928. The place became the beating heart of her universe, a home she saw as the perfect place for a life in which she envisaged bringing up children and living out her life. So when Keith died in 1952, and people advised that she sell up and move somewhere less isolated and 'more manageable', she would have none of it. This she tells in the brusque, businesslike voice that must have made her determination very plain. The same timbre in her voice comes through when there are questions she does not intend to answer, although my abiding memory is of this elegantly-featured woman with the sharpest blue eyes, being utterly gracious, making it known that I really am welcome in her home. There is no pressure to leave before we chose to do so.

'How could I have upped and left a home which was the centre of my family's life? A home so full of memories of the most important parts of my life.' She turns a face of wrinkles soft as puppy skin, towards the window which looks out on the garden of giant eucalyptus, broad oaks, cypresses, wattles, and a weeping elm where the children, when young, made their den. The flowerbeds and carefully tended borders are alive with hydrangeas, agapanthus, vivid orange day lilies and a mass of roses including one named after Dame Elisabeth.

This set her to musing on the young years of her three daughters Helen, Anne, Janet and her one son Rupert.

'Keith and I always saw Cruden Farm as a place for children. They had such physical freedom and it was wonderful to see them running, climbing trees, inventing games by the lake.'

Helen, interviewed before she died recently, recalled a very happy time, 'Rupert and I spent our life in the garden. We had ponies and we went fishing in a small boat with our father, on the lake'. They would go off for picnics in the horse and cart with hampers of food, and Elisabeth played cricket with them.' Helen had recalled the intimacy of life at home. How for she and Rupert 'the idea of heaven' was to get on the bed with their parents in the morning, while they had breakfast and read the papers.

'This home has been the centre of my life since the first day when we drove up and it was only a little cottage with a suburban garden which we set to renovating. It is the place I have been my happiest sharing my family's growing years, and it is remains a centre for them.'

This organic, accessible home life, Rupert and his sisters went on being close to and involved with into adulthood, and then with their own families. This embracing home-life was very abruptly taken from Rupert, however. When he was aged 21, a Labour supporter studying PPE at Oxford University, his father died and he returned to Australia – Adelaide – to take charge of the family newspaper business and before very long turned the Adelaide News into a major success working with the single-minded, ferocity for which he has become famous.

Yet I find myself pausing to think how it must have been for this young man to have had to grieve his father's death so far away from his family and home, at a time when those things are what most of us would need. Indeed Michael Wolff in his biography of Rupert Murdoch *The Man Who Owns The News*, mentions his subject's loneliness in Adelaide. Yet there was no question but that Murdoch must take on his father's mantle. That had been made clear the time, when Murdoch was 16, and his father gave him a 'tutorial' in how the business was run. Nevertheless this still green-behind-the-ears chap, parachuted in from a British university life, may have been greeted with less than enthusiasm by the long-standing, matured newspaper team over whom he must take control.

The idea that Murdoch is entitled to compassion, does not sit easy at a time when the stunning intrusiveness at best, cruelty at worst, of the hacking scandal that has been the stuff of Murdoch's press in the UK recently, is still much in the news. All the same as the subject of this book is home and its meaning for us, I do find myself feeling sympathy and compassion for that young man, on the cusp of adult maturity, being forced to harden himself against grief and sentiment, in order to do as required. Isn't it possible that Murdoch's driven, relentless, tough-nut approach to life has at least some of its genesis in the loss of a home that might have supported him emotionally when he so urgently needed it?

The Value of Home

Home is a word I love. It rolls in the mouth, voluptuous and evocative, pushing the lips into a sensual round before popping out, stating our claim to a little piece of the universe in which we can be our private, authentic selves.

The place we see as home may be a basic hand-crafted shelter on a scrubby patch of land, an extravagant mansion in rolling grounds, or one of the umpteen other styles of abode we have made the place to hang our hats. Whichever, a home – a shelter, a refuge – is viewed as a basic need and one we go to considerable lengths to achieve. When we are homeless it is by and large a wretched, destructive situation. Home has been a bedrock of our way of life as long as human behaviour has been recorded.

A reason, possibly *the* reason, that in earlier times home was considered so vital to us for our psychological and spiritual wellbeing, as well as our physical protection, is that it was the place perceived as most real. The writer and artist John Berger brought his elegant thoughts to bear on this idea in an essay *The Meaning of Home*. It sets one thinking how far our contemporary culture has journeyed from the idea of home being most real because it was a refuge from the surrounding chaos of the outside world. These days we are surrounded by people who appear to do all they can to embrace the chaos of life – at least when it represents something more dazzling than the thought of hugger-buggering up in a domestic nest.

Yet it seems to me vitally important that we learn to re-imagine the value of home, because in losing touch with what it can be, at best nurturing relationships, providing children with a contained world in which to develop, offering a private domain in which to work out what kind of sexual behaviour and structure is life-enhancing for you, and so on.

In this chapter my aim is to get down to the detail of how and why home matters to us. To hear the different ways in which people cherish home, including how that value may become particularly poignant, tugging at the heart-strings with a quite unexpected intensity if we have to move.

Home becomes so much the fabric of life that, although we may fret about practical issues, questions of bricks and mortar, upgrading or downsizing, we are far less inclined to stop and contemplate what home truly means to us, or to think beyond the seeming mundanity of repetitive chores. Yet the philosopher Alain de Botton suggests there is a deeper, more elemental meaning for us to consider in his analysis of the many ways architecture and its deeper meanings (*The Architecture of Happiness*, Hamish Hamilton) affect our sensory lives.

'Home constitutes, for almost all of us, simple rituals that link us with sequences of the day and patterns of time. The rituals that surround gathering food, cooking for ourselves or our families, washing, eating, sleeping and cleaning connect us to almost all of humanity yet we do very little to celebrate or pay tribute to those rituals that centre around, and link us to the diverse but collective experience, of 'home'.

Why is that? Perhaps, because the pace of life means we often perform the tasks and rituals on auto drive, less aware of what we are doing than the need to get done. Or we may employ somebody else to carry them out, to be in our homes while we are away from them, becoming familiar with the way light slants through a window on a dazzling winter's day, the vagaries of the washing machine; what it takes to make our potted plants cheerful; comparing notes with others linked into the activities of home to get a great recipe for chocolate cake, to please children arriving home from school. Finding surprising pleasure in stopping to chat with an elderly neighbour who lives alone.

And if we pause to look back at the meaning of home through the immense tunnel of history, artist and writer John Berger suggests that people understood that the strength we need to deal with the challenges, demands, delights, unpredictability of the world outside came from having our sanctuary. 'Without a home everything was fragmentation' Berger says.

A fragmentation we see acted out very graphically these days in the collapse of relationships, which leads to the desecration of home very often, blotting out an understanding of the vital role home may have played in life, and what might be salvaged from that, but all too often the *denouement* is a bitter wrangle over who gets what of its material value.

Fragmentation of the soul and psyche takes place in other circumstances, of course. In the worst of homes which may remain intact when it could be a lot better if they did not. Places that are not a private retreat but a private hell, mocking the notion of the place being a homely shelter. If we can survive what happens in such an environment we may, as memoirist Maya Angelou does, recognize with an anguished urgency what we need home to be.

'The ache for home lives in all of us, the safe place where we can go as we are and not be questioned.'

Our experience of home is, of course, as different as we

are, as varied as the experiences that have taken place there, as disparate as our personalities. A home that conjures cheerful, cherished memories will be for some of us a reflection of uncomplicated, sequestered childhood, relationships that have flourished within the walls of home. But home need not necessarily have been a place of perfect idyll or unblemished joyfulness for it to be or have been integral. Indeed we can be powerfully attached to a home and all it embodies, have had some of the best of times, while other times have been marked with resentment, rage, conflict, disaffection, and many other uncomfortable emotions.

So it was for Adam Nicholson, whose growing up at Sissinghurst, a place of exquisite beauty was alive with memories of magical times there with his father. Yet no less vividly expressed in Nicholson's memoir of the place *Sissinghurst An Unfinished History* (Harper Press) is the inability of his father to express love and the pain it caused, which was the other side of the experience.

Yet never lost was the deep meaning of Sissinghurst as the root to Nicholson's life. It remained intact so that as an adult he returned with his family, to live there, determined to reinvigorate the human heart of Sissinghurst Castle now owned by the National Trust. At the end of Nicholson's first year there he is alone in contemplation: 'I sit beside the barn… and look at the clouds streaming away in front of me to the northeast. That is what the future looks like too: avenues of bubbled possibility.'

Yet that connection with a sustaining past is too often a casualty of the so called progress of developed countries believes Barbara Bonner editor of a collection of essays, *Sacred Space* (Milkweed). Here she inveighs against how, increasingly, we are allowing the significance of home to be blotted out by the many conflicting activities, distractions, temptations there are in life today. She believes we might just glimpse what a bad bargain we are making when we trade the time we might have to care for and appreciate home, for all the external temptations on offer in our consumerist culture. If home becomes too much a bit part player in life what is lost? She asks us to pause and consider, 'what is the essence of home?'

'Here I Belong'

One response comes from a project worker with a housing charity who had interviewed many very different people, asking them what home meant to them. Once she had sifted through the replies, she distilled the responses, 'Our literal home is a 'sacred' mythic place, even for non-religious people. We all believe in a special place beyond our own doorsills that simply cannot be violated. This is my place where I can close the door on chaos and find some kind of cosmos, peace, assurance of purpose. Here I belong.'

At the turn of the century, the Arts and Crafts Movement was much concerned with decorative aesthetics but also the idea of shutting out chaos. For Architects Philip Webb and M.H. Baillie Scott, for example, one of the most important elements of the houses they designed was a heavy oak door, quite possibly studded, to accentuate the notion of safety and privacy within.

The intrusions of the outside world were anathema to Joel Chandler Harris, author of the Uncle Remus folk tales which included the picaresque exploits of Bre'er Rabbit, Bre'er Fox and Tar Baby. Home, he declared was the fortress that protected him from those encroaches. He told this to Erastus Brainerd who interviewed Harris at home in West Point Atlanta. Home was 'a neat cottage which nestles near the bosom of a grove of sweet gum and pine trees. In the grove a mocking-bird family sings.' In the 1888 anthology *Authors at Home* (Cassell) we hear how Harris was 'devoted to his family, which consists of his mother, his wife, four exceedingly bright boys and a girl, and the flock of mocking-birds that winters in his garden'.

Home and family were what he wanted in life and the small talk of society had no attractions for him. Brainerd explained of Harris, 'his home is enough. When his children are tired and sleepy and are put to bed, he writes at the fireside where they have been sitting. So strong is his domestic instinct that although he had a room built specially as a study, he soon deserted its lonely cheerlessness for the comforts of his home.'

This provokes an eye-tingling nostalgia in me. It sounds so comforting compared with the vision we so often have of today's lives packed tight with competing stimuli, preoccupations, stresses, aspirations, networking, so that home as a place of such sweet relaxation gets a scant look in. We've come to accept that our homesteads are subject to the law of diminishing returns. An alien popping in would conclude that today's homes are far from being the centre of the world for us.

The 19th-century architect C.F.A. Voysey had a notion of the house as 'a frame to its inmates', and within that frame, writes Isabelle Anscombe (*Arts and Crafts Style*, Phaidon), Voysey believed there should be 'Repose, Cheerfulness, Simplicity... Quietness in a Storm...' Home to Voysey should be a place where you are, 'free as a bird to wander in the sunshine or storm of your own thoughts'.

My own memories of childhood are like photos stacked up against each other, and as I pull one out to return to a moment in time, I realise that all the most affecting images are centred around the home in which I grew up.

The memories are a bit higgledy piggeldy, not by any means always chronological, but they are the narrative of a life shared as a kid with my brother and parents. The most vivid memory-snapshots depict the human stew of emotions that gave substance to home life.

I see loving delight, sentiment, joy, the roller-coaster stuff of intimacy, rollicking shared activities, dissent, mickey-taking, the *Sturm and Drang* of sudden raging disputes.

There is the 'snapshot' of me and my brother on the lawn of our house on a modern red-brick estate in Buckinghamshire when I was five, he three. My face is streaked with tears but captured set firm in defiant glee as my brother, who had been howling just minutes before in protest at a protracted bout of bullying by me, was yelling at our mother 'Don't bang Angie's bottom!' She had taken a quick swipe at my backside, in the interests of protecting my brother. She would tell me years later, laughing as she said it, how she had told my brother, 'that's the last time I stand up for you!'

Or the photo of my brother, well cultured into obeying the wishes of his older sister, sitting at a doll's tea-party his face a huge plea for rescue. His memory which nudges itself into my memory album is of me forcing him to eat mud pies as a punishment for something or other. It may be apocryphal but my brother still, jestingly, uses it as demonstration of my fundamental delight in power.

My childhood Christmases, are a set of vivid pictures that never fade. It was a time when my mother's special friend Anne (a former girlfriend of my father who by now had a far richer, girlie relationship with my Mum) and her family arrived. Anne and my mother immediately scuttled off to the kitchen and got outrageously tipsy on VP sherry, making merry indeed of the domestic chores. While Anne's husband and my father, two diametrically different personalities, sat by the fire lost for conversation.

The next morning our father would gather my brother and me up for the ritual visit to the mental hospital where he worked as a psychiatrist, to wish his patients cheery festivities. We would trail him around the wards where I recollect an enormous black woman in shocking pink satin embracing my father so he could scarcely breathe, and a tiny shrunken man with a messianic grim who insisted my father listen while he described making corsets for Queen Mary. At the end of it all the wiry Irish matron, who had something of a crush on my Dad, would ply him with rather better sherry than we had at home.

While all this was going on my mother and Anne would be preparing lunch and not to be outdone, they too had reached for a small glass of 'eau de vie'.

Arriving home we would be assailed with glorious meaty, fruity, roasting smells in the kitchen. The blue-leather topped table in the dining room – too best to be used except on very special occasions – was laid with some ornate cutlery only ever dug out for this festive meal and there were red crackers plump as dowagers, belted with sprigs of plastic holly, beside the plates.

Not all the gallery of memory pictures are so sanguine. I recall one particularly where I am standing on the lawn, a plump pubescent, in a dress with a full gathered skirt of white poplin over my already too full shape. My face is a black reflection of the discomfort I felt with myself. There are other sulky images from the teenage years when I was fretful, bleak and perverse. Overburdened with a grandiose sense of how little anyone understood. At this time I lived at home and was, at a level not to be admitted, glad of the embracing certainties it offered. Overtly, however, I was often positively hostile towards home life.

Interior décor, creating homes with the height of fashionable ideas on display, that will be showcases bringing us admiration, has been big business the past few decades. And I am the first to know that doing up our homes as a reflection of ourselves is enjoyable and rewarding. Yet somewhere there is, I feel, a disconnect if we call in the specialists, the professionals, the experts to create the effect for us, to be the source of our design ideas, as though we have no faith in creating a home for ourselves.

It brings to mind a time many years back when I went to interview a TV star who had recently moved into a smart apartment block. Buzzing around her were a team of interior design people telling her 'Oh Amy you just *have* to have a blue lamp here, a midnight blue carpet, moon grey curtains in raw silk…' If she demurred she was treated to a faintly indulgent suggestion that she was best to leave the total effect to them.

It set me wondering how far we can be ourselves if our environment is so thoroughly constructed around what is deemed to be right, according to the mores of the day, or some designers' mind set, rather than our own picking and choosing, trial and error. Isn't making home a place to be a personal, organic process? Rather than a matter of spending mega bucks on the 'safety' of having your intimate living space created for you?

That said, one of the ways home certainly reflects who we are and what we want to display of our own taste, comes with the objects we put into it; those things we gather through the course of living life. Penny Mansfield, director of the One Plus One relationships research organisation, describes how the decorated china plates her mother had collected and loved, were special enough to her that they came to her own family home after her mother died. The council house of my friend Ruth is a dazzle of odd items gathered for little cost, but with sharp eyes, which each have a meaningful story to them.

I look around my own sitting room and imagine how antipathetic it would be to a purist interior designer with the sequined Chinese wedding dress I bought in Hong Kong hanging on display alongside a t-shirt I bought because it amused me with its slogan asking for a good woman whose overarching attribute would be possessing a sports' car. There is the enormous picture of implacable faces, I bought on impulse because I knew it would go on posing interesting questions; a marble topped table with half the inlaid stones dug out by my brother and me as kids, an Art Deco lamp bought from Argentina, on line because I love the flowing forms of that era and the Bakelite radio Olly bought me, with a lunatic fluffy wolf draped over it which unzips to reveal a sheep inside, given by Andrew. The long wooden dining table Olly and I commissioned when we moved into our pub conversion because we intended large dinner parties and many other mementoes of a life lived.

The things we put into our homes, the weekends we spend decorating or re-organising the way we live in our homes, are all emblematic of emotional investment of creating a place that reflects who we are, and want to be, and this is why the individual ideas, taste, gathering that go into the creation of our environment are important.

Yet investing emotionally in home may be difficult if you have not known it as a place where it is judicious to give of the heart.

An unloving father who later committed suicide, and a broken home during her childhood, did not make it easy for novelist Julie Myerson to see home as a happily reliable place. The reviewer Nicholas Clegg observed when interviewing her, that Myerson writes about domesticity but without cosiness.

So it took her by surprise to find she felt contentedly 'at home' in the house she and her husband Jonathan bought together more than a decade and a half ago. In the charmingly evocative opening to her book *House* Myerson describes realizing that her rootedness had crept up on her, quite stealthily.

'I am perfectly, unquestioningly at home in this house. I loved Lilieshall Rd. from the start, but I was never someone who thought she'd stay anywhere long. And then one day it dawned on me that I had been here ten years and might actually be here another ten. Might even grow old here. I was surprised that the thought didn't frighten me. In fact far from it – it was oddly comforting.'

The Caribbean trainee nurse, newly arrived in the UK, when asked to describe his home lowered his head to hide damp eyes as he talked of a small brick building surrounded by thick foliage and a yard out the front where he, his mother, grandmother and siblings would sit in the evenings eating their meal, chewing the cud.

'For me it is a place that has known so much of my life, some very sad times we have shared, and the happiest times we have spent together as a family. I feel my strongest there.'

The importance of such memories is not simply agreeable sentiment. If we have grown up in a home with the assuredness that here who and what we are is valued it goes a long way towards helping us carry a template of what it means to be 'at home'. I became very aware of the significance of this template when pregnant, and I realized that I had in mind a picture of how I wanted my own children's home life to be, very closely modelled on my childhood experience.

Likewise, Olly's experiences meant that he carried, although in a less formulated way than I, an idea of what it meant to experience home as a place to be 'at home' with people among whom there was mutual caring. His dream of how home should be came from the straightforward, uncomplicated love of an extended family living hugger bugger in the same neighbourhood, treating each others' homes like an extension of their own.

Olly's home was a tiny, very basic two-bed house in a squat

small terrace in Amsterdam. What our homes had in common is that they were full of heart. And we have no doubts about how fortunate we were in that.

The buildings in which my brother and I grew up were very different. When I was seven we moved to a double-fronted Victorian house of sizeable rooms shot-through with icy draughts in winter. My father thought he could deal with these with his own 'double glazing' – plastic bags from Marks and Spencer stamped with St. Michael adorned just about every pane. But even St. Michael wasn't saintly enough to keep the cold out and I have abiding memory of shivering through winters with hideously chilblained fingers.

The house on three levels had large bedrooms, and a main room like a dance hall with parquet flooring and a veranda leading on to an extensive garden. It felt immense. That my family only had money to patch up its problems superficially at that time, my mother defiantly painting blueberry coloured paint around the kitchen, when the order of the day was cream, beige or off-white, mattered not a hoot, we had space to roam, play hide and seek, get lost and have friends for pyjama parties.

Yet although my home and Olly's were physically very different, when it came to creating a home for our young we were like-minded in wanting our boys to experience, as we had, the knowledge that home was about them, for them, reflecting them. We wanted them to know a careless experience of growing up with unspoken for time in which to be inventive. To experience what the poet Philip Larkin referred to as 'forgotten boredom' within the safe confines of our caring.

More important than eau de nil leather sofas, pale minimalism, easily breakable objects, was a robust place, an environment that would not be not harmed by messy games. No impermissible places, no more rules than necessary and we wanted them to be sure that approval and uncompromised affection could be relied on like air breathed.

Moving Home

If homes have the portentous role as 'guardian of identity', as de Botton proposes, then no wonder moving home can stir up infinitely more anguish than was ever anticipated. In the scheme of things it is listed as the third most traumatic event after bereavement and divorce, and perhaps that is not so surprising. If you have put down roots, played out the story of life there, had it bear witness to a gamut of emotions, conflicts and rapprochements, why should we be surprised that it is no casual matter upping sticks.

There will, evidently, be times when moving is something that must be done, or when it offers an obviously sensible solution to other issues. For example in the case of our own first house. We had a mortgage with interest rates that had headed skyward during Mrs Thatcher's reign. Olly and I both worked freelance which meant we could never be sure of what our earnings would be and we lived perilously close to vertiginous debt. Selling the home in which our children had grown to young adulthood, reduced us all to a state of wretched melancholy, but it was nevertheless the right thing to do if we wanted our future years to be less financially fraught.

The stress of keeping that home going was worth it while the children were young and so loved the sense of freedom they had in our ever half completed building, and the long shaggy garden which became every kind of haunt in the imagining of their games. But then as they were reaching the age to head off for gap years, university we began to wonder how wise it was to keep spending all we could earn on a house that would be far bigger than our needs. The roof of the house would soon need some £30,000 worth of repair; other parts of the building cried out for aid, the heating bills were monumental, and so on.

Even so I hadn't anticipated what a business it would be. I detested anyone who came to see it and who didn't instantly swoon with delight at the place, and the things we had done to it.

We had the good, the bad and the ugly tramp through the place each acting as though it were just any old house, talking as though we had no feelings about it.

Douglas Adams of Hitchhiker's Guide to the Galaxy came with his wife to view, and they were charming and managed not to offend our house's feelings while discussing its shortcomings for them. On the other hand the house, I could just feel, detested the prissy businesswoman in a tartan kilt, who almost held her nose as she looked around and kept saying 'it would need stripping out completely. *Everything* needs doing!' as much as I did.

What remains, powerfully, is the memory of my sons' faces when we told them we were selling the house in which they had lived for almost all their childhoods. We explained logically, pleadingly, that it was, really, the right thing to do. Our new home would be lovely too…

Oh yeah? Their looks conveyed, unequivocally, what our sons thought of this. What compensation could there be for loss of familiar shambolic bedrooms, morphing through the years from places for bedtime stories and pictures of Thomas the Tank Engine, to teenage dens where hair gel, music posters and secrets took over? The sitting room where a sofa, bounced and played on through years, had ended its days with the stuffing spewing out; the grimy finger-prints and childhood squiggles on the walls, which were somehow never painted over and had assumed a kind of Picasso-esque allure.

Selling up and moving house is something that caught Sue

Peart, editor of the *Mail on Sunday*'s *You* magazine, broadsides. She is a woman well used to handling crises with her sharp intelligence and impeccable charm, yet when, 'for very sensible reasons' she decided to sell the home she had lived in so long, it hit her, with a startling ferocity, how much she cared for the place.

How could she bear to lose the large light rooms, the garden lovingly tended through the years? This place that had welcomed the pictures and photos she had hung, the ornaments she had chosen because they caught her fancy, and were mementos of special trips and holidays. This place which had seen her through the tough aftermath of divorce and which she had re-shaped around herself and her daughter supporting them with its homeliness.

But of course sense must prevail, she told herself. The house was too large for her now her daughter would be going to boarding school then university and afterwards who knew where. It needed work – quite a bit of work and that would be a financial stretch.

On the day Sue had moved she came to dinner and sat across the table from me telling, in a carefully controlled voice, that she was 'in shock'. Yet she treated the deeply significant business of leaving her beloved home with the throwaway humour we so often feel is called for in the face of what could be seen as foolish sentimentality.

'I know women do crazy things at this time of life… cast off husbands, travel around the world, take up hula dancing… well I cast off a home that has looked after me so well for 21 years and given me no grief whatsoever apart from the occasional leaky gutter… What a cruel person I am!'

Then later, more quietly reflective she emailed me to say, 'In the end, the person I hurt was myself because I didn't realise that homes are like people – you love them just as much and come to accept their idiosyncrasies. Like people, you don't realise how much they meant to you till they're gone!'

The daughter of Barry made clear, very graphically just how terrifying it was for her to feel she was being forced from the security of her familiar home.

'When we moved, Louisa was so upset, she locked herself in the attic of our old house and wept, and wouldn't come out. Awful. And she was, I think quite depressed for the first month or so. Her mother and I later found in her bedroom a spare front door key for the old house. She had smuggled it out – as if it was her magic key, to take her back to her old life.'

The degree of homeliness we feel in a place is not, of course, necessarily defined by how long we stay in one place. Indeed, for generations still growing into adulthood, impermanence can seem adventurous, bold, a way of not belonging, and the absence of an encumbering home can seem very liberating.

Yet it is surprising for how many the home in which they grew up remains the container in which their sense of having a place in the universe is firmly rooted. This, very often, is what gives the confidence to spread wings and head for autonomy and worldly experience.

That is very different to how it may be, however, for children obliged to move home at a time not of their choosing and when it is not at all what they want. A study published in early 2012 in the *Journal of Epidemiology and Community Health*, found that if children frequently move house before the age of 18, it can affect, negatively, psychological and physical health. The study followed 850 people over 20 years with 59 percent moving once or twice, while one in five had moved at least three times during childhood. It may not always be possible to avoid this kind of constant coming and going for children, but then it is important to understand how it may feel for them; how they may need our particular effort to help them feel that at least the quality of home life will remain, that their security is not under threat.

The writer Harriet Lane, described how she grew up in a diplomatic family, moving home and frequently country too, every year or so. People, she says, envied her existence.

'It's odd how many people assume this sort of nomadic childhood must be endlessly fun and exciting.' In fact forever having to learn to know a new home, make friends, adjust to a new school, caused her considerable unhappiness. She is elegiac in expressing it, 'All these cities, all these houses. They were home... then we would move away.'

Now she is a mother to two children and she holds dear the importance of a home life with an unchanging, rooted existence. Her children, she tells stoutly, live in the home they were brought to from the maternity ward. They have been always at the same primary school.

'My children cleave to what they know... We walk home through the park with my parents, through the cycles of crocuses and conkers. My children are changing all the time, so they want the things around them to stay constant. I think I understand that.'

The grace of novelist Annie Proulx's prose in no way disguises the upset it caused her to live in 20 different homes during her childhood; to be subject to her father's single-minded use of moving to serve his purpose, regardless of how it felt for his children.

'My father... was always moving up the various ladders of his ambition... A large part of the reason for constantly moving was my father's obsessive desire to reinvent himself as a New England Yankee, to escape working-class poverty, to achieve financial success. Over the years we lived in dozens of houses.'

For all her discontent at this Proulx fell into the same pattern and moved 'countless times' in her adult years. Yet for her it was a search for the ideal house. Finding the 'final home of which I had dreamed' became a defining goal. She had not succeeded at the time she wrote her memoir *Bird Cloud* (Simon and Schuster), when she believed she had found the desired destination. Even so finding 'the final home of which I had dreamed' remains compelling.

When a child has been unable to feel they can be at home, that home is there for them, there may be a compulsion to return to their childhood homes, seeking reassurance that there is still, somehow, a route back to what the remembered home meant to them.

Clare Moynihan, now 70, sits on a deep sofa in the tiny flat she rents, where silk and decorated cushions surround her. On the floor are patterned carpets, on the walls, photographs, hangings and many elliptical pictures painted by her mother in law Elinor Bellingham-Smith. Her home is a homage to the importance she attaches to home – 'I fall in love with my homes and never want to leave them'. She traces it back to a fractured home life during her childhood in India.

A childhood where home was the ecstatic centre of the universe, and yet, sent to boarding school from the age of four, she was forever being forced away from the place she so wanted to stay.

Three times Clare has made a journey back to Assam to return to this place that was home, seeking that old connection. Reassurance.

As she describes this to me, she is back in the low, thatched building with its veranda looking out over a lake, and to the side there is jungle where the monkeys chatter carelessly. There are trees around the house, the tea-garden in the distance, the colours, the cascading bougainvillea, the scented mimosa, aromas filling the air, mist rising off the grass first thing in the morning, and then the heat spreading itself across the day. There are the servants, 'our friends. We adored them and they us. When my sister and I visited some years ago they all came over to greet us'.

It was a magical home full of love, and yet aged four Clare was dispatched to a convent in the hills, returning just for the holidays. Then at the age of 11 she was sent to boarding school in England, returning home to India just once a year.

'I have wondered how my parents could have sent me away, I couldn't have done it with my children, but it was what happened to all children of ex-pats living in India. It had nothing to do with not loving or wanting the children – I always knew my parents loved us – but they followed convention unquestioningly.'

Home became a mythical, hankered-after place.

'I felt so excluded and abandoned, so far away from my home which seemed protective and nurturing, yet was not there for me. I was sad all the time and now I believe it was profoundly damaging being kept away from home with all that made me feel safe and loved there. As an adult I have resented my parents for this.'

She also believes the experience has undermined the trust she feels in relationships, has made her guarded about commitment even though she has had a marriage and sustained relationships.

So Clare has determinedly made homes for herself and her family, in which she invests passion, commitment and the determination that these homes will provide reliable succour for herself and her children.

'Home is the most important thing for me, when something goes wrong with my home, as happened fairly recently, it destroys me.'

It was an attempt to undo some of the psychological destruction and sense of sadness for that distant time that took Clare and her sister back to their childhood home. Each time has been difficult because things have changed, but until this last time enough was the same that Clare could leave, reassured, that it was still there for her.

Then, when, in 2010 she and her sister returned, dramatic alteration had taken place. The house was now owned by an old friend of their father who had replaced the thatched roof with corrugated iron; the lake had gone and in its place was, 'a hideous swimming pool made of bright blue tiles'. Trees and the terraced garden had been removed and a 19-hole golf course was being built in the tea garden. Then there was the house. Their mother's coolly elegant and understated sitting room had been re-done with, 'garish shiny tiles, huge drapes with pleats, at the windows. Everywhere contemporary furnishings.'

The upset in Clare's voice is palpable as she tells this.

'The place has been violated. The precious memories are ruined, Our special home has been done up as a rest house for tourists, to make money.'

The first evening spent there she talks of a raging anguish and hysterics.

'It felt as though my childhood had been rubbed out. I was bereft.'

Her sister left and did not return. Clare did not feel that she could just leave.

'So next day I went back by myself, quite alone. I was able then to sense something of the house, the old feeling. That was good. It was the thing you get with an old friend not seen in years, and in the time they have changed out of recognition, but as you sit with them, very slowly you see the familiar face coming through. I was glad of that, but I shall not return.'

Hearing how, in different ways, people feel so deeply about their homes gives a very real importance to contemplating how a home can be made to nourish and uplift our spirits. Author Jeanette Winterson who has written a good deal about her own childhood believes there are quintessential things we should focus on in order to create a place of sanctuary and where we feel at home, whether it is a modest place or something lavish, a permanent place or a sometime resting place.

'It is important to make some rules for yourself about your home and you inside it, and if you live by those rules, they will work for you. This takes thought, planning, self-awareness, courage, and a sense of humour. You don't need a big budget or a TV show that helps you 'create your space'. Rather, you need a space inside to project on to the space outside. Inner houses, outer houses, as my Jewish friends tell me. Happy/normal. Normal/happy. Home is where the questions are answered well.'

So back to Barbara Bonner and her quest for the essence of home, her question in *Sacred Space*, 'why has it become less certain for us?'

She refers to the seven hundred submissions she received for the book which were perturbing, 'Loss is what seems to be on the minds of writers these days. Their stories showed overwhelmingly the social, spiritual and emotional dislocations we have suffered. It is clear that the issue of home strikes troubling chords in our society.'

Could it be that the answers to what we need, fundamentally, viscerally, are not being adequately answered in our homes?

This is something to think about. In this chapter we have had a glimpse of the importance home may have for us, the feelings of often profound loss when for whatever reason home is not available to us in a secure and reliable way. And if Confucius got it right when he declared that the strength of a nation derives from the integrity of the home, then we have every reason to invest in our homes, body and soul.

3

TRADING UP

Tiger Woods and Elin Nordegren did romance superlatively in a ceremony costing $1.5 million when, on October 5th, 2004 they made their vows under a pagoda reputedly decorated with 10,000 black roses, and later fireworks lit up the coastline, at Sandy Lane Beach in Barbados. Even the powers-that-be welcomed their promises to love and to cherish, with a rainbow arching over the luxury yacht on which the couple spent their wedding night.

This, and the honeymoon were, of course, the precursor to moving into a home that would suitably demonstrate what the couple were worth in every sense. Home was a three-storey 6,692 square foot edifice with eight bedrooms, nine bathrooms and a boat dock, in the exclusive gated community in Isleworth, Florida. That was for starters, but greater splendour was planned for another move to a waterfront estate on Jupiter Island, Florida (where inhabitants have the highest per capita income in the US), that the couple bought in 2006, reputedly for a sum nudging $40,000. It was to be re-modelled to their own high spec. desires.

A home chosen as the base for embarking on a lifelong commitment is important to most of us. We want it to echo and reinforce our sense of being united in dreams of a future. But get into celebrity homes and you are talking of a significance and meaning that has as much to do with being recognized for having achieved success and status, as being a place to build an intimate nest. Los Angeles writer Carl Braeden puts it simply when she observes that, 'there's nothing better defines the Hollywood lifestyle than the lavish, luxurious mansions celebs call home'.

The pressure of standing out, being noticed, in a world which as Leo Braudy, author of *The Frenzy of Renown – Fame And Its History* (Vintage Books) notes is, 'overcrowded with people, places, things, ideas', is great indeed. So getting a home to fit the picture really matters as one Hollywood real-estate commentator I came across made clear.

'Sure celebrities tend to cluster with people of like minds and incomes... that means the Malibu buffs, Aspen slopes, Hamptons beaches and Miami waterfront.'

Just being nice guys with simple, straightforward tastes and values won't do. You have to live in a mansion, ranch house, a turreted castle-style affair, the faux-Italian villa, the ultra-modern glass and steel edifice, with huge rooms, umpteen en-suite bedrooms, sumptuously landscaped gardens, the follies, the carports, swimming pools, cinema centres, servant quarters and of course luxurious rooms for entertaining. Oh yes, and usually enough private land to house a small African village.

So being seen to be worth it is one thing. But, observing all this, it seems to me there is a dimension that goes beyond the desire and the necessity of a celebrity to let us know their worth through their material pile. When somebody spends gargantuan sums on their home, it seems likely that at some level is the idea that in doing this you are also buying a quality of joy that that is of an exalted dimension. So home, the long-term extension of the 'happiest couple in the world' wedding, carries very great expectations for the quality of happy-ever-after that it must deliver.

Isn't that what Jennifer Aniston and Brad Pitt were telling us, albeit subconsciously, when they moved into their huge, Wallace-Neff designed estate in Beverley Hills? Ashley and Cheryl Cole with their £6 million Surrey mansion? Kate Winslet and Sam Mendes with the honey-coloured Cotswolds home valued now at £8 million, which they were so thrilled to get, and then spent a fortune to make fit their dreams?

The Perfect Life

Delusional it may seem to us more ordinary mortals, but that is not entirely the fault of celebrities' disturbed minds. The notion that a super-real quality of happiness is what fame and wealth bring is not incidental, simply an act of faith by individual celebrities. It is a belief system beamed at us from ubiquitous screens, from umpteen glossy magazines, vast billboards. We are bombarded with the 'because you are worth it' message of the L'Oreal advertisements. And as the line between objective reporting, infotainment and advertising has ever narrowed, so breathless articles are produced by journalists with not even a hint of irony, an askance lifted eyebrow, for every kind of publication, including serious broadsheet newspapers. Once our elitist celebs have moved into their residences, we get the spreads of photos showing what an enviable family life they have, the photographer leading us into homes where celebrities are to be seen, reclining in deep, soft sofas, flitting through a kitchen fitted with state of the art gadgetry, reclining on a tree-shadowed lawn that seems to stretch forever, assuring us with their beatific smiles that they do, indeed, have the perfect life. The glimpse we get is fleeting, but just long enough to stoke up the belief that if only we could live like that, we too would be perpetually wreathed in blissful smiles.

Except that, it is not quite like that as we can hardly fail to know, given the *schadenfreude* of a media that reports with zeal when celebrity relationships hit the dark side. The homily about money not buying you happiness, becomes the next instalment in the saga. As the myth comes tumbling down in this pampered world it is frequently replaced with a good deal of hell-hath-no-fury stuff around the value of the very home that was to be such romantic superglue. It morphs from the fairy-palace promising eternal magic to having no more meaning than as a pricey bit of real estate.

If this were a moral drama we should see easily the medium's message, that believing material goods and image-making are the things that answer our need for a rooted contentment or that they can provide the kind of sustenance relationships need to prosper, is misguided. But we live in an advanced capitalist economy and that thought is counter-intuitive to its need for us to be endlessly seduced by the need for lavish consumption.

In the past three decades a great deal of money has been made very quickly, and the 'Greed is Good' mantra of Gordon Gekko, the ruthless stockbroker in the film *Wall Street*, has infiltrated the collective psyche. Consuming, whether was clothes, cars, state of the art high tech gadgets, expensive meals out or property, was ever more compelling and addictive. Observing the excesses political commentator Neal Lawson talked of 'turbo consumers'.

So enter celebrities as main players in the business of stimulating consumer demand. They have been marketed to become the people we most want to be like, their tastes in everything from fashion and jewellery to how they live are reproduced to make enormous profits. Publicists and PRs labour prodigiously, often earning a great deal for dedicating their working lives to selling celebrities' lifestyles as infinitely desirable. This after all is a prime function of celebrities. It is not only their talents but their ability to inspire envy and desire that designers, manufacturers, advertisers, publicists exploit. The fashion, accessories, jewellery, shoes, bags worn by celebrities from Christina Aguilera and Robert Pattinson to those who seem to have morphed into celebrities with a conspicuous absence of talent or even native sense – Katie Price, Paris Hilton, Lindsay Lohan come to mind – are instantly interpreted for the mass market. Even stars who have earned their status through hard work and real ability now celebrit-ise their faces and bodies. David Beckham, Jude Law, Sarah Jessica Parker, Julia Roberts are among the many who have greeted us from billboards and screens giving their mark of approval to consumer goods.

Nor, for all the evidence of a long economic downturn, serious unemployment and considerable hardship, is there any sign that encouraging people to want these inessentials is causing pause. Promotional subliminal strategies, far more powerful than Vance Packard ever dreamed of when he wrote his seminal book *The Hidden Persuaders*, continue inexorably. Indeed the power of the celebrity market is such that the New York Times in 2010 ran a lengthy article describing how internet users go to celebrity sites like, INFDaily or CelebStyle to see what kind of clothes Jessica Biel, Nicole Richie, Justin Timberlake and other such arbiters of fashion are wearing and where to buy them. The consensus of fashion marketers, we are told, is that celebrities are more effective than models now in imprinting a brand in the customer's mind. And those involved are laughing all the way to the bank.

Just cock an ear to branding strategist Eli Portnoy, 'They (the consumers) live vicariously through the products and services that those celebrities are tied to. Years from now, our descendants may look at us and say "God these were the most gullible people who ever lived."

What I am saying may not appear to have much to do with celebrities' homes, but in fact where they choose to live, and what we learn of their lifestyles, has become an integral ingredient in making sure brand celeb. keeps its place in the market. So the exposure goes into the one place these people, whose public lives are incessantly recorded by paparazzi, might retreat and have private time for their relationships and children. All too often homes are not sacred spaces but another commercial opportunity. So much so that you can now purchase the ultimate vicarious experience.

One of the newest trends for those who yearn to be touched by celebrity is to get a taste of celebrity lifestyle by actually living in their homes. Mushrooming websites advertise celebrity properties to rent. So you can imagine yourself being Mick Jagger at his six-bedroom Caribbean retreat knowing that everything from the tin-opener to the Jeep you have at your disposal, has been used by Jagger himself. Leonardo Di Caprio lets out his holiday home Encinal Bluffs in Malibu; you can make yourself at home in the private domains of Christie Brinkley, Keith Richards, Bruce Willis. Impoverished wannabes, however, are strictly excluded by prices spiralling into many, many thousands of dollars.

In this world where money talks, if you have wealth enough you can take on celebrity by osmosis in a permanent home now that a fair number of celebs are, it seems, having to sell their piles. Worth checking the karma first, though. Shortly after Charlie Sheen put his home on the market he was charged with domestic violence.

What, of course, no-one bothers to tell, is how often the gilded lives are in fact much tougher, more disappointing and disillusioning than we imagine. Over and over the celebrities confess all in print, on screen, telling how wretched she or he feels or has felt, how all that they have has not, in fact, been the answer. That is the danger, believes actress Mary Steenburgen, who has been around the celebrity circuit, but maintaining a discrete profile, long enough to have understood how danger-ous colluding in the hyped up mythology and distancing your-self from the demands, challenges and efforts that are the stuff of keeping the human soul intact, can be. 'We are not taking out the trash. We're not cooking dinner. We're not yelling at the gas company because they didn't fill the gas tank. Somebody else is making your bed. You're basically a big baby. If you fall in love with those circumstances, you have to be very careful to ask yourself how real is this'.

Elaine Lipworth experienced the seduction of L.A's 'aggres-sively materialistic society'. They lived here with their two daughters and saw the girls seduced by the allure of aspira-tional partying: Bar Mitzvahs on yachts at $100,000 'a pop', were the norm Lipworth tells. There were birthday celebrations in chauffeured party buses rented at $2,000 an evening fitted out with TV screens and dance floors. One friend of their daughter invited her to a sleepover at the $600 a night Chateau Marmot hotel in Hollywood.

Parental anxiety grew as the couple recognized that 'nothing we do can ever match up.'

These lives of pampered unreality, that have succeeded in drawing an almost surreal amount of awe and desire to belong in their orbit, has led to a 'cognitive malaise' in the view of physician and author Raymond Tallis. He believes 'The heart of celebrity culture is an individual emptiness gawped at by a collective emptiness... Preoccupation with celebrities is an appalling squandering of human consciousness.'

'The Affluenza Virus'

I hadn't thought of it quite that way, but Tallis' words have a resonance that should be heeded. It is time for a reality check on the acquisitive, money-driven values that have taken such a grip on developed Western countries in recent decades. Not least if we want to confront the malaise that psychologist Oliver James. In his book *Affluenza* (Vermillion) identifies. He talks of a society which worships affluence to the extent that it has become a virus, infecting large parts of the world and accounting for the ever growing numbers of people suffering psychological distress and mental health problems.

'The Affluenza virus is a set of values which increase our vulnerability to psychological distress: placing a high value on acquiring money and possessions, looking good in the eyes of others and wanting to be famous. Many studies have shown that infection with the virus increases your susceptibility to the commonest mental illnesses: depression, anxiety, substance abuse and personality disorder. We have become absolutely obsessed with measuring ourselves through the distorted lens of Affluenza values'.

With the result that from top to bottom of society, indiscriminately rattling through the class and economic hierarchy, we try to deal with these disordered feelings by buying something or things which we believe will make us feel better – haven't we all been the retail therapy route? I know I have and yes, there is a brief buzz but when that is gone the world isn't a happier place. Indeed the follow on, I find, is frequently a hollowing in the gut realising how I've pushed myself into spending more than is sensible once again.

Yet, if we follow James's line, and I find it compelling, those of us in pursuit of goods to enhance our public image – the biggest, best, most expensive homes are an ultimate feature of this – we are pursuing false gods. Drawing on his years of clinical psychological work, James talks of how far we have got from fulfilling fundamental human needs which seem to exist in every society.

But we are far from meeting these needs: security (emotional and material), connectedness to others, authenticity and autonomy, and feeling competent James says. Demonstrated in the fact that one in four people in English-speaking countries suffered a mental illness in 2006 compared to 11.5 per cent of mainland Western Europeans. These findings from the World Health Organisation include being anxious, becoming phobic, hysterical, obsessional or depressed. As well as using drugs and alcohol. And we know from the incessant revelatory interviews given by celebrities, the rich and famous, how prone they are to all these. As I write this, the news of Whitney Houston's death is announced, and with it the wretched story of how her glittering life took the familiar route of drugs and desperation until death.

It is the subconscious motivation that drives the desire to be recognised as significant through the purchases we can put on show, like children holding out toys they hope will buy them friends, that interests psychologists Glenn Wilson and Andrew Evans. They talk of how this behaviour reflects a deep fragility of the ego. Exploring the psycho-dynamics at work here, in their book *Fame* (Satin Publications Ltd), they describe how as humans we have a basic need to find something that refutes 'our primal fear of disappearing forever into an unknown void. What we try to create, therefore, is some illusion of permanence.' It is very easy to see how a home can appear to be a very graphic and reassuring symbol of permanence. An anchor in solid form, for a life that must at times feel very ephemeral.

Was this, as I suspect, the demon driving Barbara Amiel, the journalist from the East End of London who was described as developing 'a ferocious social climb to a life of unrestricted luxury.' Her fourth marriage was, famously, to the newspaper tycoon Conrad Black and she lived a life thenceforward of exemplary moneyed flamboyance. The homes from which they moved one to the other, were centrepieces. These homes were a stately double-fronted house in Kensington with a vast ballroom, a huge flat in Manhattan and a 22-room mansion overlooking the sea in Palm Springs.

It was suggested, by Geoffrey Levy in the *Daily Mail* that Amiel always had a desire to be envied as well as admired. There was a feverish need to live as a billionaire, while Lord Black was worth only millions. So there was speculation as to how she would cope psychologically as well as materially when Black was imprisoned for fraud in 2008, and the family wealth so diminished Amiel had to move into 'a modest rented flat in the Florida town of Lady Lake and make do with a cook, a maid and a chauffeur'. Tales of how desperately hard she took the fall from grace were pitiful. And you cannot help imagining how far her previous lifestyle and values will probably have distanced her from less exalted new neighbours.

Yet Amiel's tale is instructive. Her father left her mother for another woman during her childhood and she was uprooted from her smart private school and taken to Canada when her mother re-married. Then when she was 14 she arrived home to find all her possessions packed in boxes, described writer Sarah Sands. There was a letter from her mother explaining that she and Amiel's stepfather could not cope with her and she must move out. Her father, in the UK, committed suicide. You see how deeply the conviction that the possibility of having every material goodie you might want, may be found in earlier desperation, an enduring hunger for security and love that it is very hard to ever trust. Material goods become the most accessible surrogate when a reliable home is not available.

Segregation

Alienation is what happens when we consciously remove ourselves from the normality, the interaction, the aggravations, the supportiveness and humanity, found at best in community. And you hear that in the words of Amiel after Black was imprisoned. She described herself as like the Wandering Jew, 'I'm Lady Black of no fixed address.' It was not, of course, true, but it is a vivid cry of how she felt.

I am reminded, writing this, of the question a little Indian boy in an orphanage, in the Danish film *After the Wedding*, asks Jacob who looks after him. 'Is it because their houses are separate that they (the wealthy) are separate?' It is something that has been more and more evident in our atomised lives where individualism and privacy have become the things to aspire to. And where there is so often no time, nor maybe inclination, to become involved with immediate neighbours and our neighbourhood.

For what are we saying when home is a gated, guarded, locked-in world designed to isolate you from the rest of society? That we need to protect ourselves from the threatening 'other', that those outside fortress home may wish to do us harm. And that may be true. If you have a great deal in a world where there are others with very little except a constant awareness of the gulf between, then they may well want what you have.

This is the ironic product of the very envy and covetousness that we set out to inspire with our conspicuous consumption, whether as celebs or anyone else. Alienation is felt as powerfully by those who cannot possess the most desirable goodies as it is experienced by those who have everything and feel threatened by the envious.

It is what Karl Marx talked of when he described how the lives of workers are connected to the wealthy ruling classes only by the goods and services they produce for them to consume. Yet these workers are unknown as fellow humans, non-existent as anything but the means of production. It is hardly surprising they may feel hostile and alienated towards those people whose lives thrive in a culture that so restricts and limits their own.

It brings to mind a lad of 17 I interviewed in prison He had broken into one of the elegant Georgian houses a stone's throw, but also an immeasurable distance, from the degraded terraced house where he and his family lived. He had stolen goods worth around £100 and was given a prison sentence. He accepted doing his time as one of those things (it wasn't his first stint) but the thing that really delighted him was thinking about how, 'that geezer (the man whose home he broke into) must have been ranting around the place cursing whoever nicked his stuff. And that was me. It was the only way I could ever have got that man to know that I exist.'

Richard Wilkinson, author of many books on the physical and mental effects of social segregation, and Kate Pickett, a Professor of Epidemiology, drew together some 200 research papers looking at the impact of inequality related to wealth in society. In their book *The Spirit Level* (Penguin) the authors demonstrate something that, recently, has been echoed in an ever growing number of studies. That in countries where wealth inequality was greatest – and the UK and America are among the most unequal – everyone top and bottom of the economic scale suffers more social ills than in countries where the difference is far less. Wilkinson and Pickett talk of 'the life-diminishing results of valuing growth above equality in rich societies' and how the results can be seen all around us. Inequality causes shorter, unhealthier and unhappier lives; it increases the rate of teenage pregnancy, violence, obesity, imprisonment and addiction; it destroys relationships between individuals born in the same society but into different classes; and its function as a driver of consumption depletes the planet's resources.

But that does not leave the most well off consuming extravagantly and often carelessly, untouched. They must either shut off any acceptance that it matters or use psychological defence mechanisms to deal with their guilt and these, the authors suggest, have a very clear link to unhappiness, mental health problems, clinical depression.

My point has been to show how the desire to be famous because of what it appears to offer is compelling, as is the need to get self-esteem feedback from putting our status on show. There is, however, another dimension to all this which, too, is corrosive of home being able to be a place of respite ; a place where we can ground relationships and replenish our energy by being our unadorned authentic selves. That is the process required to gain fame, wealth, celebrity and to hold on to it. To do this will very often mean dedicating time and energy to mixing with people who will help your progress, being seen at the appropriate social events and parties, particularly in the case of celebrities, networking, socialising at fashionable restaurants and clubs. That on top of the time taken up by doing the work that being a celebrity requires. All this eats into time that would otherwise have been available for the home, family, friends and neighbours. For engaging in the stuff of human contact whether sharing a good meal and drink, conversation, arguments, passions, domesticity. The stuff that builds human bonds within the domestic sphere, rather than it gathering dust from underuse while we put ourselves out there.

At which point I am going to get personal, for although I have never been within a giant's howl of experiencing a full-blown celebrity lifestyle nor reached a boardroom or executive chair demanding the vast bulk of my waking hours, I have experienced on a minor but nevertheless significant level, the way we will put a desire for the recognition and approval of a public world over home life.

My Separate Life

The 'celeb effect' in my life occurred during the five years I spent as fashion editor of the *Guardian*. I was young and dazzled by the sudden fame and desirability I had acquired by virtue of my job. I became the toast of PRs, invitations came to delightful foreign publicity occasions, I could have bathed (without Johnny Depp sadly) in champagne, the amount that was offered by just about every designer grand, or insignificant, when I attended the collections. At parties I was charmed when people recognised my name from the hefty by-lines I got in print. Suddenly I was not just a small time feature writer, lost among many others, as I had been writing about ordinary issues. I had acquired a curious aura of glamour. The irony was I had never wanted to be a fashion journalist. But when I was offered the I accepted as a way of getting to work for the *Guardian*. The price was giving up writing about social issues, human foibles and humanitarian matters, and getting to understand the difference between culottes and a liberty bodice. The reward was that the world seemed to be chock-a-block with people who thought me worth their time and attention.

This was heady stuff for a 30-year-old with memories of

being a shy and ungainly teenager who had had little confidence about her own worth. So the point is that I found myself becoming hooked on all this. I wanted to be out and about at the events I was invited to, the boozy lunches that left me a drained-out rag by the time I got home, the networking sessions at some watering hole that so often took place at the end of a working day.

Which would all have been fine enough except that I had a small child at home with his Dad, waiting for me to get back, to be pleased to be with him, have energy for a game, a bath, a book. I adored my little boy, but even so the seductive pull of raising my profile in the outside world by accepting a drink, some 'quick' coffee break or other, was persuasive. So much of the networking stuff went on after working hours.

Getting home to a familiar domestic routine which would fill the evening, somehow didn't match up. Without the 'interference' of the opportunities in the world outside our West London flat, being at home with Olly and my baby son would have made me perfectly content. Instead I determinedly pursued my separate life, so that home life got the bare minimum and I felt much of the time as though I was living in a food processor. I didn't want to see it but my son was suffering. I, who had given birth to him, was elusive both physically and emotionally. He became clingy, crying a lot, angry and demanding. It was frankly easier to hand him over to his Dad and the child-minder than recognize what was going on.

So I regard it as fortuitous that, thanks to a bit of backroom dealing by a features' editor who didn't rate me, I was not given a promotion that had been promised. I would probably have swallowed hard, kicked the cat and stayed on at the *Guardian* even so, if I had not seen at that moment what I was sacrificing for the sake of a career that was not that wedded to me.

I was making home the disposable part of my life because

working for a quality paper was satisfying as a journalist, and carried considerable status. Reasons that would be sympathized with in our present value system, but which were draining off the quality of life at home. I resigned and went freelance, and within months the PRs who had courted me so eagerly were conspicuously not eager to spend time with me. The glitzy invitations petered out. Working from a little office at home I was no longer invited to join after work social networking sessions.

In other words without my 'fame' I had lost my value in a world that judges your worth that way. Happily I got a good deal of freelance work, but I still was able to pick my son up from the baby-minder and later from school; early evenings I had time and energy for games, to let my boy help with cooking supper, to relax in front of a children's cartoon with him, and then when he had gone to bed Olly and I would have a bit of chatting time – before I had usually been collapsing by this stage.

I remember years later reading an article that Gaby Hinsliff, political editor on the *Observer* wrote about choosing to leave her coveted job because of the stresses and pressures it was putting on her life as a wife and mother. She went on to expand the idea in her book *Half A Wife*. But the words that particularly struck me were: 'the thing I was missing out on was home'.

When I made the decision to invest more in home and less in personal progress it felt surprisingly comfortable. I found, to my surprise, that I really didn't mind about the loss of 'fame', and the bonus was I enjoyed my home in a way that had been impossible when I was perpetually spinning through it. I spent time relaxing with friends over a cup of coffee when they brought their children around, doing laundry (almost therapeutic), collecting my then two sons from playgroup and school and larking with them. I spent time in the garden and discovered the pleasure my mother used to take in digging, planting, plucking, crooning over a suddenly blooming plant. I had time to kick a ball with Olly and the kids before supper, or play some board-game which would probably end in family warfare.

My son's tearful distress subsided and there was far more laughter, although a residual uncertainty and anxiety remained in Zek for a long while. Olly too was happier. Having created a home that he loved for his family, he took it hard when I had chosen to be away from it for so much time. As I now spent time enjoying the place, he felt validated and valued. I became part of my local community, bumping into people on the street and finding friendships forming. I looked forward to the playground encounters as we parents waited for the children to come out in a rush of flailing limbs and billowing shouts. I had what I did not before, which was a comforting home life.

Yet I suspect if I had got that promotion at the *Guardian* the story would have been very different. I'd have gone on as I was and in the process I would, very probably, have been increasingly alienated from, and alien within, my home.

The Profit Motive

This is a personal digression and I want to return to the bigger picture of how our homes are traduced by the profit motive. The housing boom dealt the idea of home as a place treasured for its emotional content and human history, a belly blow.

As the brittle, brutal culture of the Thatcher years took root – times during which those without money and power acquired the charmless soubriquet the 'underclass', while making money – lots of it – became a defining goal. Children in their early teens told surveys that their ambitions were to be rich and famous. Buying and selling property was suddenly the way of making a fast, and often substantial, buck if you had the means to do so in the first place. Properties were traded within hours, if not minutes, of coming on the market. Competition was feverish, stock was scarce and the sense that your home was your goldmine became conventional wisdom.

Newspapers and magazines spawned supplements and advertising spreads featuring infinitely tempting properties and articles talking every which way about the benefits of buying and selling, of trading up. Not surprisingly people without much disposable wealth wanted some of the spoils of this boom-time and money was borrowed, mortgages raised against whatever homes people already had and never mind that the payments required sent shivers down the spine. All would be well when the profit came in. How true was Jeremy Paxman's observation in his wry book *The English* that those who borrowed money saw the bricks and mortar working for them. To suggest that this modus operandi could actually make your life less good, not better, was dismissed as the wilder shores of counter-intuitive thinking.

So it was no good being sentimental about your home. No use allowing in the sickening sense of something treasured becoming a cool-headed commercial proposition.

The Sampsons lived this way for twenty years during which they had two children and moved eight times. Each time, just as they had done up the home they were in, got to know the neighbours, chatted about how much they liked the area, an 'unmissable opportunity' would come up and they would be off.

Louisa Sampson, wife of James and mother of two small sons says now, 'I lived on valium through the days when the houses were packed up and the removal men arrived. I found it painful every time and so did James, but we were so bound up in the idea that we would make the money we needed to live a good life, that we kept on. I had to completely harden my heart over the things I really cared about in a home, and often it was silly things like a drawing one of the boys had made behind the bath, or the way the light fell into our bedroom. I learned to blot out what bereft felt like.'

Then she seems close to tears. 'But it's the boys who really paid the price. They hated the upheaval, the emptiness of their homes as we left, and they always hated the new place for quite a while. It seems now that we were really neglectful of their need for security, friends around the corner, a sense of belonging somewhere. The other day my eldest son who is married and has a small child and has bought his first house, told me he was never going to move. He so wanted to be somewhere that felt like a home to rely on.'

So the value of home lay in what it represented as a capital asset. Homes were not valued for how they would feel to live in, but became a favourite object of investment. Among the most avid of these are celebrities who often put their money into property. I was struck by reading how the actor Daniel Radcliffe, scarcely out of short pants, having made his millions in the Harry Potter films has amassed a £10 million pound portfolio in the US and a flat in London in the UK, and it may well be more by now. While Madonna famously, buys property as others buy paperbacks. There is, or was, Ashcombe Manor, former home of photographer Cecil Beaton, in Wiltshire, with a 1,000 acre estate. At least half a dozen properties in central London worth many millions. With ex-husband Guy Ritchie there was an £8 million house in Beverley Hills.

Fashion designer Diane von Furstenberg describes her 'favourite home' as her 200-year-old farm in Connecticut with five houses on land of fields, woods, rivers, waterfalls. But there are others: an apartment in Paris on the Left Bank, a 'beautiful little house on the pink sand of Harbour Island' in the Bahamas, and a home in New York.

In the world around me, for those without wealth, a very different situation was emerging. As house prices rose people who had saved to buy a house found they could no longer afford it. Or else they were given, with few questions asked, mortgages they would have the greatest difficulty paying off.

I saw people doing as Andrew Oswald, Professor of Economics at Warwick University describes, treating homes as 'a giant piggy bank', becoming mini-speculators and borrowing all they could to sink into their home. But then mid-2000s the trading bonanza stopped delivering the goods. Prices began to sink and people found their piggy banks were not only empty but had IOU notes inside them. The tragic consequence of the hyped-up idea that property was a guaranteed earner turned into a very sick joke as mortgage companies that had seemed gloriously unconcerned about lending 100 per cent on a property, became tough with borrowers who found they could not pay, and there was none of the leeway there had been before the credit crunch. By 2008 a record numbers of homes were being repossessed. According to the Council of Mortgage Lenders in the UK some 27,100 homes were repossessed – a rise of 21 per cent on the year before, with a warning that the numbers would probably rise further.

By 2009 in the UK around 900,000 homeowners were going into negative equity as a result of falling house prices, with some people owing many thousands more than their homes were worth. In America in the same year homes in negative equity made up 24 percent – more than 11 million of all residential properties with a mortgage.

Behind these statistics is the human story so many of us dread – that we would be forced to leave our home and find ourselves adrift without its securing arm around our lives. Dwelling on this the psychiatrist Keith Ablow sees, as Oliver

James does, how pursuing wealth as life's goal without concern for the emotional dimension, takes us far from meeting our deepest needs. We cannot afford to treat something with the emotional meaning of home as 'simply a financial asset'. Ablow has seen how profoundly damaging are the consequences. 'The distressing number of foreclosures on property means economic conditions translate into a public health concern. Those losing homes can feel like failures, that they have let down families, been losers in the eyes of the community. There is the crumbling of the home-based relationships with a perfect storm of lowered self-esteem and perceived loss of face. Perfect conditions leading to breakdown of families.'

A situation seen visibly real in a study carried out by economists at St Andrews University, Scotland, based on extensive historical analysis of fluctuations in property values and divorce rates. They found at the end of 2008, that an extra 50,000 Scottish couples were at risk of splitting up in 2009 as a direct result of the slump in the property prices. Evidence showed that for every 10 per cent drop in house prices in Scotland there is a 5 per cent increase in separations. It was most likely to happen to couples with young children.

So in this chapter I have set out to show how far we are taken from being able to appreciate and enjoy home whether large or small, grand or shabby, when all around us our homes are held up as a symbol of our worth as a person.

4

A HELL OF A HOME

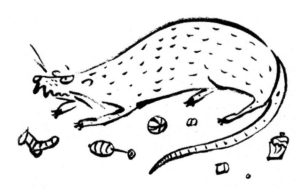

The tower block stood in a pool of oily water, an island in the scrubby grassland stretching towards seemingly endless blocks of flats – humongous slabs of despair against the granite skyline. It was mid-morning and eerily quiet.

I was, frankly, jittery at the prospect of going up to the 19th floor where I was to meet Mary in her home. The choice was between filthy concrete stairs with the cliché of hypodermic needles discarded among the litter in the stairwell; the smell of urine and the insubstantial looking metal lift which, had it jammed on its journey to the 26th floor, would have made for an experience beyond terrifying. I opted for the stairs, pausing on the half landings of the stairwell to listen for sounds of people coming, sounds that might indicate whether they would ignore me, be friendly or dangerously hostile. In fact I reached the 19th floor without meeting anyone.

Mary had the chain on the door and she opened it very

slightly to peer at me, then asked me to recite my name and who had sent me, before the door was opened fully. She could have been a strikingly attractive 24-year-old if her long dark curls had been glossy not lusterless and matted, if the pale complexion had had colour, her blue eyes a spark of animation. In fact she looked weary and depressed beyond measure.

The apartment – home to Mary and her two sons four and six-years-old, was a single floor with a narrow hallway off which were two small bedrooms and a living room with a kitchen where a grease ingrained kitchen equipped with a cooker circa 1960s and chipboard cupboards worn away at the edges of the doors which scarcely clutched their hinges. The paintwork on the walls had dark mucky patches, as though blisters had burst on them; a window in the living room was broken and patched up with a sheet of cardboard; damp mould clumped around the ceiling of the bathroom; the boys' bedroom smelt of damp too.

Once Mary began talking she couldn't stop, a deluge of words telling how she had lived here three years; how the council never responded to her pleas for them to fix the window and the damp. How she was scared to go out after 5p.m. And in fact it was difficult to go out any time she had the children – who would look after them? To my enquiry, didn't she know other mothers in the block willing to share a bit of childcare, she gave me a look of pure panic. 'I wouldn't trust anyone here. No not the other mums, neither.'

I met Mary when writing an article for the Evening Standard about those whom Shelter, the housing charity, described as the homeless homed. In other words they have shelter of a sort but not for Mary. and too many others in equally grim circumstances, did home equate with safety and nurture. How could anyone say that their accommodation aids their ability to thrive, as the World Health Organisation believes housing should do?

Mary's husband had gone out one evening a year ago and never come back. Her sons had veered between aggression and depression. Today, the elder, inclined to hyperactivity she told, was running up and down the hall, in and out the bedrooms, impervious to Mary's weary demands that he stop.

'Welcome to my home, welcome to my hell', was what she said.

How could I have failed to see that the efforts of this young woman, struggling to bring up her children, were impeded rather than helped by the place she called home. This dismal nest, perched high in the squalid warehouse of similarly ghetto-ised inhabitants felt so devoid of anything you could call homely, of any aspect that might nourish the soul.

Is it really surprising that, when something as central to our lives as home is effectively a mockery of the word, a satire on the cosy pictures children are encouraged to draw, of rooms populated by calmly joyous families, that something feels painfully amiss?

Do we think it right that the most marginalised in our society, when it comes to wealth, employment, health, should also be deprived of what the philosopher Gaston Bachelard in his work *The Poetics of Space* (Beacon) spoke of as absolutely central to our emotional and psychic well-being?

'The importance of home as a place to dream, a place where the imagination can stretch itself outwards, upwards, supple as a gymnast's body. Our house is our corner of the world.… It is our first universe, a real cosmos in every sense of the word.… If I were asked to name the chief benefit of the house, I should say: the house shelters day-dreaming, the house protects the dreamer, the house allows one to dream in peace… I must show that the house is one of the greatest powers of integration for the thoughts, memories and dreams of mankind.' Without an adequate home, 'man would be a dispersed being. It maintains him through the storms of the heavens and through those of life'.

'Underclass'

As I was writing this police sirens were shrieking on the streets. It was the second day of the summer 2011 riots which erupted into several days of destruction and devastation – vandalism, looting and death. This began in the Tottenham area of London and spread to various London boroughs, then other major cities. What we saw was looting of small local shops, as well as theft from larger electronic, food and drink and clothes shops. Along with theft, muggings, carjackings and in the midst of all this, dreadfully, several people died.

There were among the rioters, certainly, the egregiously bad: career criminals and callous opportunists and such like, driving from their own areas outside, into the riot-wrecked areas to vandalise the stores with goods worth selling, then loading up as many as possible and driving off. It would be difficult to disagree with the many and vociferous critics who condemned them for pure criminality. But let's then pause, as others suggested at the time, to think about those young men, women and children from the areas in which they ran amok terrifying their neighbourhoods, committing criminal acts too. And, bizarrely it would seem, they burned down homes, razing, in the briefest time, the places where their own neighbours, people they had possibly grown up among, also lived.

But is it so strange? Or were we being given a powerful clue by the rioters, albeit unconscious or inchoate, into the reason these young from some of the most degraded areas in

Britain, desecrated the very places they belong. Writing, as I am, about the meaning of home in our lives, I have found myself dwelling on this and wondering how far these destructive, impulsive actions were a very graphic howl of rage against the meaning of these rioter's lives, emphasised by the places they call home.

When the link between poverty, deprivation and anti-social behaviour is made, as it is over and over and over in significant pieces of research, the homes in which the protagonists live are rarely mentioned specifically. Yet how can we fail to know, if we bother to look at our society with any kind of will to learn, how damaging the worst of housing and home environments can be? Can we really ignore the evidence pointing to how destructive the worst of homes and their environments of insecure housing so often are to the will to be a social citizen, a productive member of society, to have mental well-being.

Lynsey Hanley grew up on one of Europe's largest council estates – a cluster of inhospitable, high-rise flats outside Birmingham. And there are no sentimental memories, 'it can sap the spirit, suck out hope and ambition, and draw in apathy and nihilism'.

The experience was sufficiently searing, and created such political fury that Hanley, in her 20s, translated emotion into words writing an exploration of just what it means to grow up in housing so clearly labelling you as the least significant cog in society. To be seen as the group Charles Murray, researching working class Britain, and later Mrs Thatcher condemned as the lowest of people. The book Hanley wrote, *Estates* (Granta), is a beautifully crafted, visceral document, that no outside-looking-in sociologist could have produced. She understands with acuity what was happening to Mary and the thousands of others similarly housed around the country in squalid and unsafe high-rise flats, estates, terraces where danger and despair lurk.

Hanley, now in her 30s, is sweet-faced, with impressive composure, but it is the ferocity in her brushed-steel Birmingham accent that lets you know the seriousness of what she has to say. Sitting with me, in my home, where I am sharply aware of how much my life has been enriched by the aesthetically pleasing homes I have lived in, she is explaining that it is not just the quality of the physical home itself, but the poverty that is implicit in the bottom layer of housing, that smashes the spirit.

'It's four years since I wrote *Estates* and I was writing from a place of deep anger which I still have' Hanley tells. 'As a child I did a lot of observing and I saw an immense amount of frustration… I saw endless struggles about money, frustration at working so hard but not even managing to meet bills. There was massive stress. A friend of my mother's had loud music and stomping upstairs and drug dealers coming around but nobody would do anything about it. There was the way family relationships broke down under the consuming and ever-present anxiety over money. I saw people aging early and dying young. And collectively we saw no way things were likely to improve.'

'One of the things that defined my experience of growing up on the estate was going to school there. I had the chance to do a scholarship and go to one of the grammar schools in Birmingham, but I didn't take it. I was too young to know what it meant. I wound up going to a school that was at the bottom of the pile.'

Hanley describes the enormous fatalism in the community she grew up among. 'It really contradicts what Left wing people like to believe about working class people, which is that they are the agents of change if they did but know it. Endless poverty just makes you want to give up.'

Overcrowding

So let's step for a moment into such a life. Imagine how it would feel to know that if you lived on the lowest of incomes and were reliant on social housing, your children would probably be top of the list for the worst of everything. *The Family and Children's Longitudinal Study* (commissioned by the Department of Work and Pensions) conducted over 2001-05, found children living in the 20 most deprived areas in England, were the most likely to experience homes seriously in need of repair – here we are talking rats, mice, mites, crumbling masonry, dilapidated interiors, rising damp, mould, windows falling from their frames and so on – and to know how powerless you were to change things.

Shouldn't it shock us, in 2011, living in an affluent country, to learn from Shelter, the housing charity, of more than one million children living in overcrowded homes – a rise of 54,000 over two years from 2007 to 2009. In their later Full House report they revealed a quarter of children sleeping in living and dining rooms. As the bottom line for homes that enable us to thrive Shelter lists, 'privacy, security, adequate space, affordable costs…' In 2011 some 7.4 million homes in England failed to meet the government's own Decent Homes Standard.

When we talk of overcrowding it is not the kind of temporary squash we have with Christmas guests, an extended family stay, or a temporary student flat with shared rooms. We are talking about an inescapable 365 days a year of people existing in cramped proximity, with no place for solitude, for tranquil reflection, no play space for children, and where in too many cases teenagers of different gender share a bedroom. Where it is heard of for a broom cupboard under the stairs to double up as sleeping space.

One fifth of the teenagers of the opposite sex, surveyed, must share a room. What this means is no privacy – ever. At worst it ups the chance of sex abuse by siblings, something we now know is uncomfortably prevalent although not confined to those in cramped homes. At best it means nowhere quiet to study or think, fat chance of peace. It's hardly surprising to learn that such conditions make it tough for children to perform well at school, and plenty of reports link educational failure with poverty.

It was reported in February of 2012 that more than a quarter of children in the UK are not reaching their potential at school because of poor living conditions and unwell parents.

Researchers from the University of London's Institute of Education and the University of Sussex analysed the intellectual development of 18,000 children between the ages of nine months and five years.

They found that children were likely to have stunted intellectual development if they were exposed to two or more disadvantages, one is living in an overcrowded home. Even so politicians are mercilessly quick to turn their backs on such findings and instead see not reaching potential at school as a failure of the child, or possibly the teacher, but not society.

School is one thing, but the importance of strong and supportive family bonds cannot be over-estimated, and this, of course, is something the Coalition Government is quick to stress. So should they ignore the fact that growing children thrust into such proximity, and in circumstances where frustrations and stress are hot-housed, often feel unhappy with their families? More than three quarters of families claimed their relationships were affected by living conditions. Not for them the tender sense of a home built with care and concern that Alain de Botton conjures in *The Architecture of Happiness* (Hamish Hamilton).

'It has provided not only physical but also psychological sanctuary. It has been the guardian of identity... It's rooms... give evidence of a happiness to which architecture has made its distinctive contribution.'

Danny Dorling at the University of Sheffield has done studies demonstrating that the place a person is born remains the key thing in determining their future, status, health and wealth. As was the case with Lynsey Hanley, Danny Dorling has been much influenced by personal experience. He told the *Guardian* newspaper how his views were shaped by growing up on an estate on the fringes of Oxford.

'I thought as a child that what people did or where they got to depended on the estate where they lived.'

That childish thought was translated into science by the adult who worked on a study led by George Davey Smith, professor of clinical epidemiology at the University of Bristol. This work revealed huge differences in life chances depending on where in the country, or where within a single city, people lived. People in deprived areas were not only dying prematurely but the gap in life expectancy between rich and poor – a key indicator of progress – was widening.'

It hardly comes as a surprise to learn that everyone's health suffers in such conditions, and especially that of children. Those living in overcrowded conditions (*Chance Of A Lifetime*, Shelter) are ten times more likely to contract meningitis than others. There is a direct link between childhood tuberculosis and overcrowding, children in these conditions are more likely than their well-housed peers to have respiratory illnesses and their growth is often impaired.

In 2011 the Child Poverty Action Group produced chilling

figures illustrating how things have not changed. How from birth, life expectancy is impacted upon by social class – that is if the child lives. In the lower social group (routine and manual occupations) infant mortality is 5.9 infant deaths per 1,000 live births. This is 20 per cent higher than the average 4.9 per 1,000 babies born alive.

The poorer a child, and the less health-supporting the home, the poorer their health is likely to be into adulthood. For instance three year olds in households with an income below £10,000 are 2.5 times more likely to suffer chronic illness than children in households with incomes over £52,000.

But how much do we care? The Black report of the expert committee into health inequality in the UK, published by the government in 1980, found a great difference between the health of the haves and the have-nots – economic inequality was overwhelmingly the reason and they found the gap widening. You might expect that to have been a wake-up call for a society that prides itself on being humane, and espousing equal opportunities, but how much pressure has been put, collectively, on governments to radically reform those things, and at the centre of them, social housing, responsible for this health profile?

The Child Poverty Action Group concluded, 'poverty makes people's lives shorter and more brutal than they need to be. Poverty is not simply about being on a low income and doing without – it is also about being denied power, respect, good health, education, housing, basic self-esteem to participate in social activities.' And every one of these is intimately tied to the kind of home you live in.

Larry sees how true this was for his second son, Brian who was taken into care after years of an ultimately unsuccessful struggle by Larry and his mother to find a way to show him love and discipline, to keep him from rejecting them, in favour of the street group he was associating with.

'He didn't want us, or life at home. He was moody, hostile telling us we were nothing, we hadn't made anything of our lives. And home was a part of it all right. He used to tell us he hated living in a box where he couldn't have a life of his own, couldn't bring friends home because with just the sitting room they had to sit with us. So he went out, and we couldn't stop him. He just walked, and then he started getting picked up for petty crime. In the end social services decided he was out of control. Only then he cried and said he wanted to be home with us'.

Yet even if the young living at the bottom of the housing scale do have a particularly tough lot and feel bad about it, surely this does not excuse the outrageous behaviour we saw in the 2011 riots? Isn't the idea that we understand a little more and condemn a little less vacuous marshmallow liberal posturing? A stance likely to encourage yet more anarchy? I hear the voices raised making these points, pointing out how just last generation people lived with over-crowding, falling-down, infested homes, and yet they seemed to find a way to live with dignity and bring up social-minded children. It is of course a distinctly partial truth – there were plenty who did not manage so well and where all kinds of physical and psychological torment went on behind doors and curtains.

Pause to watch a couple of Dennis Potter's studies of domestic life to get the idea. Think Lipstick on Your Collar, Pennies From Heaven, John Braine's Look Back In Anger, a sharply autobiographical piece of writing, where the cramped one-room flat – 'unspeakably dirty and squalid' as one reviewer put it, in which a stifled Jimmy Porter lived and fought with his classy wife Alison.

In his film Time and City, we see Terence Davies's raging, albeit with lyrical shots and poetic script, at memories of his

Liverpool childhood. He evokes the cramped, cobblestone, smoke-filled streets of back-to-back terraces, decaying brick tenements and children playing in squalid rubble-filled lots. Davies saw these homes as so lacking in inspiration or elevation of the spirit that he felt he lived 'a slow death'. He saw how those in charge of social housing promised housing estates as the offer of something better, that 'a New Jerusalem was going to arise'. But instead those with least clout in society were once again led to understand that they were not worth much. 'They (council estates) were built shoddily demonstrating the British genius for creating the dismal. They were slums in the making, despite the government's commitment to improve lives.'

Besides, life is different today. The gilded memories Davies has from his years between 7 and 11 had much to do with the closeness of neighbourhood, games on the street, things that mitigated his father's violence, his own sense of being trapped in slums that could never improve lives. But these days, as is so often pointed out, the close-knit threads of community have been pulled loose by social mobility, a pace of life and aspirations that leave little time or often inclination for dallying on the doorstep having a chat, listening to a downtrodden neighbour's woes, for visiting an elderly neighbour. What we have replaced this with is a culture that encourages us to devote our time to finding common cause with the well to do, the famous, those we feel reflect well on who we are, and to develop a passion for wealth and a sense of entitlement.

Peter Oborne, columnist for the *Daily Telegraph*, stood out against a simplistic popular raging against the rioters as collectively an amoral lot, giving his analysis of the double standards and hypocrisy that was distorting Britain's values.

'I believe the criminality in our streets cannot be dissociated from the moral disintegration in the highest ranks of modern British society. The last two decades have seen a terrifying decline in standards among the British governing elite. It has become acceptable for our politicians to lie and to cheat. An almost universal culture of selfishness and greed has grown up'

Which brings us back to David Cameron, by this time Prime Minister, stating without missing a beat, that a looter who had taken a plasma TV set was simply a thief because he had not saved up for it as other people do.

As his children will be asked to do when they want a telly, do we presume?

You can hear approval from the auditorium at this black and white morality, but it suggests mighty little empathy with the reality of living on a very low income. There is usually a minute margin – if any – for saving up. So let's take that idea further. Take someone like Tom who so hated his home on a tough estate, feared the older boys lurking everywhere it seemed, getting their fun from intimidating kids like him, that he would go almost anywhere else but home after school. Should we expect him and those like him to save up for homes in the safer, more attractive areas, if that is what they want?

An Imaginative Approach

Oborne was describing the distortion wreaked by inequality of wealth that Kate Wilkinson and Richard Pickett pointed in their book *The Spirit Level*. Here they surveyed a number of countries comparable to the UK and the US, showing the way in which inequality of wealth affects every measure of well-being. The greater the inequality the greater the actual disadvantage as well as the disaffection of the people. And Britain has one of the highest levels of wealth inequality.

Every day in every way we are told, and shown, that those

in the classes where there is wealth, where privilege rules with homes a very visible symbol of status, are the superiors in a meretricious society.

Nor can those who live in what could be called a parallel social universe, expect to gain entrée to such a world. For most the chances to get on their bikes and seek improvement are pitifully small. Employment might well make a good deal of difference to how they behave, but work is often very hard to get, or as we saw with high unemployment in 2011 and 2012, borderline impossible for many. And who can doubt there are employers who would put an application with school and home in the worst postcode areas, into the rubbish bin?

Nor will bad school grades get much of a look in. Yet can we really wonder that children living with the kind of deprivation talked about here do not function well? That they fall behind at school, fail to get homework done, are often too tired or stressed to concentrate and may well have behavioural problems? Yet we see politicians becoming ever more punitive towards these children, wanting tougher teaching, stringent higher standards demanded, greater discipline to deal with the fall-out from our least fortunate children's behaviour. As I write I hear Education Minister Michael Gove talking of schools being taught by military men, as a way of instilling good behaviour. Is this really the best a man whose job it is to understand the reasons behind educational and behavioural problems in the classroom, can come up with?

In fact it is others, outside the myopia of government-think who are taking a successfully imaginative approach to some of the problems that manifest so often in school and at home. Ruth Ibegbuna runs the innovative Reclaim project in Manchester, working with the most alienated young to find ways to improve their lives and prospects. She sees daily how: 'the impact of poor housing and disorganised households can certainly make life much harder for vulnerable youngsters. Often the confusion, conflict and chaos that characterises their mind-set is a direct reflection of the interior of their homes. Many children at home struggle to find a safe, calm space to call their own.'

Ibegbuna is a strikingly handsome, fierce-minded Nigerian woman who chose to work with the young she saw as both most desperate and most abused by an outside world, and most notably attacked by a media, that can be merciless in condemning them as the lowest of low. I have known Ruth for some years and been to see where she works. I have sat in on a seminar about her programme of focused discussion, activities, tasks designed to create a sense of self worth and autonomy in the young recruits.

I have met some of the youngsters severely at risk, teetering on the brink of falling into the prison system, acting out their sense of impotence, insecurity, despair in bizarrely unhelpful ways. I listened to her talking of the girls in a dedicated group that she runs who are 'sweary, smokey, loud-mouthed, promiscuous – and under it all so often just kids in need of emotional support.'

The homes they might turn to are very often part of the problem Ibegbuna says, telling of a 13-year-old girl who was hanging out in the local park night after night because she didn't want to be at home. She was beginning to go off with boys and Ruth, assuming her family would do something, rang home. The girl's mother answered, listened and then told Ruth to stop interfering and get out of her life.

That is one tale, and there are plenty more of parents whose own loveless, careless lives – lives of depression and apathy, drug and alcohol habits – are too regularly linked with living in the twilight zone of life. Living in a way that can strip them of the ability or the will to parent their children or provide a save haven for them. Parents who have known nothing but deprivation and too much rejection themselves, and who cannot galvanise the optimism or faith to believe they could make it otherwise for their young.

To make the point she drives me from the smartly rehabilitated centre of Manchester with its streets of stylish shops, an overflow of up-market coffee houses and little indication that Britain is in recession, on to the main arterial road out of town. The houses here become steadily more decrepit; some are burnt-out shells, others boarded up. We reach Gorton, once a place of vibrant industry, but now that is gone it has become one of the area's most deprived districts. We reach a terrace of houses with battered paintwork on windows and doors, rubbish piled into the tiny front gardens of many, an air of neglect.

The home of Liz, whom Ruth and I are visiting, is different. The garden is neat with flowers planted and inside the small sitting room has papered walls and fresh white paintwork. There are pictures and photographs on the wall.

Liz has a face of strong bones and a steely look, but then comes the enormous smile and gritty laugh. She and her husband of 22-years, father to Damian, 15 and Jason,18, moved here reluctantly, ten years ago, when they were rehoused. She recalls

'It was a run down shack and the area was very grim with the houses run to rack and ruin, drug dealers on the streets, syringes in the gardens, and parents who didn't seem to give a monkeys about their kids so they have no respect because they get no respect. I soon realized there was no cohesion, no community. The kids protect themselves by forming gangs from about the age of ten, and when you intervene if they are picking on the little 'uns you get the gun sign.'

She describes the despair she and her husband felt: 'We

wanted our boys to have a nice home and feel safe. We've always been a close family doing things together even if it was only shopping or going to a park. We always eat together and if the kids seem worried we talk to them. But it was very clear what a challenge this area would be. Doing up the house was one thing but helping Jason when his nose was broken by a couple of kids as he was walking home at 7p.m. one evening was another.'

Once he started secondary school Damian started looking on the internet at guns, he knew the names of all class A drugs and would stand around on the streets talking with dealers. He bunked off school regularly and Liz says, 'he got worse mouthing off at us and walking out the house. I got to the point of asking the police to speak to him but he didn't like that and my husband and I were seriously wondering whether we would have to put him into care to get him out of the environment.'

It was at this point that Damian's school asked if they could enrol him on the Reclaim programme – Ibegbuna had visited with some of her 'graduates' – they had been as out of control as Damian – who were talking about how the programme had helped them change and had involved their families in the process. Liz smiles, 'Agreeing to that was the best thing we ever did. Damian was given a mentor who really took trouble with him. Some of the activities at Reclaim were based around trying to improve the neighbourhood, asking local people what they would like to see. Damian made friends with other kids who were questioning how they could improve their life chances and because he has seen how the community police try to help people, and particularly the kids, he has decided that is what he would like to do. He began studying again and started wanting to be home with us.'

Liz, offering a large, striped mug of coffee, knows this

sounds like a 'miracle tale' and obviously she says, it took time for Damian 'to begin to see that there were opportunities for him in life. One of the troubles with living in an area like Gorton is that so many people feel abandoned and hopeless. But now the boys spend a lot of time with us, and I am like a Rottweiler if I think anyone is trying to seduce my kids back into a bad life.'

Clearly Liz's sons have a home life where, even against tough odds, their parents have struggled to protect and care for them. Without that and when life gets too tough in too many ways, mental health issues at times closely linked to anti-social and criminal behaviour may be the thing we notice.

Environmental Impact on Mental Health

So here we come full circle once more to the matter of how the dismal, spirit-draining and insecure kind of homes and environments we have been discussing, can have a profoundly damaging impact on mental health.

There's a pretty unequivocal statement from Professor Louis Appleby, former National Clinical Director of Mental Health, 'Employment, housing... are as important to people's mental health as the treatment they receive...'

None of this is a secret to the Department of Health which in 2009 published *New Horizons: A Shared Vision for Mental Health* in which they too pointed out the relationship between poor housing and environment and mental health problems particularly in the young. Indeed successive governments have commissioned enough research into this relationship to paper the walls of Downing Street yet little seems to change.

Gina's story is an example of how a parent's mental health state, worsened by housing, may impact profoundly on children.

'I am a single parent and yet no consideration was given to my mental health issues, even though they had taken me to the doctor several times. My flat was on an estate renown in the area for being isolated, dirty and the flat itself smaller than a usual one-bed flat with no storage space. The walls were paper thin so there was constant noise from neighbours. I cannot sleep or function in this rabbit hutch but the housing association say I am adequately housed. I feel suicidal at times and I am in danger of losing my daughter forever because of what my housing circumstances are doing to me.'

When I sat on the landings of young offender institutions interviewing boys and girls, young men and women, about where they had ended up in life, for my book *Locked In – Locked Out – The Experience of Young Offenders in Prison and Out of Society* (Gulbenkian Foundation), it seemed very clear how much their disturbed and distorted mental health had played its part in the impulsive, irresponsible, dangerous, devil-may-care crimes they had committed, and on the other side how little ability they had to find a way to deal with their mental health problems.

Housing was certainly not the whole story, but I did recognise how the place many of these youngsters lived, what they could expect when they crossed the threshold into home, the knowledge engraved into their psyches that this place was good enough for them, made its mark. As did the setting for home in which they knew that they would have to deal with the mean streets that those of us living in better areas are able to avoid. There is the ever-present knowledge of danger and threat, along with the awareness that, when it comes to affiliations and gangs you are, to borrow George W. Bush's memorable phrase, 'with us, or against us'. There is the boredom of a place where open space has been sold off. In one of many such cases a makeshift football pitch was turned into a rubbish tip by the council, sports grounds which may have been the only bit of open space for frolicking and letting loose without some voice or notice forbidding it.

At the School of Psychology, University of East London, Dr Tom Dickins has studied what may be going on with young people 'stressed out and struggling'. Their mental health disorders, he contends, may be an adapted response to stress with depression, anxiety, poor control of emotions and behaviour simply at the extreme end of normal. For example, he explains, cortisol is a useful stress hormone that aids the production of glucose to increase energy used in flight or fight responses to threat or competition in extreme situations. But high levels of cortisol, and when it is called on too often, has negative consequences longer term for mental and cardiac health.

It's not difficult to see how life circumstances would have played its part in the case of Zakk Sackett, jailed in 2011 for the catastrophic rape and murder of Jessie Wright, a girl he had known from childhood. He grew up on the notorious North London Bemerton Estate, surrounded by alienated gangs, a good deal of bullying of the least able. It was after Zackett had committed his gruesome crime, was arrested then convicted, that shocked concern beamed down on Sackett's grim homeland, its culture, and Sackett himself.

We learnt that he had a low IQ, 'complex emotional needs' and his childhood had been a grim distortion of care and sanctuary. His father left home when he was little, his mother was stabbed to death by another woman at a party. He watched as his grandfather was brutally knifed and beaten to death. Foster placements broke down with saddening predictability. Neighbours on the estate talked of how people were scared of Sackett, even his youth worker. He committed a number of crimes from theft to violent assaults against women, and even the police could not get control over him.

The irony is that, in the midst of all this, Jessie had

befriended Sackett, but he was beyond understanding what straightforward friendship meant.

Perhaps it was growing up with a forensic psychiatrist for a father, reading his 1950s study of psychopathology *The Mind of the Murderer*, that has led my work towards understanding the motivations of our behaviour, and particularly the most unacceptable behaviour, the story behind the surface events. So I listened with interest to Dr Dickins describe, at a seminar organised by the young people's mental health charity YoungMinds, responses to stress of many kinds. He pointed to the kind of impulsive, eruptive behaviour characterised in the 2011 riots, but also in the regular seemingly random, violent crimes on the streets and estates, particularly of the most embattled areas. Areas where, very often that word 'respect' has assumed a mythical status, becoming a measure of worth when where you live, where you are educated, who will mix with you, so often label you without value.

The quest for respect is, of course, the underbelly to competition. A competition to be top dog, to have power and control, to be admired. All of which means we would do well to listen when Dr Dickins says that studies show how social status and subordination affect cortisol levels, very possibly pushing our mental state out of kilter.

'The Logic of Discontent'

It doesn't take a great stretch of the imagination to see how living in a comfortless home which seems not a root but a trap can easily exacerbate this. Philip Slater, a former professor of Sociology and author of The Pursuit of Loneliness, his contemplation of a competitive and atomised society, sees the bottom line as the if-you-don't-belong-to-society-it-can't-hurt-you approach. While Richard Sennett and Jonathan Cobb who have devoted long careers to the study of working class culture make an interesting point in their book *The Hidden Injuries of Class* that links directly back to the rioting in communities that we saw in the summer of 2011: 'the logic of discontent leads people to turn on each other rather than on the "system".'

This may be an own goal but it's an accessible form of protest, on familiar territory, whereas it is harder to turn on the parts of society who appear to be well insulated by the comparative palaces which they own. Yet surely there is nothing neutral about knowing you can scarcely walk past the best appointed houses without being moved on as a potentially dishonest loiterer, that to live in a place you want to escape from rather than being a place to which you wish to retreat.

The way Andrea Dunbar, whose life was re-evoked in the new millennium with Clio Barnard's film about her, *The Arbor*, can be seen as an own goal too. But little addles the brain, pushes askew the mental compass, in the way that abuse does. Whether it is physical, emotional or sexual abuse it pollutes and poisons, creating a domestic hell.

You see this vividly portrayed in the tale of Andrea Dunbar's short life lived on the notoriously grim, racist Buttershaw Estate in Bradford, Yorkshire. Her enormous talent surfaced while she was still at school, where she wrote her first play, *The Arbor*, aged 15. She went on to have three plays performed at the prestigious Royal Court Theatre before she died in 1990 aged 20.

Dunbar was one of eight children with an abusive father and a life – the subject of her plays which include Rita, Sue and Bob too – where a pattern of addiction, violence and racism were how it was. She had three children by different men, and as a teenage single mother spent 18 months in a refuge for battered women after leaving the Pakistani father of her first daughter Lorraine. *The Arbor* was a chilling illustration of how, in the family, the cycle of deprivation can run through generations.

Lorraine, through whom the story of *The Arbor* is told, grew up in a community where people would not acknowledge her half-Pakistani identity. Although Barnard put it on record that the neighbours did what they could to support Lorraine and her siblings after Andrea died, when Lorraine was just nine.

From then on her merciless life crashed downwards. Lorraine was raped aged 14, exposed early to crack and heroin. The men she took up with were often violent and she endured prostitution.

The cycle of deprivation stopped for Lorraine's five-year-old son Harris when in 2006 he died after ingesting his mother's methadone. She was given a long custodial sentence and it says something about what home had meant in her life that she told the only place she had a roof over her head and felt safe was in prison.

That is a dreadful reflection on how far, as a society, we care about lives characterised by the environmental, physical and sexual abuse that young people in our country endure. It is so often wrapped into home life, private life not to be revealed to the outside world, and of course children are especially prone to fear of what will happen to them should they tell the family secrets.

Shut up, Put up

Abuse, of course, happens in all kinds of homes and is by no means confined to the lowest socio-economic classes. Domestic violence, sexual abuse, relentless mental cruelty create emotional havoc in every part of the social scale, for both genders and all ages. The feelings of shame and desire for secrecy may be even greater in homes where these things are not supposed to happen. Keep the drapes closed, the front door with its tasteful Farrow and Ball paintwork, firmly locked. Shut up, put up and possibly dull things a bit with the gin bottle, is the best way.

That's how it was for Suzanne who grew up in the most apparently embracing of homes with pale, sunlit rooms, a spacious kitchen in which everyone could gather, a garden of well tended lawn stretching towards a fishpond. The well planted herbaceous borders and flower beds dazzled with every shade of blue and purple bloom. It was commuter-belt Home Counties where neighbours were friendly on a day to day basis, enjoying an aperitif together later in the day, at weekends the men headed for the links, the women held coffee mornings. Everything in its place. The children, publically biddable and quiet, played together, and if anybody spotted Suzanne's anguish, it was never mentioned.

From when she was four years Suzanne's father would tell his wife, whom she remembers always nodding compliantly, that he would put their daughter to bed. And so he did, getting her into her nightdress, tucking her into the crisp sheets, with a little pat. 'That was the signal to let me know he was going to get in beside me. It happened five nights a week, and the only time I was safe was when we went on a family camping holiday with my brothers, and all slept in one tent. I hated what he did, the pain, the weight of him, the sticky wetness he left behind, but if I asked him not to do it he just laughed and said 'now why wouldn't you enjoy this? It's what grown-ups like to do.' And then the warning that Mummy would be cross with me if she knew.

'Some years on when I was at puberty, and desperate, not wanting to be in my home, but not knowing where else I could go, I told my mother. I hoped she would stop it, but she was angry with me. Very angry.'

Even so Suzanne's parents split up, and for a brief time alone with her mother and brothers, her father gone from the house, Suzanne was at peace.

Then her mother re-married and although her step-father did not sexually abuse her, he hit her – often – when she displeased him. Her loathing of him showed, she recalls and, 'when I was sixteen he threw me out of home. I went to stay with a relative until I was old enough to get a flat myself, but I never said a word. I had learned that my experiences were unacceptable. But when people used to come to the house and say 'what a lovely home you have, aren't you lucky?' I wanted to scream 'it's a poisonous home. Home is the place you can be tortured.'

Years later, with several abusive relationships and a broken marriage behind her, Suzanne is telling me she has no feelings for her second husband, she cannot bear the idea of sex with him and in spite of their having five children, wants to leave him. And yet there are tears in her eyes as she says this, and then she is pouring it all out, how he's not a bad man, he has wanted to be there for her, but she is the one who has drawn away and shut off all feelings.

She recalls how thoroughly she defended herself against her father by cutting off all emotions, how his kissing her on the lips was as bad as anything, and she cannot now tolerate this with her husband. Yes, they had good sex in the beginning, and being pregnant was a happy preoccupation, but now the children are grown up and she can no longer be the mother creating a safe and happy home for them. She is a woman whose emotions have been so cauterised by life growing up in an unsafe, abusive home that she wonders how she might learn to bring them to life again. Wonders if she can ever make a relationship work.

Molly Reisman was not beaten by the husband she married, but he became increasingly mentally cruel to her when she changed from being a housewife, ever at home, to a student. It was then he started rubbishing her friends.

'I had always felt ugly as a girl and I was grateful he wanted to marry me. Things became difficult when I decided I wanted to get a degree with a view to working in finance. It was hard study and he became very resentful of my involvement. So I went to watch him play rugby at weekends, I learned to cook properly and do dinner parties and to show there was time for his wishes at home. But it was never enough, he was always angry with me although he didn't hurt me physically, but I lived in fear of the contempt he heaped on me.

Then he became obsessed with having a bigger house and that meant that all our money went towards the mortgage, we never went out or had any money to spend on enjoying ourselves at home and when I begged for us to go out he would be very cold and refuse.'

Aged 30 Molly had their first child but found it hard to engage with the baby. 'My emotions were so cut off but my being tied with the children – we had three very quickly – gave him power. He was very critical of me for always being tired, I got very confused trying not to anger him because then he shouted at me. Friends used to ask why I put up with it but I could see no way out. He was also very hard on the children, believing they must be controlled from very early on, so they didn't feel at ease in the home either. They were very wary of their father.'

When the children were at school she defied her husband and got a job which was, she says, 'a wonderful break from the oppressiveness at home, but I felt nervous all the time. My husband hated me working, but he accepted we needed the money.'

The pressure of trying to keep the home as her husband wanted it, and do her job proved too much. Molly had a breakdown and quit her job. She remembers vividly her husband saying, 'see, I always said you had madness in you.' In between crying fits she worked maniacally at home trying to prove her worth. 'We had 160 roses and they all had greenfly. I felt I must get rid of it. He insisted I should get weeds from between the paving stones. I ironed his shirts on Sunday.'

Then came the day she argued with her husband and he shut her out of the house. 'After that I decided I couldn't go on. I told him I had to leave but he then locked me in the house and tried to strangle me with a tie. My eldest son heard and was petrified, and my husband then threatened to kill himself which was terrifying for the children. I knew I just had to get out.' In fact she didn't go but life fell into 'complete chaos'. The central heating stopped working, the roof began leaking, the washing machine flooded and she heard that her husband was having an affair.

'It was as though my internal state was mirrored in the house. Any sense of it being a home in the sense of a safe and happy place was completely ended. I was committed to a psychiatric hospital because I just couldn't function.'

It was when she came out that Molly realized she could cope with working and got a cherished job using her degree training. 'I decided to divorce my husband because it seemed the only way I could keep a grip on myself. Moving house seemed a vital part of removing myself from the force field of my husband's controlling behaviour. I was warned I wouldn't get the children and as my husband had told me over and over that I was a crap mother I believed this. But I got custody. We moved into a much smaller place and we were very hard up, so it was not all easy but I felt I could make the home I wanted at last. We got cats and later a dog, the kids had their friends to play a lot. I could have my friends around in the evening to for a drink and a laugh.'

That felt like a happy home, but not as much so as the place Molly moved to, in Glasgow, when her children left home. She got a job there, got divorced and had a 'lovely flat with big Georgian windows in a bohemian area. I was aware of this being a place I could call home and feel at peace.'

Although women are the most likely to suffer domestic violence of one kind and another so that home becomes a place of demolition of the spirit, they are not the only ones. Some two in five of all men are victims of domestic violence according to the campaigning equal rights group Parity, quoting Home Office statistics and the British Crime Survey. As has often been said men may feel too ashamed to tell what is happening, or they are not always taken seriously by the police, so the figures are not entirely reliable except to do away with the myth that women do not abuse their men.

At the Mankind organization, which runs a helpline, they tell what they encounter.

'We receive calls from male victims across all age ranges and professions. From dustmen and doctors, bankers to builders. From men in their 20s to men in their 80s and from across England, Northern Ireland, Scotland and Wales.'

For Steven Bennett home became a place of anguished confusion, he could not grasp why things went wrong, in the way they did. But like many men, he felt too uncomfortable about admitting he was the victim of a woman's abuse to do anything, so there was a silence around his domestic life.

'The relationship between me and my wife had been of the whirlwind variety: passionate, tactile, and intense. At the start we made a positive impression wherever we went – a beautiful happy couple, for whom anything seemed possible. We were a radiant pair.'

They married about a month after the birth of their son. Steven is aware now that, 'I ought possibly to have thought more about whether our relationship really was healthy before we tied the knot. I preferred to believe that any cracks and imperfections would be resolved by the fairy-tale ending of a wedding.'

He had preferred not to believe the changes that took place when they discovered that a baby was on the way, were significant.

'I was delighted. My wife was distraught. She began to behave oddly and a nasty, dark side of her character emerged. She told me that I did not earn enough to keep her, and that I had trapped her. Then I heard that I was not good looking enough, that I was too old for her. This gradually devolved into aggressive verbal outbursts about my odour, my physique and perceived lack of muscle. Derision of my sexual prowess followed, and odious comparisons with that of her former lover. During her pregnancy she declared that she was revolted by the fact that something of me – my son – was actually alive inside her.'

Steven says he took this in his stride and put it down to hormonal imbalances due to the pregnancy and the post-natal depression that followed. Life improved and their son was born. They got married. He got a new job with a 35 per cent salary rise and assumed this would make his wife happy.

'The job required that we move to London from abroad, where we'd lived when we met. We settled on a three storey town house in a leafy road in SW London which she wanted and I knew it was important she should have a home that felt right.

I encouraged her to socialise, to meet people in the area, and suggested that she might like to meet a woman of her own nationality whom I'd met at work. She too had recently come to England and said she'd be glad to make a new friend and to chat in her own language. But my wife reacted badly and coarsely suggested that I was having sex with the woman.'

Steven tells that his wife became physically abusive but would not explain what was wrong. He was kicked and scratched. 'Objects were thrown at me – dinner plates, ornaments, anything that lay to hand. Books were ripped up. I was told that my son was not mine.

'My wife seemed to be on a quest to prove that anything and everything I did was wrong and as home was where she spent a lot of time, much centred on that. The house had too many stairs; the garden was too small; it was too far from my office so I was gone too long during the day; she was lonely and had no friends; I didn't put enough effort into looking after my son '

One day, Steven relates, his wife, 'hit me so hard on the shin with a solid object (I'm not even sure what it was) that I could see the bone through the wound. I told lies about how it had happened.'

In due course they separated. Steven went regularly to visit his son. 'I would stay at her flat, initially in his bedroom on a mattress on the floor. We enjoyed time alone in the mornings when he woke early, and we developed a routine of games on the floor, bath and then breakfast.

On one occasion we went with my son to a restaurant. There was an atmosphere due to some issue my wife had raised about insufficient money being paid to her I was already sending her a third of my salary every month, but she was becoming aggressive. It was evidently not enough. I asked her to calm down and not to make a scene. She promptly poured beer over my pizza and spat in my face. My son, who was aged two at the time, mimicked her; he poured his orange juice over the table and also spat in my face. She laughed, applauded him, picked him up, and left the restaurant. She probably laughed again when she picked up 95 per cent of my assets five years later after our divorce settlement.'

He kept quiet about all that was going on and, 'I remained loyal to my little dysfunctional family and kept things to myself. This persisted until our separation, and inevitable acrimonious divorce. Despite all the attempts I made for the sake of my son to keep the relationship from becoming a battlefield, I have now not seen him for over 10 years.'

Steven is regretful that he didn't attempt to get help for himself and his wife, 'had we tackled the issues earlier, many arguments might have been avoided. Had I approached it all differently I might even have retained contact with my son. Now, looking back, I realise that it did not have to be that way. I should have jumped over my pride and asked for help.'

The Place2Be

Even the mildest abuse at home can make it feel like a place to escape from, but there is little worse than children being abused and with no idea that they might be able to do anything about it. How well Benita Refson, director of the charity The Place2Be which works with disturbed and disturbing children in schools, understands how home may be 'unsafe, lacking in warmth and the nurture needed to survive', for children. She may be elegant, stylish, her gleaming blonde hair beautifully styled in a way that seems well suited to the fashion world, but she has never waivered in believing she made the right choice in turning her career in this direction.

As a 20-yearold, fresh out of Rodean and the Sorbonne, Benita was offered an assistant editor job on Vogue magazine. It was a much coveted post, she knew, but her real wish was to work with children with mental health problems. So she joined

The Place2Be, started by Camilla Batmangelidjh, of Kid's Company, and in due course took over as director. The organisation takes counselling into nearly 150 of Britain's schools, where they are 'embedded' with rooms and highly trained staff, giving one to one counselling. They see many of the 80 per cent of children in these schools with desperately impoverished backgrounds and behavioural difficulties.

Benita reflects: 'our brief is to deal with the wellbeing of children and their families because that way we may be able to find ways to make things better at home. The children we work with have all sorts of worries from friendships to bereavement, domestic violence, gang culture or crime.'

Luke was a 10-year-old boy who caused concern at school because of frequent absences and lateness. The school learnt of his mother's mental health problems, including panic attacks, depression and alcohol misuse. Luke had been separated both from his sibling (who was placed in care some years earlier) and from his father, who was living out of the city with another partner and who was chronically unwell. It is not difficult to see how home felt very unsafe both because of his mother's problems and the fear that he too could be taken away, as his sibling had been.

Luke was a very lonely child. He had few friends. The Place2Be provided one-to-one counselling for Luke to give him space and positive attention. His mother, for all her own difficulties, became very supportive of this referral and was able to come into school twice to talk about it (after a two-year period before this when she did not once come to the school). In order to be fully involved with Luke's needs, the counsellor went to case meetings with the Children & Families Department and had regular contact with the Head, Deputy Head and class teacher to consider what was happening for Luke at home as well as at school. He made very good use of the weekly sessions although there was a difficult start where he missed a few, but he then began to arrive at school every day on time, and the fact his mother was involved, too, made home life with her easier.

Stephen Langley Adams is the regional manager at The Place2Be and has been involved in evaluating their school based help. He says, 'In the children whose behaviour is seriously of concern and where they are exhibiting conduct disorder, severe behavioural problems, and are at risk of exclusion, we see clearly a link between home and home circumstances and how the children conduct themselves. We work with children to try to mitigate their problems, but it would be so much better if the fundamental structure of their lives were sorted out.'

A Congregation of Negatives

Which takes us back to research available to help the government get a grasp on reality. In the summer of 2011 the Institute for Social and Economic Research (ISER), based at Essex University, talked of 'the magnitude of inequalities in the pre-school year occurring in the UK today… of the poorest families who are seven to eight times more likely than their more advantaged peers to exhibit serious social and emotional problems requiring clinical attention.

Might we be helped to grasp it a little better if we heard what Dr. Martin Teicher, an associate professor of psychiatry at Harvard and director of the Biopsychiatry Research Program at McLean Hospital in Belmont, has to say? He has been at the forefront of new research linking abuse to brain-wave abnormalities.

In one of the first major studies in the field published in *The Journal of Neuropsychiatry and Clinical Neurosciences* in 1993, Teicher described reviewing the records of 115 consecutive admissions to a child and adolescent psychiatric hospital. He found brain wave abnormalities in 54 percent of patients with an abuse history, but in only 27 percent of non-abused patients. And 72 percent of the patients in the sample with a history of both physical and sexual abuse had these neurological abnormalities.

These neurobiological findings show that trauma – physical abuse, sexual abuse and neglect – dramatically affect both the structure and chemistry of the developing brain thus very possibly contributing to the behavioural and learning problems that plague about three-quarters of children he describes as, 'mired in the child welfare system. Although these brain changes aren't necessarily permanent, and interventions in time can help rewire the brain and put psychological development back on track.'

It would be hard to disagree with the social services commissioner Harry Spence when he adds to this, "Neuroscience has helped to clarify our mission. We must do more than just protect children after the brain damage has been done. We must also provide loving environments because they are fundamental to healing on a physiological level'.

I sometimes contemplate how much, much harder it would have been to provide a loving environment if I had been living in a place that was not only aesthetically ugly, but where life was lived on the edge, where risk stalked the streets, where there seemed little to look forward to. Because, after all, the love one pours into an environment is a product of feeling good about oneself and if we are talking about children, the faith we have in our ability to be good parents.

This can be a tough call for all kinds of parents. Post-natal depression, the recognition of how much of yourself you must give up to children's needs and so on can get in the way of creating a reliable, unconditional loving. But add hardship, an environment that sticks two fingers up in your face, to these factors and it may be tougher by a broad margin.

Harder still for people who are homeless, or the homed homeless in such accommodation as Mary had, bed and breakfast or some other transient, inadequate dwelling. You may love your children as powerfully as anyone but overcoming the urgency of poverty, of housing that feels unhygienic, unsafe, unhospitable, can get in the way of translating that into a home where secure loving is the fabric of a child's life, can be almost impossibly hard.

Risk of Eviction

All of which makes a mystery of the singularly savage measures being brought in by a Coalition government that makes much of its wish to support the family, to do all it can to provide a stable fundamental life for our young, while putting in place measures that will do a great deal to ruin that bedrock of family life, a secure and decent home base.

At the end of 2011 those living in one in every 111 homes were at risk of eviction from unpaid mortgage lenders or landlords. A report that almost seven million people were relying on credit to try to keep their homes, resorting to payday loans, unauthorised overdrafts and credit cards, shows the lengths that desperation and fear drives people to.

Even so, by the end of 2011, the number of households declared homeless was up 13 per cent on the year before, according to government figures and over the months since there has been a shocking number of reports of people's homes being lost, their lives turned upside down because the cut in housing benefit, brought in, means they can no longer afford to live in the place that may have been home for many years. An article in the *Observer* talked of some of the 'London homeless' being moved as far away as Hull, while Islington, my local council, has talked of a regular stream of people for whom there is not affordable housing in the borough, being moved out.

One housing charity raged at the illogicality of measures that will put enormous strains on to family lives that are often already fragile saying, 'We know from the people we see every day that living with the constant threat of losing your home puts enormous pressure on family life. Research has shown that the threat of homelessness is seen as more severe than being assaulted, burgled or going through a divorce involving a custody dispute'.

A poignant report talked of children at a London primary school being so disturbed at the idea they may have to move that they are asking their teachers if they can find them a home. There are, in fact, plenty of schools adding attempts to help families avoid being evicted, to their already pressed schedules. Others are hearing how families cut down on food in order to be able to pay their rents.

And although house repossessions were down at the end of 2011, the Council of Mortgage lenders warned that higher unemployment means a likely rise again in 2012 with all the homelessness, distress, disruption that means.

There was a time when my children were little, when Olly and I both freelance and with mortgage rates under Mrs Thatcher's government risen to 12 per cent, that I seriously wondered if we would be able to go on paying. I imagined then how it would be if our home were re-possessed. What mayhem would descend, how our lives would cease to be our own as we became utterly dependent on what the state would offer us.

We were fortunate. It didn't happen, but I know people to whom it has happened and I have watched how their lives have shuddered and in some cases split apart. A report compiled by researchers at the University of York and Heriot-Watt University showed in summer 2011 councils reporting 44,000 people newly accepted as homeless, an increase on the previous year – in fact the first increase in almost a decade.

Which makes you wonder as unemployment rises inexorably how much we will witness re-enactment of what Ken Loach depicted in his film Cathy Come Home, which drew 12 million viewers. We saw how mercilessly a young couple attempting to bring up their children as a family, had that possibility ripped from them. We saw how homelessness is not a result of fecklessness and foolishness, but the grimmest of fate that can all too easily happen to any of us if, through no fault of our own, circumstances change.

The 1966 drama, filmed in gritty, grainy documentary style, is a salutary tale of Cathy and Reg, an attractive young couple, with dreams and aspirations. He has a good job and, happily together, they have a child and move into a smart maisonette. But when Reg is injured, he loses his well-paid job and unable to pay their mortgage they end up evicted by bailiffs from when their life careers inexorably downwards so that they fall into poverty, live in vermin infested homes, squat empty houses illegally and eventually Cathy, after being moved from hostel to hostel, so that she is increasingly unable to cope, has her children taken away by social services.

I remember well how heart-breakingly shocking that film was, how we talked about there being something wrong that this could happen in an affluent country like Britain, that there should be protections for people whose lives pitched them into misfortune and gave them no way of helping themselves. And here we are now with Libby Brooks, in *the Guardian*, pointing out how this story could all too easily be set in the here and now. '40 years on, Shelter is once again dealing with the consequences of a housing crisis in this country', she writes starkly.

From time to time small initiatives spring up to try to provide housing for those in need, and some are admirable, but they will not be able to solve the enormity of the need. And anyway, surely we should be able to turn to government to prioritise creating enough homes for all those who need them and homes built in ways that encourage a sense of wellbeing and neighbourliness. Not the sort of place in which Mary lives.

Neighbourly Initiatives

There was nothing neighbourly or wellbeing-provoking about the Old Blurton Estate in Stoke on Trent where Nina Hulse grew up. Through the years she watched things get progressively worse. Then, in her 50s, her children grown up and gone, she set about transforming Old Blurton – one of those estates people moved heaven and earth to avoid being moved to, and where she has lived for many years.

I interviewed Nina, a tiny, feisty pensioner, her fine-boned face, lined with a tale of tough times, for Comic Relief which funded some of the initiatives she and her team were working on at the beginning of the new millennium.

By 1999 many of the 300 red-brick houses on Old Blurton were boarded up and had been taken over by drug dealers. Others were unsightly with grubby curtains at windows, rubbish in the front gardens and other indicators of the hopelessness residents felt. Violent crime and intimidation ruled the streets; members of the criminal groups were regularly escorted off the estate by the police.

Nina, who left school at 15 and went to work in a factory, brought up four children of her own, as a single parent, on the Old Blurton estate and she has seen a generation of kids terrorising the streets from when they were still in short pants. She was one of many who lived in fear. She shrugs delicate shoulders and shakes her head of bobbed hair to demonstrate just how bleak it was.

'I wouldn't even walk to see my daughter-in-law who lives three minutes away, if it was after five in the evening. There would be gangs of lads on the street, the young ones were drug runners for older dealers and that got them into the criminal way. The house next to mine was firebombed in a drugs' feud. A mature man more or less ran the estate with his girlfriend. Nobody ever tackled him – the price was too high.

'Nobody, but nobody, wanted to live here. We couldn't imagine ever having a Centre as a heart for the community' Nina recollects. It was the offer of funding from Comic Relief that led singer Robbie Williams, a local lad, to add £160,000 to the funds. Nina explains, 'Robbie grew up close to here. He knows the problems, and he was in a position to understand what was needed to build the Centre we had in mind.'

Nina had convened a group of residents who shared the feeling that 'enough is enough' and composed a 'sort of petition', sending a copy to their MP and putting one up in the local post office. They got more than 300 signatures.'

So when the council called a meeting to explain that they were planning to demolish some houses, and refurbish others spending £400,000 so that 'nice people' would want to live there, the reaction was immediate. Nina's voice is a mix of irony and outrage.

'We said yes, and what about us. New people getting done-up houses won't be made welcome if you don't do something for the rest of us, too.

'I told the council they should upgrade homes for everyone with the money they had and they did so. It did a lot to boost morale on the estate. Then I learned of their scheme for a car park where some houses would be demolished.

'That showed how little they understood this estate! They

didn't realise that a dark car park at night would become a magnet for drug dealing.'

She chortles: 'We won that one. It's now a much used toddler's playground.'

The local council was inspired enough by Nina's vision that it gave the OBCA, of which Nina was chair, money for neighbourhood renewal, an architect, and project manager for the building of the Centre. She, in turn, embarked on a steep learning curve to make sure their Centre would work. She did a computer course, business management, first aid, health and safety, child protection. She learned how to manage databases and broadsheets. She gives a hoarse guffaw, 'I didn't know a thing about how to organise a budget or organise our finances. A council youth employee knocked up a constitution for us and that evolved. For the rest we've learnt on the job. Most of us are Mums so we know about being frugal and I'm proud that we have done good. We are never in the red!'

Even so there has been much 'arguing the toss' with the council in the years since they began, and Nina describes herself as a thorn in their side. Others describe her as a pit bull because she is relentless in battling on for the Old Blurton residents. Her success is seen in the fact that the Centre has become a magnet for all generations with activities of all kinds and a sports centre. It delights Nina that the young regard it as 'their place'.

'People ask how I discipline these kids and it's straightforward. I tell them 'if you mess things up you answer to me.' They get the sharp end if they are bad. I've chased youngsters with a bucket of cold water before now. But they respond well to someone caring about how they behave – there's not enough of that in many of their homes. They get fed erratically, they are kicked out at nights and nobody cares what they are up to. There are not enough decent role models, and the kind of entertainment out there for society is just not affordable for people living here.'

At the youth centre they try to steer teenagers away if they are 'getting on to a bad track, and we persuade some back to school, or into further education. For a time we were able to have teachers here working with kids out of mainstream school, but then the government took over city councils' education departments and that ended. Makes me spit blood. But I regard as my big achievement a lad who was expelled from school who spent a good deal of time with us, and he's now qualified as a plumber. Another troublemaker is doing an apprenticeship which we helped him to get.'

And has all she has achieved given Nina an easier life?' In her amused, throaty voice she answers, 'Good God no. I work harder than I've ever worked in my life. But the council are better at engaging with the community than they were ten years ago and there is a waiting list to move on to the estate. Perhaps the best measure of success is that the buzz is out saying Old Blurton centre is a cool place to go.'

When someone like Liz in Gorton impressively beats the odds or a Nina Hulse, a Ruth Ibegbuna helps people to help themselves, we admire them. They will be held up as proof positive that it is possible to overcome the toughest of odds. The flipside of that admiration, however, is that those who cannot or will not do so are despised. Thus there is every chance that each generation acquires another level of hope-lessness, apathy, fury, dysfunction.

Lynsey Hanley found a way to take control of her destiny. Aged 16, she decided that she was 'going to become middle class' by going on to college to do further education. She explains, 'I realised this was the chance I'd been waiting for, a chance to feel at home among people and take control of aspects of my own life. I realised if I stayed in the same place certain aspects of my life would always be out of my control and I would be eternally frustrated, angry, fatalistic'.

Yet even though Hanley had advantages: loving parents, stability at home she found that determination to become socially mobile came at a price.

'I had a nervous breakdown aged 17 when I was at college because of the sheer dislocation of what I had at home and what I was having at college. I didn't see it in other children. The dislocation was that I knew I could not be at home in my own environment because I had come so far with my education. At sixth form I realised how utterly cut off I was on the estate where I grew up, from all the things people around me expected as a given – it was transformative. I was able to make the step I desperately wanted.'

Whatever class Hanley sees herself inhabiting now, she acknowledges with an eyebrow-raising laugh that, as the author of *Estates* a hugely successful, intellectual book, and with another on the way, as well as being asked, regularly, to write for the *Guardian* (among other prestigious publications), she might be viewed as having become middle-class. Nor does the irony of getting commissions from papers that, for years, she felt she was not 'equipped' to read, escape her.

Even so, she says emphatically, she will never escape the stigma of growing up with poverty, in a ghetto designated for those society values least. She describes it simply as 'the wall inside your head.' At which point she ponders whether, 'the stigma of coming from a council estate is ever turned to an advantage'.

This question lies at the heart of the work done by Richard Sennett, Professor of Sociology and the Humanities at New York University, and Jonathon Cobb, a former associate of the Centre for the Study of Public Policy, Cambridge, Massachusetts. In their book *The Hidden Injuries of Class* (W.W.

Norton), they record the depth of immutable alienation – 'wound' – they found among American men whose origins were the bottom of the social pile, no matter how successfully they apparently shifted into a higher socio-economic class with access to a middle-class lifestyle.

One of their interviewees Frank Rissarro a butcher who achieved a job working on loan applications, got himself a suburban home and rented a country cottage can surely be seen as a success story. Yet, explain Sennett and Cobb, he was never able to see himself as having achieved legitimacy in rising above his working class origins. He could never believe he was worthy of a status above this, having grown up understanding that he and his peers were qualitatively different to those up the socio-economic and social scale.

Rissarro with his success conspicuously displayed in bricks and mortar, the car in his drive, the school his children can attend nevertheless feels, 'illegitimate, a pushy intruder, in his entrance to the middle-class world of neat suburban towns, peaceable families, happy friendships... He doesn't believe he deserves to be respected.'

Home, as I have discussed throughout this book, is such a vital place, so thoroughly a thing which at best helps us stay anchored and able to function well in life, that it is surely one of the most important things for us to press our leaders to prioritise.

It does none of us good to have people living in circumstances which have them wounded, angry and unhappy throughout their lives. And Lynsey Hanley tells us very plainly what the price of growing up in the meanest of streets and estates means.

'Although I have been away from home for over a third of my life now, it continues to shape the way I think about the world outside... It's a lifelong state of mind.'

5

A HOME TO BE IN

We were sitting on the porch of my brother's clapperboard house in Virginia, USA. The backdrop a softly focused silhouette of the Blue Ridge Mountains, in front of us meadows and flowerbeds of gladioli, lilies and roses, sloping down to a small lake, and it was here we came to chat about the directions our lives had taken as adults.

As the conversation turned to how home life – family life – had mapped out for us both my brother seemed to unravel in words, telling of his marriage to an American woman who persuaded him to live in her country, and how it had foundered. He explained, with the same wobbly, shy grin he had as a small boy, the irony of he and Robin, his wife, having bought this dream house – he swings an arm out to indicate the big airy kitchen from which you can watch humming birds feeding, the shadowy rooms, the double bedroom with its view of the vegetable garden his new wife, Paula, cultivates, and the fir trees my brother planted for Christmases.

He talked of how he and Robin worked on making it a place they felt reflected them both. They raised the money to build on the big kitchen; they had a swimming pool put in. Yet somehow they never seemed to make time to be together at home, in loose-limbed, relaxed time. Somehow there was not much space for the emotional stuff of a new marriage. For celebrating good times together, having fun, working through the difficulties, the misunderstandings, stopping to talk long enough to recognise where compromise would have been a healthy thing.

And when, say at weekends or holidays, there could have been time enough to just be together, organically, doing whatever felt companionable and pleasing, or just to be enjoying their first child together, they always found 'things that must be done'.

He reflects on all this. 'Robin and I met and married quickly, really knowing very little of each other, but we were both quite needy. I had lost my two parents fairly recently and was feeling very lost in life; she had her issues with her family. I fell in love with her because, I think, she seemed a solution, and I saw America as a place I could make a new life. I had always dreamed of having a place in the country – a beautiful, rural space for children to grow up able to have chickens, animals and the great spaces in America seemed somewhere we could create a place of permanency, a home for generations. So when we found here – Belle Hill – and moved in I felt I had my piece of paradise.

He pauses, there has been time and therapy since their marriage blew apart two decades ago.

'I see now I really hadn't understood that Robin was a much more urban person than I, and although she had agreed this house would be good for children, and that it was lovely, we had never really talked about what she would be giving up. She'd had a job in New York and it was quite a sacrifice for her to lose that and with it her identity as a journalist.

'In due course we had a second daughter and Robin chose not to take a job away from home. I was working as a doctor locally and I was hard at it all day, stuck indoors, so when I got home at the end of the day all I wanted was to be out in the garden doing things I enjoyed. Robin, who had been all day at home with our two children, and felt quite isolated, found that very hard. She wanted me to spend time with her indoors, she wanted conversation, time focused on us and our relationship. She made it clear she didn't want to be outside fitting into whatever I chose to do.

'I don't think I understood well enough how important that was to her, and she wasn't good at asking for what she wanted in a direct way. It usually came out as an accusation that I was always 'running away' from her even though we were at home together. This is just one of many examples but I think the point is that although we had this wonderful home, what we weren't good at was making time for ourselves, or using the free time we had to do things that would bond us. More and more we had our separate activities done in parallel which was not good for intimacy. We never really learnt how to understand what we were each feeling. In the end it was as though all the good feelings we had begun with were crushed by our recriminations and our strong sense that the other person was being unreasonable. I remember so often feeling towards the end that it was just another shitty day in paradise.'

As is true of so many of us, my brother had not been able to see that the home he believed would be an answer in itself to a happy family relationship, had very different meanings for him and his partner. What a home represents for each person is not necessarily an unspoken mutuality but may need articulating and recognizing. Professor Clare Cooper Marcus who has spent decades studying how people feel about their homes from design to the psychology of being in them, observes in her paper *The House As Symbol of Self,* 'It may be that what a home symbolizes for each person is more critical than almost any other issue. In all the conversations I had with couples who were comfortably making and sharing a home together, they all seemed to be in accord over the basic function and meaning of home. Concerns over privacy, territory and personal space can usually be negotiated or made to work'

But it is when partners have a different concept of what home is for, the part it plays in their relationship, that it may no longer support them. For example, says Cooper Marcus 'If one perceives the home principally as a symbol of status, the other as a nurturing vessel for family life, or if one cares deeply about homemaking while the other seems to just use the place as somewhere to sleep without appreciation for the partner's efforts, it may be difficult to avoid resentment and conflict.'

So what the story of my brother and the thoughts of Cooper Marcus help us grasp is that home may be the place where we believe we belong; a place of sanctuary, refuge, intimacy. But these things can be turned on their head, home may become a place we dread being, or at least dread being in with the person we set out to share it with. For if we do not recognize the dissonance that may step through the door when we have not organized with one another what we want from our home, the place is little more than a structure into which we have put ourselves, rather than a nourishing environment.

Time for Intimacy

So often, in the tales people have told me for this book of the way their homes and relationships do and do not interface, I see how important time is. Yet time can feel like mercury on a board, forever slipping away. And when there is not enough time for souls to touch base at home, without some elastic time for being companionably close, or for a bit of private intimacy, relationships may find themselves stripped to the bone.

This is how Esme Solanger believes it was for her and Ben Laithwaite, 'He and I had only recently met and we were planning to live separately, but one weekend we were alone, without the children from my marriage, and we saw an advertisement for a house that sounded so wonderful we decided we must go immediately to see it. When we got there it was quite magical with big, high-ceilinged rooms, lots of light and airiness and a garden that stretched out with a huge pear tree. It needed quite a lot of work but Ben was an architect and full of ideas for what we could do to the house. We decided then and there to buy it.

'We revelled in the house at first. Ben had all these ideas and would sit with papers all around him, drawing plans and I felt very excited about creating our custom-designed nest. My children liked the house and it was a pleasure to be in. We gave great supper parties there, and it seemed the house had come to us, as a way of enhancing our relationship.'

Gradually, difficulties began to creep in.

'We had moved North from West London and my son didn't want to leave his primary school, so he had to be got across town every day. I was going to psychotherapy three times a week in West London, and doing a university degree. I was also working part-time as a medical sociologist, and collecting the children from their schools.

Ben was an academic and less busy than me but still I seemed to be the one doing the chores, and we never got down to working out that it would be fairer and we could have more time for ourselves, if he did more of the domestic work.'

The sense of closeness, being in their own intimate world at home, shifted.

'Ben would make more plans for the house which never got done, I felt angry with him, and that he didn't understand how stretched my life was. He, I think, was feeling neglected and he was often cross. I remember a work colleague saying to me that he saw the relationship disintegrating because I couldn't give him my undivided attention. He would do things like start to make love to me in the mornings when he knew I had to be at psychotherapy at seven o'clock and be back in time to take the kids to school. Then I would get carried away and be late for everything. I am sure now it was utterly contrived. Then if I got home late from work Ben would make a point of leaving to go off and get drunk, complaining that I was never at home.'

They were together three years during which time the relationship disintegrated in the house which, Esme now suspects, had represented a fantasy life for them.

'He felt that as he was doing up the house I would be rooted in it and there for him when he wanted. But of course the reality of our life just didn't make that possible, and my loving the house was not enough for Ben. Then he began neglecting the house as a way of saying he didn't care.

'Things came to a head when I took the children to France on my own – he was working – and when I got back there was a heap of decaying rubbish on the top step of the house, as though to say 'fuck you' to me. His ex-wife clearly knew that things were not good. She had always been very jealous of the house, seeing it as more of a commitment than if we had had a child, because for her it had all the symbolism of togetherness. Looking back I think she tried to sabotage Ben's and my life in it by phoning at three in the morning saying she needed him to fix lights, or some such thing, and he would always go. In the end he had an affair then went back to his ex-wife and we sold the house.'

So was this a fundamentally flawed relationship or could buying their dream house, and believing their love was a durable thing, have worked? Could things have been organized differently to allow for enough intimate time for Ben to have felt 'at home' with Esme?

She contemplates this. 'I think part of the problem was that we just fell into the situation, impulsively buying the house when we really didn't know each other very well, and believing it had the power to be more than was possible in our lives. Perhaps I could have altered my very busy life a bit to make more time at home, and Ben could have seen that if he had helped in caring for my children it would have left us more time, and we might have relaxed more in the house if we had got it done up and not had things forever needing to be done. If our circumstances had been different, and if we had been able to come together and understand what was going on, we could have been more protective of the relationship. We never paid enough attention to the logistics of our relationship and as I see it now we were waiting for the house to somehow make our relationship okay.'

We live in a world where time is so often a commodity in short supply. Work means, for a great many people, spending the most vigorous and productive hours of the day away from home and family.

But we choose to give time, very willingly these days, to the idea that the exhilarating and fun times are very often to be found outside the home. If you want stimulus forget domesticity or flopping around in relaxing clothes. Snuggling into bed with a book can very easily seem less the way to spend our time than heading off for drinks with mates, eating out, dancing. Social events and parties of the kind that feature in glossy magazines are the places to be seen and heard if you want a high profile; you certainly won't make it into *Hello* or *OK* sitting at home with the kids of an evening.

Being out and about, sampling what is on offer in the bigger world certainly has its place but too much time spent this way may also displace home as somewhere to find an un-crowded, just-hanging-out kind of intimacy. The low-key pleasure of just being in the home we have created – reading, chatting, viewing, cooking and so on – is all too easily debased when the alternative is some external pleasure, a chance to dress up, to meet new people, to see and be seen in an unaccustomed milieu. May not home, then, be seriously at risk of being seen as the scrag end of our existence?

Determined Solipsism

The cult of individualism has done its bit to undermine home life, encouraging us to see giving up autonomy as losing our own identity or as oppression. An approach that, carried to extreme, leaves scant space for considering how we might be sharing and caring with the others with whom we have chosen to make our lives. How loudly the mantras about self-fulfilment, finding oneself, communing with that pesky inner child, doing right by yourself, putting number one at the centre of the universe, have resounded over the past three decades. And this determined solipsism has paraded hand in hand with the whole consumerism, exhibitionist, personal best culture that has so dominated.

Was this the pull for the high-flown professional mother of three, whose husband talked of her as being 'a restless socialite' during the weekday evenings because she was out just about every weekday evening after work. So not much time for getting down on the rug playing Lego with the kids, or a cosy time *a deux* with the partner.

We do know – indeed a myriad of magazine and newspaper 'agony' columns, shelves in bookshops almost collapsing under the weight of relationship self-help books – let us know that couples need time together if their couple-ship is to develop a durable quality and not just be a lusty fair-weather affair. There again although being 'at home' is frequently mentioned, home is rarely pitched as being central. Yet a home which we have created together as a container for lives we have chosen to spend with each other, is surely the place in which to fertilise relationships as a conscious choice. Being in your own home, embedded in the history you have created, the dreams of future that you have spun, sharing enjoyment in the style and taste you have brought to your nest, has a very particular meaning.

A meaning in which home needs us as much as we need it. The poet Gaston Bachelard took as read that home is 'the place we love", but equally he is clear that it risks being an 'inert box' if we do not inhabit in a lively and appreciative way.

When home is drained of liveliness it too easily becomes downgraded in the mind to seem dreary, the opposite of sexy – that catch-all word used to depict a contrast with conspicuously tedious. Instead of being a place that may be busy, demanding, full of children's needs, yet a place you feel the stresses of the outside world at least diminishing, and the being around people for whom you care gladdens the heart

Alienation from home may become still greater, as I well know, if we have children there but are all too often stressed, weary and very probably guilt-ridden at not being a more enthusiastic parent. Children's antennae may pick up how we feel almost before we know it ourselves, and they may well be demanding, challenging, trying to get us to demonstrate that we do want to be with them, but, oh gosh, can they have a taxing way of asking us to read their signals. And so the idea of getting home to that all too easily assumes the proportions of a situation you cannot face.

What about the male employees who seemed suddenly wildly enthusiastic about putting in long hours at work when their city boss offered the chance to go home early on the day before Christmas eve. As one after the other found a reason they couldn't go home yet, it struck him that they preferred being at work to at home. He concluded that being at work was more soothing for the ego – the men understood and knew how to deal with the demands. They found it far tougher, they were less sure-footed, being at home helping the wife with home-based chores, bathing and bedding children.

Working Mothers

Allison Pearson, the columnist and novelist told me a similar story of a high-flying woman executive who could have organized her life to be home for her children's supper but she told how she delayed going home, sitting drinking in a wine bar, until she knew the nanny would have the children in bed and asleep. Allison, who talked of her own guilt at not having had enough free-wheeling time available for her two children during their young years, even though she worked in the home, analysed what she believed was going on with this executive.

'She had lost touch with her children to the extent that she was actually afraid of them… That is the new kind of home-lessness.'

It is an astute observation and one that lay, unarticulated, at the root of her own crisis in 2011 when the centre stopped holding suddenly, shockingly. Why should it have happened?

Theoretically Allison has the ideal situation. She is not tied into long away from home hours, but works in an office at the top of her 1930's house in Cambridge, alongside that of her husband Anthony Lane who writes film reviews for the *New Yorker* and with whom she has a daughter and a son. Mention her name and people are inclined to sigh with envy. She in constant demand to write columns and features in newspapers, has written a successful best-selling novel *I Don't Know How She Does It*, parodying the women-can-have-it-all idea and this summer her second *I Think I Love You* was published.

Even though Allison's popularity was such you would have imagined she could moderate the amount she worked, turning down jobs when they threatened overload, but not so. She had the difficulty so many freelancers experience finding it fearsome to turn work away. So she found herself constantly overwhelmed with deadlines for her columns, for articles she had agreed to do, books to be delivered. It meant, she says reflectively, that she was as fraught, time-panicked and emotionally absent for her children as if she had been in an office job. But for all that she was aware of the stretch and stress she had faith in her ability to cope no matter what.

Sitting in the main family room – an expansive kitchen and sitting room opening on to a garden of abundant green, and mysterious corners – as she prepares a beverage for us, you imagine her work life merging fluidly with a rich and vigorous family life.

A few days earlier, however, Allison had been publicly bold and brave, telling in a newspaper article in a frank, undefended way of the depressive break-down she had been going through. The glossy Allison, much photographed for different publications through the years, her lustrous blonde hair coiffed and flicked-up, her smiling mouth voluptuously coloured, her expression, with a whisper of the sardonic about it, endearingly girlish, appeared now to have been overlaid with a pale melancholy.

She spoke to me in a manner that was welcoming and entertaining, her sharp wit intact, as ever. But it was as though she were hanging on hard to what vivacity she could while being pole-axed by what had been happening. The absolute collapse of all her erstwhile certainty, the realization that the high-achieving woman of enormous chutzpah who had coped impressively for so long, had suddenly ditched her.

We had moved to a table at the top of her garden to drink our coffee. Sunshine cool and pale as lemon sorbet spread over the grass, laced through the trees.

'The depression was terrifying because it stopped me so thoroughly in my tracks. I felt I couldn't go on with anything. Simple things loomed large. Like having to get the clothes from the washing machine and hang them up. When you are brought up not to go to bed at night until the dishes are done you have a great fear of domestic disorder.'

She talks thoughtfully but there is the sense of panic surfacing as she describes how it distresses her to watch situations of chaos in the home on TV for instance, and she ponders whether 'those of us who stretch too far don't feel they can create an adequate holding place, a home as they want it. Does it represent internal chaos?'

That, however, is a different order of panic to the fear-fuelled distress she pitched into believing she had lost the ability to work.

'I couldn't imagine how I would ever be able to work again. I was barely able to leave the house... I hit a point where it was like driving a car, I put my foot on the accelerator pedal and there was nothing there. The engine was going but the car wouldn't move. It was unbelievably scary because work, the only thing I could do, was being taken away from me. I had quite a hard upbringing and my escape has always been hard work and I had always been able to rely on myself as a machine for work.'

Growing up in working class Wales, Allison was aware how tight money always was. They had no car, the phone bill was a perpetual anxiety and so on. Then she saw her mother 'left high and dry by divorce' with the result, 'I was very determined to always make my own money, have my own pay cheque. The underlying fear of being high and dry is with me to this day.'

Her immediate situation, the depressive collapse, came to a head, Allison says, 'when a lovely friend said she would do a chart and divide it into my activities. Then when she asked how much leisure time I had, I burst into tears and said, 'I've got nothing. There is nothing.

'I was confronted so starkly with how work had been everything and I felt – feel – I have missed a big chunk of my children's childhood. When the therapist I went to said I needed to remove the causes of stress from my life, I felt like saying 'it would be easier to remove my life from my stress '– there being so little of the former for so long. When you work as I have been, all the things that might be a priority when you leave work and get home, like giving attention to your partner, go right down the drain. I do agree with Anthony, my husband, that the actual heart of the home is the loving relationship and the children being happy.'

Now, with life re-shaped to avoid the over-stretched urgency that led to her breakdown, Allison says very firmly that she is much more with her children in a just 'being present' way so that there is 'kicking around time, time lying on the sofa. Discussing stuff around the kitchen table when they are doing homework. Things come out in that precious down-time.'

She is aware these days of being drawn to words like *gezellig* from the Dutch, *heimlich* from the German which describe a welcoming homeliness. She sees them as very much about what home represents. While in her second novel *I Think I Love You*, based on her own upbringing in Wales she sees the word *hiareth* which, in Welsh, means a longing for home, as 'the thrust of the book, looking at what home means'.

She reflects on the path she has taken for her adult life. Like so many women of her generation (she is 50), she watched the way it was for her mother who stayed at home. Just as she remembers a friend who described her mother pacing the kitchen like a caged animal being driven mad and she considers, 'My mother was a much happier person when she went back to work when I was about 11.' Before that she is sure her own mother was depressed and this was another reason she felt so fearful at the idea that depression had taken her over.

'Being raised by a depressed mother is very damaging, and I think that has to be put into my equation, so I would never say women shouldn't work. What I do think is that we need to recognize what home represents as well.'

Care as a Commodity

Arlie Russell Hochschild, Professor of Sociology at the University of California, and author of a number of books, experienced the painful power her mother's depression inflicted on her. She describes how it was in her book *The Commercialization of Intimate Life* (University of California Press), a series of essays exploring how globalised capitalist has increasingly made care yet another commodity to be purchased and often as cheaply as possible at whatever human cost, and the problematic impact this has on intimacy, family and who cares for our homes and children.

Hochschild began to wonder what 'hidden compass' in her own personal life might account for her strong interest in the business of caring, but with the paradox that, 'like so many middle-class women in the 1960s' she became a 'migrant' from the emotional culture of her mother built around doing the home-based caring.

'My mother was a full-time homemaker who raised my brother Paul, and myself, volunteered for the PTA and helped start a preschool program in Montgomery County, Maryland, all the while supporting my father's career. It was she who deciphered some intention in our chaotic finger paintings and she who reassured us that scary monsters go 'back home' so we could sleep in peace at night. She gave us many gifts of love, but each with a touch of sadness.'

By contrast Hochschild saw her father's demean as jaunty, happy, 'skip-stepping down a long flight of stairs'. But 'he wasn't the caring one'. Knowing her parents loved each other, hearing them laughing and joking made Hochschild aware that her mother wasn't sad about her husband, and he wasn't sad at all, so her mother's moods which led her to 'see the world darkly' could have just one cause, 'I concluded that mother wasn't sad about her husband, just about her motherhood.' Which meant that, 'early on I developed the simple, mistaken, idea that staying home to care for children was sad and going to work was happy.'

It was, of course, this equation and what it meant in terms of our – women's – right to a jaunty, fulfilling world, rather than one bounded by depression and very limited self-worth as full-time carers in the home, that was a touchstone of 1960's feminism.

Both Allison and Hochschild were living through the years of new wave feminism with its determination that women should not be caged lions – their intellects and capacities for tasks other than the domestic kept in check. The mood was compelling, convincing young women such as myself, in the '70s and Allison more than a decade later, that they could equal men in the public sphere, and be competent caring mothers when at home. I, like many others, relied through the years on the caring labour of young women, sometimes from less wealthy countries or backgrounds than mine, who needed the work. Several homes along the road had housekeepers and nannies from South East Asia, some of whom had left families of their own to earn money looking after our children and homes.

The energetic bid for women's liberation, through two decades, energized many of us, so that we had a sense of destiny. It was as though a curtain had been torn from covering a picture displaying the way men's wishes, beliefs and authority were accepted as the way the world should be run. Our world.

The heady idealism, the ambitions born of the new feminism, dealt a body blow to the idea of home as a place where women might be content to be wives and mothers. Who among us hadn't read Betty Friedan's excoriation of the lot of women in the 'concentration camps' that were the traditional home? Her book *The Feminine Mystique*, based on many interviews, showed how little autonomy women who relied on their men for all their needs, believed they were entitled to. The popular *Mad Men* series has painted a deeply ironic picture of the 'perfect' lives of the doll-like obeisant wives exemplified in the decorative Betty, initially moulding life around the pleasure and advancement of her ambitious husband Don Draper.

Going out to work as we, an educated generation, realized we could do, was not just a choice about the right to have a career if we wished, it was also a political gesture. We recognized that if we had children the challenge was to combine this seamlessly with our work. It was no good pleading too many broken nights if we showed signs of not matching up; heaven forbid that anyone should see the milk stains on my tee-shirt from milk aching to be released from engorged breasts. An unwell or needy baby did not cut the mustard as an excuse for too many late mornings or missed days. And so on.

Those of us who had partners sharing domesticity and childcare, had a better chance of coping without too much anguish. And, as I found with Olly, it was possible to keep a wry dialogue going some of the time, at least, about how impossible it was to have any 'us' time. Others, with partners who didn't seem to realize their women had actually got two jobs and were reeling under this load, couldn't quite fathom why their relationships were creaking under the strain, and by no means all survived it.

The importance of human rights work convinced lawyer Helena Kennedy (she became a QC, and received a life peerage for her work in 1997), that she must continue the work that felt so integral a part of who she is, even when she had young children at home.

'One of the things I have wanted to pass on, as a woman, to both my daughter and sons is that it is possible to have a career and work hard, but for my family to be valued highly as well.'

Her daughter Clio was home from university where she was studying anthropology when I visited, and the three of us talked about the role of home with Helena, and her surgeon father Iain Hutchinson. What Clio had to say was a touching picture of the effort she felt her mother had made to be present in a full-throttle way.

'When I was little I always knew when Mum had come home because I would hear her bangles jangling. It meant that at any minute I would see her.

She has always had to work long hours and people sometimes ask if I didn't miss out because of this, but my memories are of Mum being very much around because once she was home she spent her time with me and my brothers. She's always been a very lively, involved mother playing games, reading and larking around with us. There was the time when we were in Brighton and she sat with us for hours in a cupboard, lighting matches, singing and then blowing them out. Mum is particularly good at treasure hunts and I remember one Easter when we were on holiday with all our cousins and she had written lots and lots of little clues in rhyming limericks sending us scurrying all over the place. Another time, in Scotland on holiday, she read us a book about the Second World War and she joined in with us playing all the characters, escaping across the border and going into the forest.'

She goes on to describe Helena snuggling up in bed with her 'being cuddly'', when she was home from university, talking about everything from Clio's boyfriends to politics and Helena's cases. 'Sometimes Dad will wake me in the morning and suggest I go and get into bed with Mum.'

Not that it has been as effortless as this may sound, Helena is quick to interject. Indeed she was brought up sharply on one occasion, realizing that being determined her family were central to her life, might mean considering what work she could and could not take on.

'On one occasion I was doing a murder trial of a battered woman who had killed her husband. The case was in Sheffield and I got a call from our nanny saying Clio was running a very high temperature and the nanny wasn't able to get it down. I immediately thought meningitis and I felt desperate. I couldn't walk out on the trial but how could I not be home with my sick child? This is where I am so grateful for my fantastic gang of women friends. I phone up one and she went straight around to the house, phoned a doctor who came at once. It turned out not to be so serious but I felt such guilt at not being there and decided I must not have cases so far away in future.'

Guilt. Guilt. Guilt. It scarred so many of us attempting to juggle home-life and work-life in a way that did not make our loved ones pay the price, yet which also didn't demand that we sacrifice talents and abilities we wanted to use in the outside world. We began to see a number of remarkably successful career women often with equally successful husbands who could certainly afford the best of care for their children, choosing to leave their full-time jobs in order to be home more. Of course the wanting to be at home more with the family, is a well-known euphemism trotted out by male politicians as a matter of course when their careers take a downturn. But with these women – and there are less noted men I am sure who did the same – it was different. These mothers were, quite simply, missing being with the children to whom they had given life, but who were spending the bulk of their growing years with somebody paid to care for them, in the hope these carers would love them too.

The Nourishment of Time

So often in the beginning when we choose to set up home with someone, we plant our relationships like springy saplings, embodying our dreams that they will become weathered old trees, our lives intertwined in their limbs. We may envisage all this in the same home. There is, after all, a pleasing sentiment in that idea. But without the nourishment of time dedicated to building their strength and solidity these saplings may well not make it.

I think of early times in my relationship with Olly. We had come together as amateurs in the business of building a relationship envisaged as long-term, within a home. How little we understood about the need to be available to explore the texture and tenor of what went on between us, to chew the cud over matters of the spirit as well as the practical issues of whether we needed to replace a shower head. I remember how isolated I felt at times, when it was clear we had evolved no real skills for being able to express the things we wanted the other to hear. How being too busy with work and children became convenient ways of deflecting from the risk of saying things that would make us feel vulnerable, might be misconstrued, could lead to rejection.

The writer Alain de Botton evokes in his novel *Essays in Love*, the way time enough in our private domain, creates the place to find safe emotional expression. He depicts for us the progress of his protagonist's affair with Chloe.

'We could lie together on a hot summer evening without reference to our nakedness. We could risk intervals of silence, we were no longer paranoid talkers, unwilling to let the conversation drop… We grew assured of ourselves in the other's mind, rendering perpetual seduction obsolete.'

De Botton makes us voyeurs to a relationship where layers of supportive strength are being built, because the couple have unfettered intimate time. So within the intimacy, rather than instead of it, their relationship had a space for individual pursuits: 'but they came back to each other, bringing the fruits of the individualistic foray, the threats of the outside were shared on a common bed. Chloe became the final repository of my judgements on the world… But the intimate time was not just lived and lost, it was converted into the story Chloe and I told ourselves about ourselves, the self-referential narrative of our love….'

Home is indeed the place where we need emotional space to negotiate the trickier bits of our domestic lives, when they go through times of upheaval, misunderstanding, hostility. We need time to work through conflicts so that they don't become running sores, and when disagreements are building to a crescendo. With time we may be able to take pause rather than becoming hysterical, seeing the family member as a conspirator against us. With time we can be like surfers learning to roll with the curlers when our greatest inclination is to run scared. In the doing, and the coming out in one piece, we emerge with a greater knowledge of our ability to survive, greater skills in dealing, and a willingness to risk it again

We might take the steady failure of marriage (and cohabitation does worse) as a way of measuring the limited life those saplings have. On average marriage may last eleven years, with the numbers collapsing at that stage or sooner climbing steadily from the 1960s. Although making it that far looks like a minor miracle when you glimpse at the length of time some well known characters have mode their marriages last. Think Rudolph Valentino and Jean Acker six hours, Zsa Zsa Gabor and Felipe De Alba one day, Michelle Phillips and Dennis Hopper eight days, and Kim Kardashian and Kris Humphries who lasted a whopping 72 days. The list of those couplings lasting less than a year in celebrity-ville is mighty long.

I seem to have returned once more to celebrities, perhaps because they are instructive as the group least likely to have home as a place of mundane cosiness, so if you accept my premise that home, if we invest in it, will in turn invest in us, then it is perhaps no surprise that those with lives that delegate home to a bit part player, may not find a place to build their durable intimacy.

Our culture does little to help us think about the idea of time at home without a set purpose – poring over paint charts, zipping around with an interior designer doing something to our property – being valuable. It is not a thing we are taught but expected to intuit, which is a chancy way to model a life ahead.

Women, far more than men, are instructed in ways to please our partners as a skill for helping keep happy home life on the rails whether preparing his favourite dishes or a bit of protracted sex play. This may be no bad thing if it does not become yet another chore, but there are examples of man-pleasing that would be too demanding for most of us. I am recalling an American woman who had written a book telling how she had revived a marriage where she and her husband were mired in sullen boredom with each other. She had designed a strategy to reverse that state.

Her head of bottle gold curls shook with animation, her glossed pink lips moved rapidly, as though mechanized, as she related how the minute her husband had left home and the children were gone to school, she scampered around preparing the table with damask cloth and silverware for a dinner she would prepare painstakingly during the day. The children were fed, bathed and got to bed without fail before her husband arrived home.

She would put on a raincoat with nothing underneath, and as her husband came through the door into the room with candles lit, incense burning, she would throw open the raincoat revealing all. There was a great deal more, in similar vein, in her book and she insisted her blank-faced husband was so much happier with their home life nowadays.

'Extreme Jobs'

Work is responsible for the fact that the greatest number of adults spend their most energetic and productive hours away from home, rather than preparing elaborate meals and seductive games, and in Britain we put in more statutory hours than in other European countries. A report on the ThisMoney website noted that Britons also clocked up a great deal of unpaid overtime.

A 'juggernaut' is how Camilla Cavendish writing in the *Times* talked of this extreme working. 'Extreme jobs' she explains 'are those that entail at least ten hours a day at work, plus breakfasts or dinners, plus being available to clients and bosses at weekends and holidays. Such jobs used to be the pre-serve of bankers, CEOs and politicians. But they are spreading right across the economy into everything from law to manu-facturing.'

The notion of giving what time we can to enjoying home life would be made a great deal easier if nobody in paid employment was encouraged to work more than the 40-hour week described by a EU report published in October 2010 (*Flexible Working Time Arrangements and Gender Equality*, European Commission) as is the way in other European coun-tries.

Even better would be a wholesale acceptance of flexible working time, or part-time work, and without it being desig-nated a female choice, as is commonly the case. Men as much as women need to be able to organize lives to have comfort-able and comforting time at home with children and with part-ners.

Increasing the flexibility of working time arrangements and gender equality, are two key EU employment policies yet only in the Scandinavian states is it accepted as perfectly normal that flexible working time is how employees can be helped to func-tion healthily and happily and with rewards for society too.

Looking at the situation in America, Sylvia Ann Hewlett in 2006 produced a report showing that already up to 45 per cent of people in multinational companies had extreme jobs, with the amount of hours varying from 70 – 100 a week. Cavendish recognizes the seductiveness of a life that may, at any moment, wherever you are, whatever you are doing, issue a call to duty. 'It makes you feel terribly, terribly important. Which is why extreme working is so addictive.'

It is also lethal for relationship. Cavendish points out that a good deal of research has confirmed that working 65 – 70 hours a week makes divorce a serious risk while another study found that nearly half of all extreme workers admitted they were too tired to say anything to spouses or partners in the evenings. Others found the demands of home too much.

Companies that hand out the largest pay cheques, and with them the status we attribute to the very wealthy, also expect their employees to enter a Faustian pact where they sell their time, lives and souls to the firm. Time for being home is certainly not a priority.

So it was, writ large, for those who worked for Lehman Brothers if Vicky Ward's grimly fascinating book *Devil's Casino* (Wiley) gets it half way right. To give the idea she quotes one of the Lehman wives on how she as well as her husband became a commodity 'if you were married to a Lehmanite, you belonged to the firm. 'You could not expect your husband to be around for the birth of your children, if Lehmann's needed him, and certainly not to participate in raising them. Social life was dictated by what the company had going on and if they issued an invitation, no matter how inconvenient or unwanted, you were expected to go 'happy and pretty and smiling.'

So for these families home was forced to be the most disposable commodity.

Gaby Hinsliff, political editor of the *Observer*, feared that she was not sure she could hold everything together the way things were going. She had a job she coveted, an adored two-year-old son and a happy marriage to a man who was supportive. Yet there she was in November 2009 writing her farewell-to-all-this article in her newspaper explaining why she was leaving the job to be based at home with her small son. She followed this with her book *Half A Wife*, setting out ideas for a better way for work to be organized and with a change of perspective that recognized how important it is for father's to have time to parent fulfillingly, too.

Reading Hinsliff's thoughtful words had the effect of having entered the spool of a film reeling backwards into the land of déjà-vu. It was like watching a younger sister, stepping out on a trajectory so very similar to the one I had taken when my own first child was two-and-a-half and I decided to leave the *Guardian*. As I have talked of earlier in this book, I too made the choice to work in a job that meant I had to carve out bits of time for my child while knowing I must give what was required of it to work. The job was satisfying, and it is fortunate if you have that. But it doesn't make a jot of difference to the drought that a very demanding job can impose on relationships at home.

I identified with Gaby's description of how she dragged herself out of bed at 5.30a.m. in order to have time with her son before leaving for work. She sacrificed any evening time with family at the end of the week, because working on a Sunday newspaper as often as not meant staying in the office until past midnight. Then there were the annual three weeks away for political party conferences.

It brought back my time as fashion editor on the *Guardian*, before I turned to entirely different writing on youth crime and such like, when the collections were on and deadlines must be met no matter what; going to bi-annual fashion collections in France and Italy for several days at a time. For the first *Pret a Porter* in Paris, after I had given birth, I could not bear to leave my six-month old son, and so I employed a friend's daughter to come with me. She spent the time wheeling Zek around the Left Bank and eating with him in cafes along Boulevard de St Germaine, while my *derriere* was pinned to the saucer-sized seat of a gilt chair. I at least saw my child at the end of the day which was not different to when I was at home, although I found watching models cavort on the catwalk when I imagined being with my baby felt almost surreally daft at times.

I shared with Gaby the dichotomy: on the one hand a job I had felt so fortunate to get, because I had always wanted to work for the *Guardian*. Plus it was promising to offer me new opportunities. On the other hand was a home life, with a child I missed keenly, and who increasingly clung to me and begged me not to go when I had to leave. Olly, at that time, was often away working on films and bringing home a much needed lion's share of the bacon.

As with Gaby, having a worthwhile career had long been a guiding goal for me. Like her I had grown up in a home with a mother who understood well the importance of education for a daughter, and to work in the outside world as well as having a family. Yet here was Gaby exposing the trip wire to the 'having it all' paradigm. You might be able to fit in all the practical tasks, and cope with the stress and exhaustion, but what you couldn't have was more than snatched and constrained chunks of time for relationships located in the home.

Gaby framed this fact of life succinctly, 'I wanted to have a home not run a household.'

The sotto voce, almost apologetic way James Morton told me of his decision to turn down a more prestigious job than the middle management one he has, was a contrast in style with Gaby's, very public explanation. But it had a similar reasoning. He had realized that the new job would mean more hours away from home, less time doing up the house he had bought with his wife – he positively lit up when he described how they had re-built a fireplace together, and chosen a brightly striped carpet which they laid over one weekend. In his present job, in the rural south west of England, he got home early evening and spent the time with his three children playing football, going swimming, around the table with Monopoly or just flopping on the sofa, watching a TV programme chosen 'by the committee that is my family.'

He weighed up and says firmly, 'It was not such a hard decision, to turn down the new job. It would have been more interesting and we could well have used the extra money, but my wife and I discussed it and agreed it wasn't worth what would get lost. Home time with my family is precious and losing that was too high a price.'

Not that having languorous time at home guarantees intimate interaction of course. It is all too easy to be in the same room as others and as far away as can be.

Technological Distractions

How often do we go into a home – our own perhaps – and find someone engrossed in conversation on a phone, another attending to emails, the imperative ping of a message arriving which must be obeyed?. In between all this the odd question or remark may be thrown out, but family interaction and communication on any substantial scale, are very easily given short measure as ever more sophisticated techno sirens compete for our precious time. Rituals and bonding time are all too easily subsumed in the compelling distraction of computers, video games, a zillion TV channels sucking us into ersatz worlds.

How, too, can the daily chitter chatter, the exchanging of small details of life with our immediate family, compete with the allure of online friendships ? These can offer easy-going interaction, while it may be a lot more challenging to negotiate the good, the bad and the ugly with a flesh and blood family.

The ubiquitous mobile phone is no longer a convenience with added apps but a life support system for many. They ring and tinkle, exude whole melodies vibrating constantly in the home. This is concern enough that Sherry Turkle, director of the Massachusetts Institute of Technology Initiative of

Technology and Self, has been studying how parental use of technology affects children and young adults. After five years and 300 interviews she has found that feelings of hurt, jealousy and competition are widespread when communication with technology gets precedence over them.

There is now a syndrome known as smart phone orphans where children cannot get their parents' attention for any length of time before the demands of the phone cut in. You can well imagine the frustration, the sense of being belittled for a child who finds the interest in their conversation evaporates at the demanding ring of a phone.

There was a report in a paper not long ago of a small girl whose mother talked incessantly on the mobile and nothing her daughter did seemed to make any difference. Eventually the girl sunk her teeth deep into her mother's leg and bit hard.

Of course this level of compulsive neglect may require catharsis, and so in *The Guardian* we read a lengthy confession by a family where they email, text and tweet each other, but scarcely speak any more.

I can't count the times I have yelled at my younger son for sitting at meal tables texting on his mobile, or Olly for becoming embroiled in a seeming love affair with his computer, which cannot be abandoned even though supper is sitting, gently congealing, on the dining table. And then, hey, I have caught myself with my iPad opened up when a friend is visiting, explaining I just have to check something while listening to what my friend is saying.

Family Mealtimes

Family meals are the place where history and tradition take their place at the table Jean-Claude Kaufmann, Professor of Sociology in Paris, tells us in *The Meaning of Cooking* (Polity

Press). Just as family meals are the place where we like to think all kinds of human interaction and communication can take place. In fact it happens less and less. The family meal can be seen as something of an endangered species with people eating at different times, grazing from the fridge, popping a ready made meal into the microwave, and consuming TV meals in front of a screen.

Thus the ritual of learning to be a social person, to use manners that make life comfortable for all, to become an adept communicator, skilled in conversing with a range of ages and personalities, is getting lost. You sense Kaufmann spitting out his words, 'The meal disappears altogether, as does the role of the cook, and in many cases the dining table itself which is reduced to being an ephemeral support for buttering bread and making snacks.'

The American Miriam Weinstein, author of *The Surprising Power of Family Meals* has no doubt we are losing more than we realise as we stop bothering with making an event of a mealtime. 'It encloses us and, for a brief time, strengthens the bonds that connect us with other members of our self-defined clan, shutting out the rest of the world.'

Weinstein wonders if we are interested to know that study after study showing the beneficial impact of family mealtimes has been demonstrated for children of all ages. Better grades, healthier eating habits, closer relationships to parents and siblings, ability to resist negative peer pressure, resilience in the face of life's problems – all these are outcomes of simply sharing dinner on a regular basis she informs.

In my own family during childhood, mealtimes were an inalienable part of the shape of life and it never occurred to my brother and I that we wouldn't attend, that we would miss out on the usually amiable argy-bargy between my parents, how they listened to what we had to tell about our day, how my mother – an avid reader – would offer thoughts on a book she was reading, my father might offer up altogether more gruesome morsels from one or other of the cases of psychopathic murderers he had interviewed to be a psychiatric expert witness.

An integral chunk of the day would have been missing without these meals, as well as the extended ones when people came to stay, or friends were invited and meals would go on and on often becoming a noisy, protracted affair.

I was determined there would be the ritual of family meals in my own home. I had few things I believed in as must-dos, but I had a Cleaver-like vision of my family around the table. My children would learn to set a table, sit down and behave in a civilised and sociable way. They would take their turns clearing and washing up afterwards.

First, however, I had to culture Olly into seeing that this was an important part of how home life impacts on relationships. He had grown up in a home where his father, a docker who quite often did two jobs, was frequently not around. While his brother, 20 years older, was already married with his own home. His nephew, more like a brother of the same age, might come to eat sometimes, but you never knew when. So meals were very much on the hoof and his mother kept a food cupboard from which she could produce a snack or meal quickly. More often than not a big tub of meatballs burbled and bubbled on the stove and people helped themselves as and when. Olly didn't quite get it when I became aerated at his lack of engagement with the whole business, my explaining the importance of having set mealtimes.

I probably nagged more than was helpful, but I also made a point of creating good food, as he does too these days, and more prettily displayed than mine. He began to see that having our children, who were like quicksilver so much of the time, reliably there for a chunk of time, was a civilising ritual.

Of course family meals can also be, at worst, the very oppo-site of a place for good communication. We have had rows ranging from childish to stratospheric, we have niggled and tetched at each other, thrown criticism around and there is no doubt it has made those mealtimes a less than civilized, indigestible affair. But nothing to match the exercises in psychological destruction that Adam Nicholson describes in his book *Sissinghurst*.

'I remember one evening at the table in the kitchen, with all of us, as well as my nanny Shirley Punnett, sitting around the scrubbed deal table, when the two of them (mother and father) began to shout at each other, from one end of the room to the other, a terrifying, exchanging shouting barrage in the air above us, as if shells were exploding inside the room, and we ran away upstairs.'

On another occasion, 'my mother threw precious plates the length of that table, beautiful nineteenth-century plates on which early balloons were painted.' His parents' marriage was not a happy one and mealtimes were just one of the times when that was acted out all too evidently.

Even when mealtimes become battlegrounds says Charlie Love, an American therapist, they are a place where family relationship is taking place. If you can keep a cool head it may well prove an occasion to work out whatever issue has exploded, rather than it festering unsaid.

As well, Love knows well how family meals may offer us a chance to pull together the bonds of family and friends, and she has chosen to focus on family meals when working with families. 'Many couples with kids eat separately. I educate them in the importance of connection around family meals and I do ask people to look at what their parents and grandparents learned about relationships through the ritual of mealtimes.'

'Emotional Terrorism'

Having talked at length about the importance of making time for our lives at home, I need, now, to acknowledge that some relationships are rotten to the core, where violence, abuse and humiliation are the daily fare, and I am not suggesting making time for them – they need to end as quickly as possible.

The temporary pall that falls over home, the dulling of cheerful vivacity that comes when home is a place of disharmony, but temporarily, is one thing. But what if home is a place where chemistry turns out not to be the glue you had envisaged, where there is a lack of fundamental shared values, when the home feels ceaselessly toxic.

Psychotherapist Michael Vincent Miller has worked over many years with couples living this way and he calls what he sees emotional terrorism. A situation where couples subject one another to extreme psychological distress. In his book *Emotional Terrorism* (Norton Books) Miller frames his thoughts.

'What you see, typically, in a relationship besieged by intimate terrorism is two people preoccupied with attacking one another's autonomy or security. Each has the aim of seizing control of the relationship'. It happens he explains because each is engulfed by anxiety at the idea they are out of control. So you witness the opposite of people allotting time to finding a way to reach each other, but who instead, 'create a regime of terror' using a whole array of behaviours from saintliness and rationality to coldness in bed, indifference and in their incomprehension of what is happening they find it harder and harder to discover a space for healthy communication. It happens, he says, most 'virulently and outrageously in the home.'

So how are our feelings about the homes we have looked to for refuge and comfort impacted on when this behaviour is

going on? I can speak for myself. On the occasions of dissonance and disruption between Olly and me, and when there
have indeed been power struggles acted out with each of us
using the best wounding techniques we could find, I would be
torn between wanting Olly out the house, and planning to leave
myself. The very walls seemed to have sucked in the ill-feelings,
the place was full of discomfort. All in all my home became a
site of aggravation, discontent, it's solid structure seeming to
mock the unsteadiness of our relationship.

Julia and Gorgio are a prime example of the way houses
reflect the emotional thermostat of a relationship explains psychotherapist Janet Reibstein, Professor of Psychology at
Exeter University. She works with couples and has written
several books on intimate relationships, including *The Best Kept
Secrets* which, through in depth interviews show how those
speaking had kept their relations alive, flourishing and intact
over the years they had been together.

'A large part of many relationships' explains Reibstein 'is
putting together a home as a way of cementing the idea that
this is a special relationship, and home can express vividly the
time when you are comfortable. But home can seem as though
it is letting you down when it no longer feels that way.

'Most people see home as a refuge and when that goes it
becomes symbolic of how the couple cannot make things right
between themselves. There is often an inclination to retreat,
and that may mean disposing of the home rather than address-
ing the flaws in their relationship. It means the home becomes
a representation of breakdown, and so in a way it becomes an
object of blame.'

It can be possible to work with the way people are using
their home to help them overcome their problems, Reibstein
suggests. Georgina and Julio went to Reibstein for help,
although with little conviction that anything could be done. She

remembers what a bad state they had reached.

'They had no sex life, no affection – all they had was fighting and kids. In the place they lived there was nowhere that
offered the chance to be together, no sofa or comfortable
chairs in the sitting room. I suggested they go and buy a sofa,
a place they could sit close and cuddle. I knew that, since they
had stopped having sex, the bedroom had become threatening
as a place where intimacy could be initiated.

'They agreed to getting the sofa and once they had that
installed in the sitting room I then got them to sit next to each
other. Later I suggested introducing a little sex play. Slowly they
began to enjoy this closeness and it led to full sexual intimacy.
The process took a bit of time but they stayed together, their
sex life came back, they saw they could trust each other to be
close, and they stopped feeling they needed therapy.'

Which brings me full circle to my brother who, with his
wife, set up a home but found no point of meeting where they
could envisage spending time adding their touches jointly, to
the place. Nor could a sofa have provided an emotional space
for being at ease together, because the disappointment over his
being out of the home too much, and his wife's sense of being
undervalued as the one who had been home all day when he
returned from work, was too great.

The happy ending here is that my brother has married a
delightful woman, Paula, whose earlier unhappy experience of
home life has given her a striking contentment with what she
now has.

We sit around a big table catching the end of a summer day
outside and Paula tells, in the kind of detail people hold when
things have been tough and confusing, of her marriage to a
controlling man. Indoors there are photographs of her looking
as young brides so often do, brimming with the idea that this
can be happy ever after. And she needed that. Her childhood

with an alcoholic mother and a father she adored but couldn't protect from her mother, had been painful. She had poured a great deal of the affection she wanted to offer into her severely handicapped sister Vicky, taking on much of the care for her as she grew up.

Paula married a man in the services and when both her parents had died, she took on Vicky at their home where she now had two young sons. She did not work away from home but took classes with the Emergency Medical Services so she could work, in due course with the Ambulance Service.

'I very much wanted to do this but my husband bitched when I went out saying I had dumped Vicky on him, and he found it an intrusion on our life that I had taken her on, but apart from going for my lessons I didn't ask him to do anything for her.

'For me having a home where, if your family needs help you give it, is very important and I had promised my father nothing would happen to Vicky when he died.'

Her husband, she tells, was the one who had a life outside, socializing, doing things he wanted in his free time. 'I was the one at home taking care of the house, our kids, his friends when he invited them over. While the children were little that was fine and when all was quiet, and Vicky not needing care, I had a place I could go and sit on the porch and be peaceful. I loved that.'

It was when their sons were at school all day that she started working with ambulances on the rescue squad. 'It gave me a great sense of self worth, but as my work outside home built my husband became very difficult. He wanted me in the house all the time even when neither he nor the kids were home. He behaved more and more pissy, he yelled at me a lot and was always telling me how useless I was. There was a very bad atmosphere at home and he started bitching at me about so many things – how I folded the clothes for instance. Before long he was accusing me of running around with other men and things got so bad we didn't sleep together or even speak.'

She pauses for a minute, then goes on in her sing-song Southern accent.

'I was so worried the children would be very upset by the atmosphere so I did what I had learned as a small girl that you have to make the best of your lot. But for me there was no sense of a home where I was emotionally safe. And my husband, whenever something displeased him, would say 'I don't have to put up with this'. One day I just said 'Fine. Don't'. So he packed and left.

'What struck me was how peaceful life was, how much easier it was at home without him, but even so it was terrible for the boys. They were in their teens. They blamed me because their father told I had thrown him out. But I had good friends in the rescue squad and they became like family to us; we had parties which was something new. And I didn't mind being on my own'.

It was some years later that she met and went on to marry my brother and move into the family home he had made with his first wife.

For both of them a huge part of the pleasure they take in the relationship is being home, doing things to the house and garden, enjoying watching each new project develop. Paula does not work outside the home, but grows vegetables which she and my brother eat throughout the year. Together they chop wood, sort out weeds in the small lake; Paula has decorated the sitting room in sun-reflecting shades, she makes the best pastry I have tasted and has been endlessly patient in finding common ground with my brother's daughters, one of whom now lives in the grounds of the house The two of them bicker amiably about where they will have their chairs in the porch as they become 'old fogies'.

So it is that Paula becomes thoughtful: 'I have a home that feels like everything a home should be, now. I have a value here, and I feel that by contributing to this home I am building together with Patrick. It feels the place to be.'

I have set out in this chapter to look at the uses and abuses of a home that, at best is a place to be, in a way that enables personal well-being, family relationships rapport with children, to thrive. At which point I will turn back to Allison Pearson who said something that seems to me absolutely integral if we are to get the best out of home.

'I want', she said, 'to be a human being not a human doing.'

6

NOT FORSAKING ALL OTHERS

Estelle is sweetly endearing the way she talks of her home situation in a gush of excitement and bravado which ends with her saying: 'I want to tell everyone that I am so happy because I live with the two people I love best in the world'.

It is trusting of her to have told me all she has, unguardedly, because it is not something she generally feels comfortable doing. In fact she tells very few people that she, Ed and Lea, three 'overweight middle Americans, given to being couch potatoes in front of the TV ', not only share a house but a king size bed as well.

She is all too aware that, in the small Texas town where she lives, the knowledge that she, her husband and lesbian lover are a proudly polyamory family, would send shock waves through the community. As well, Estelle fears, she would be fired from her employment and the knowledge would cause her parents enormous upset.

Estelle says quietly, 'I would like, so much, to be open and honest about the fact that we have such a loving, caring family and home life. But that is not what people would understand, I know they would simply condemn us as immoral, not decent people, or some such thing.'

Megh understands Estelle's dilemma very well, and what they share is the belief, increasingly gaining ground in this new century, that relationships not harnessed to vows of lifelong monogamy with a partner, may make for more sustainable relationships and less broken homes than we see at present with such a high percentage of marriages and committed relationships falling apart.

In effect what they say is, get real. In the 21st century, we recognise and largely welcome, the greater emancipation we have in a number of ways, than was he case in the post-war years. The academic Catherine Hakim argues, in her book *The New Rules* (Gibson Square) that it is our puritanical insistence on absolute fidelity that means so many marriages and long term family relationships explode in pain and fury after we learn that our partner has strayed.

When we spoke Megh, a frolicsome redhead, whose expressions change like a shaken kaleidoscope, Matt and Dave, two quieter pleasant-looking young men, were gathered in the kitchen of Megh and Matt's home for a Saturday morning breakfast. To all appearances here were three close mates enjoying food, cementing friendship and discussing things close to their hearts, while Megh and Matt's six-year-old son Tomos was out with mates

Nothing to cause a raised eyebrow you might think. It is the kind of easy-going beginning to a weekend familiar to many of us. Except that what this group were contemplating was distinctly unfamiliar, and the discussion I came in on was frankly bizarre by our communally accepted ideas on how families organise their home lives.

This threesome were giving careful consideration to whether Matt and Dave have cemented their friendship well enough, through regular meetings, whether there is adequate trust and pleasure in their rapport, for Dave to be invited to live with them. If this happens the affair Megh is having with Dave will be integrated into her married – and sexual – life with Matt.

So far Megh has been visiting Dave in his own home, but in due course she explains she and Matt agreed that if he and Dave, as the two men in her life, got along, Dave should move into their family home.

The households Estelle and Megh, describe here, are part of a slowly but steadily growing polyamory movement in Europe, the UK, the US, Canada and Australia where the basis of the home set up is acceptance of the fact that they do not want monogamy, but they do want openness and honesty. They regard themselves as flag-bearers for the idea that with these conditions infidelity need not be the destructive force it so often is.

Rethinking Fidelity

Something similar is expressed by actress Monica Belluci, although she is not looking to embrace others in her marriage. However she has said fiercely that it would be 'ridiculous of her to expect fidelity from her husband actor Vincent Cassel. They are apart for stretches of time and it is unrealistic to expect Cassel to do without sex, she says. What she does mind about is respect for each other where 'a man is not just loyal in a sex way, but will be there for you. That is more important than just fidelity.'

Can we see this as a mature, thoughtful approach to what she wants from the father of her two daughters Deva and

Leonie? Can we understand that she may well be accepting how Cassel is and not making it so unpleasant for him to go home that he pulls further and further away. We may presume that she is making a measured choice about the best way to keep strong and enticing a home life, which has already lasted more than a decade.

'Passion you can feel for the worst man you ever met' Belluci points out. 'But that has nothing to do with a deeper partnership. In such a one, passion stays, but more important is confidence, respect… It would be ridiculous to ask (fidelity) of him if I hadn't been there for two months. You can't ask such things as who has he been seeing, what has he been up to? It's more respectful and realistic to take the view that you be with me when I see you… I am talking about loyalty and, most important of all, elegance.'

I might think Belluci courageous and right in knowing what matters to her and how she maintains a marriage she values. Yet, strikingly, this frank outpouring brought forth a deluge of responses, most showing how far we are from a society that accepts a woman making such a choice or that will re-think fidelity.

When Belluci's words appeared on the celebritybitch website, many of the respondents condemned her for letting women down. One person wrote furiously, 'what kind of moron are you if you broadcast this to the whole world? Women like that bring us all down.'

There were dire warnings, 'this philosophy may work for Belluci while she's still got her looks and health, but wait ten years and see what she says when she is made aware of Cassel traipsing around with a 20-year-old… The scales will tilt against her in time as they do for most women.'

And morality, 'Sex regardless of how instinctive and ani-malistic it is, is still intimate. Viewing sex as a necessary bodily function like urinating... is demeaning to intimacy with another. Discipline and the sacrifice... are investments in an intimate relationship' While another queried, 'Why get married in the first place? How do you have respect and loyalty when your spouse cheats?'

Just a few respondents saw the point of how Belluci has chosen to play it. One wrote, 'exactly the sort of relationship I would like. Sex with someone else is only disloyal if you are breaking a promise. If you have agreed rules between yourselves that allow you both to have sex with other people, then you're not cheating unless you break those rules.'

A loosening of conventional bonds, buying into the idea that if you make the rules yourselves, agreeing that a relationship may be broadened or opened up, then it is not cheating, is the way other high profile celebrities have talked. They include Will Smith, Scarlett Johanssen and best known as someone practising non-monogamy is Tilda Swinton, who has talked very openly about having a husband and permanent younger lover.

New Monogamy

Psychologist Meg Barker at the Open University has specialised in studying relationships and refers to these arrangements between the mutually consenting as new monogamies. She co-edited with Darren Langdridge *Understanding Non Monogamies* (Routledge), a collection of essays by academics and activists exploring how polyamory and agreed open relationships work. Relationships that are, Barker believes, a way forward for the 21st century, a time when the government frantically preaches the importance of keeping homes intact, but is certainly not advocating more broad-based intimate relationships as the way.

'For so long there has been an absolute assumption that monogamy is the way it must be for a society to function well for partnerships, families and homes to hold together. But in this century we live far longer than ever before, so people might be married for 50 or so years, which makes monogamy a very daunting prospect. Is it so wrong if people want to experience more than one person, sexually, through several decades? The evidence is that they do. So shouldn't we be realistic and sympathetic to people who choose unorthodox ways if these will help homes stay together and enable people to live in way they find satisfying, provided they are not harming anyone else? In my view rather than condemning new approaches we should be open to seeing how they may meet the needs of new generations and help preserve secure homes for children.'

When Megh and Matt met 15 years ago they had the most conventional of aspirations – to marry, buy a house and have a child and this they did. But over time Megh, who had been used to a life of sexual variety and experiment realised that, much as she loves Matt, being sexually monogamous is too great a restraint for her.

Matt's expression is of intelligent thoughtfulness as he explains: 'Megh and I had a consciously unconventional relationship from the beginning. Even during the periods when we were actually monogamous, our personalities and philosophies and ideas are such that we knew we didn't want a rigid role based relationship. I had seen through a close friend how stifling that can be to love, and an independent spirit. What happens is people meet someone else, fall in love and can't be open about it, and so they see the only way as leaving, which means the primary relationship is destroyed. That didn't seem the right way to me.'

Yet a casual open relationship didn't fit their ideals either.

Megh explains: 'For us commitment and a love that is based on the idea of it lasting, being a permanent part of life, is important and I was realising that. Three years ago I met Dave and was interested in him. I knew that in a monogamous relationship that wasn't permissible, but we were getting close and I was wondering how to deal with the desire to be together and realising it was potentially a threat to my relationship with Matt.'

Matt did not immediately find the situation easy when Megh explained it, but he says: 'I recognised that Megh's new relationship was important to her and therefore I thought it worth the risk of trying to incorporate Dave into our relationship.'

He pauses for a moment, 'I guess I see what we are doing as dealing with some of the pressures that might exist in a monogamous relationship and confronting head on the reality that Megh might fall in love with Dave and chose him over me, if she had to make a choice. But because Dave and I have become close, I like and trust his integrity, I feel my life has been enhanced. I don't have anyone else I want to bring into the home, at present, but that is a possibility we all acknowledge.'

For Dave it is somewhat different, 'I came out of a 17-year monogamous relationship. I am basically monogamously hardwired, but when I met Megh I was drawn to her. I knew nothing of polyamory situations incorporating more than a single couple. Whatever, if we were to be healthy and happy in a relationship I had to meet Matt and realise what I was getting into.'

Good intentions are one thing, but making the reality work can be another. So I spoke with Megh, Matt and Dave a year later.

'We are still living and loving together. We are settled into our daily routines and have found a happy balance under one roof' was how Megh put it. 'But the moving thing was a big step because we had to work out how we would live altogether. Dave is in the basement, so I visit him there, but he comes up to Matt's and my part of the house a lot. In fact there is an easy-going flow between us all.'

Even so Matt talks of the need to 'combat any jealousy, and you understand that has required some effort for him.

'You have to cultivate an attitude of what can I give, instead of what am I losing? It's a question of shifting the usual focus. I had two brief relationships but they weren't going to work out as part of our poly family. Finding someone who will be part of the family we envisage as for the long haul is an organic process. There has to be a feeling that the other person is respectful of our relationships, and there must be a basis for friendship and a genuine sharing of values.'

Dave comes in here, 'I think of it as aesthetic consideration, thinking about how my behaviour affects Matt, and although I am only interested in a monogamous sexual relationship, I regard having Matt as part of the equation as a safety valve because I love Megh but don't want my relationship with her to become all consuming. I don't think that would work for her.'

The thing upsetting Megh most, when we first talked, was her parent's rejection of how she chose to live, and as a result the loss for her son Tomos of a relationship with his grandparents. She says, 'Matt and I were really hurt and angry at some of what had happened, the mean things said.'

So it is with touching delight that she tells in a flow of words how her parents 'have done a 180 degrees turn around. Before last autumn they decided they needed to have a different attitude or they would lose me completely as family.

'I told Matt they were reaching out in the only way they knew, saying they would meet us halfway. We said that was good and once that happened everything moved ahead and with huge benefit. They were calm when we met, not emotional and they explained how much they realised they wanted to have us as family. In fact they have built a house on the neighbouring island to us and when we visited, with Dave, she made a bed for him and we all got on wonderfully.'

Estelle, Ed and Lea did not choose to become a polyamory family as a matter of ideology. Estelle tells their tale. She and Ed were married 'very young' in 1997, but all too soon their relationship went 'off track'. There were repeated arguments, some marriage guidance counselling and they bought their own house in 2005 thinking this would improve things. It did not and a year later they decided to separate.

'We were apart for a year and during that time Ed was a serial dater' Estelle explains. 'I dated anyone I could get my hands on – including Lea.'

She and Estelle had been dating some five months when Ed came back to town and Estelle and he 'realised our affection for each other was still there and we wanted to try reconciling.'

At the same time Estelle did not want to lose Lea from her life. 'It was clearly difficult for us all. The three of us managed to hang out together and we discovered that we all got along pretty well' Estelle recollects. 'Then around the time Ed and I were moving back into the home together, Lea decided to go and live with her sister in another part of the country.'

For the following two years Ed and Estelle worked on getting their relationship back on track in a way that would endure, and in the doing she says joyfully, 'we rekindled the flame – to a point that it burned brighter than it ever had before in our relationship.' Lea visited from time to time and suddenly announced that she wanted to 'come home'. The three of them discussed this notion, and decided says Estelle, that they would, 'give the poly lifestyle a try'.

When we spoke Lea had been with them for a year and they were planning to move into a new home which they had chosen together.

Estelle and Lea were very aware of how little they understood what they had embarked upon and they knew nobody else in a threesome relationship. The two women took an adult education class in the polyamory lifestyle.

Through this they discovered a clear wish to be a 'polyfidelitous' family. This means, explains Estelle, that, 'although we aren't exactly monogamous we aren't open to additional relationships either. None of us feel we need anything beyond the three of us.'

Then she is reflective, 'although my separation from Ed, when it happened, was hard, it was probably the best thing for our marriage. We both felt that a 'reset' button had been pressed by the time we found our way back to each other.

Estelle is the one who has the most the difficulty being open about her situation, confronting the disapproval and prejudices of people who do not understand. It angers her. After all, she says, it's not that they are trampling over society's accepted norms in any other way. Indeed they are stalwarts of the local community, involving themselves in local activities and volunteering.

What she does recognise is that each has felt like the one 'left out' of intimacy from time to time, and yet she says there really haven't been problems of jealousy.

'Yes, we've found it challenging at times but we are all so close, and we all feel our arrangement is incredibly rewarding for the most part, and in many ways, from having three incomes and sharing housework, to having a referee when arguments happen, and having two people you love at home where we can all be together.'

Estelle describes herself as less 'out of the closet' than the others. 'The people we work with, and their families all pretty much know about our relationship. Eric's family is very liberal, and Lea isn't close to hers. But Estelle is very close to her largely Christian evangelical family and as she also works with some of these relatives she fears her job might be in jeopardy and that her family might be very distressed'. Yet this upsets her, 'I have a desire to be more honest. I want everyone to know that I am in love with two of the sweetest people in the world.'

Stepping Outside the Orthodox

Barker 's interest in new monogamies comes in part from personal experience of stepping outside the orthodox, yet she will not discuss how things are in her own private life. She explains that, after being interviewed on her views, in the *Guardian* newspaper, she was described as 'practising polyamory", and was shocked by the level of hostility directed at her as a result. How she was made to feel stigmatised.

Presumably this is the reason people in poly families in the UK, who write anonymously on website blogs, and meeting sites, do not wish to talk on the record about their chosen way.

So, although Barker is clear the subject needs opening up for public debate, sorry, she is not making herself the case study.

We met at the Open University one autumnal morning and, while we sat in the glasshouse café over cups of steaming coffee and hot chocolate, Barker described how polyamory – the word which only got into the English Oxford Dictionary in 2006, comes from the Greek and translates enticingly as 'many loves' – works in principle. It strikes her as a particularly promising model of new monogamy because it is generally practised within a context of rules, and understandings, mutually agreed.

The fundamental premise, Barker explained, is, 'the belief that it is acceptable or even ideal for people whether heterosexual, gay, or with particular sexual behaviour, to have more than one loving or sexual partner at the same time. It should not be confused with polygamy where men can have as many women as they wish, but women may not have other men. Both partners have the right to extra partners. We are talking equality here.'

The central focus is, generally, a 'primary partnership' – perhaps a married couple such as Megh and Matt, or a couple committed to being together for the long haul – but where they have an understanding that the essence of their intimate connection is not monogamy. If everyone is agreed it is how they want things to be, then it is workable. What is not workable is a situation when having an extra lover is a unilateral decision.

Barker also explains that one of the aims of polyamory and open relationships when everyone is a willing participant, is that it can make dealing with the destructive toxin of sexual jealousy easier. A jealousy that is experienced in bucket-loads by the involuntary victims of infidelity.

She explains it this way: 'If you are a poly family you deal with sexual jealousy, or the danger of it, differently to when, say, a partner in a monogamous relationship is unfaithful. It is not treated as a problem of betrayal and with the person who has 'done wrong' becoming the enemy. Rather the person feeling jealous takes it as their problem which they need to deal with if they are not to sabotage their poly unit. And it is talked about with everyone involved which can go a long way towards easing it.'

Indeed the cast-iron dedication to monogamy as a must-have in relationships is counter productive in today's liberated climate where there are so many opportunities for varied sexual experiences, in the view of psychotherapist Tammy Nelson author of *Getting The Sex You Want*.

'If there's anything fundamental to the meaning of marriage in Western society, it's monogamy. In fact, monogamy may be the *only* thing that remains essential to most people's idea of marriage. Given the almost universal denunciation of infidelity you'd think it must be quite rare. At least *nice* people don't do it...' Except, as we see, they do it in considerable numbers.

Infidelity and Divorce

Numbers equalling an epidemic, declares writer Angela Levin, who carried out an in-depth newspaper survey on unfaithfulness. She described us as seeming to be, 'in the middle of an infidelity epidemic'. Based on her figures eight out of ten couples will, at some time, experience infidelity. A more widely agreed figure is infidelity comes into 50 percent of marriages, the figures on cohabitees is not so clear cut. And it apparently goes up to 60 percent in the US where you might expect otherwise, with the great swathe of the country that constitutes the Bible Belt and evangelical faith. But miscreants surface fairly regularly for all that. Remember Jimmy Bakker Assemblies of God minister, and television preacher? It was revealed that he had had a sexual encounter in 1980 with a young church secretary from Massapequa, N.Y., and had paid her $265,000 to keep quiet.

The Bakker marriage ended in divorce. Unfaithfulness, with the unravelling of trust, respect and the sense of being a bonded unit that it often brings, means this is all too often the end result. Indeed Frank Pittman in his book *Grow Up* (Golden Books) has found that cheating is implicated in 90 percent of first-time divorces. On the other hand the American John Gottman, who has spent 35 years researching marriage in the greatest depth, has it that, 'only 20 percent of divorces are entirely caused by an affair'.

A UK survey earlier this decade found that adulterous behaviour accounted for 27 per cent of all divorce cases. While Levin listened to 59 percent of wives saying they would leave their marriages if they could afford to do so.

Whether it leads to divorce or a propped-up unhappy marriage, infidelity so often makes its mark on a marriage Pittman says, thinking of what he has seen in his own practice.

Day after day in his office, Pittman hears from those who have been 'messing around' leading secret lives often resulting in 'wrenching divorces', inflicting pain on their children. Or if these people do not end up in the divorce courts they stagger on in a deeply unsatisfactory way.

'They lead secret lives, as they hide themselves from their marriages. Or they make desperate, tearful, sweaty efforts at holding on to the shreds of a life they've betrayed.'

Quite possibly 'marital aids' will be called in, Pittman says, 'to keep these people company while they avoid living their life. Such practical affairs help them keep the marriage steady but distant. They thus encapsulate the marital deficiency, so the infidel can neither establish a life without the problems nor solve them. Affairs can wreck a good marriage, but can help stabilize a bad one.'

Louise de Salvo author of *Adultery* (Beacon Press) muses.

'In affairs, each gender wants to live the possibilities foreclosed to them in 'normal' marriages – women seek autonomy; men seek intimacy. Which suggests that if a marriage accommodates these behaviours there will, perhaps be less reason to stray.'

Good news if that happens, but if it doesn't, surely you shouldn't be consigned to a life of giving up on what you want, or the greater happiness that could come if you had several people in your life, who met different needs.

That is the tenor of Barker's thinking. Her gleaming smile and easy manner co-exist with a confrontational default position.

'In our society having multiple partners is usually seen in a very negative light but consider: there is such positive potential It means people needn't feel constrained, or go for endless one-night stands as a way of getting their sexual and emotional variety. With polyamory relationships and others where people invest in long-term liaisons and genuinely care for each other, it is not just about sex but it is also a way to build a community of loving relationships that ideally can support a caring home life.'

So is Barker right? If we accept that the moral superglue of an avowed marriage commitment is not holding when it comes to monogamy, should we as a society consider a tolerant and supportive attitude to those who believe they can create stronger, more enduring relationships and home bases, with sexual unorthodoxy? After all we have seen a progressive change when it comes to gay relationships. For all the opposition that seemed rooted in an inviolable moral stand, it has now come to pass that gay people can publicly celebrate with a civil union, and even marriage is under discussion.

Ménage à Trois

My own perspective has its roots in the time I became embroiled in a *ménage à trois* during the years, in my mid 20s, when I was living in Amsterdam. None of us – myself, the other woman, Els, or Ron, lover of us both – was married to each other or anyone else. But what happened did initiate me into the idea that a relationship embracing more than just two people was an idea worth considering.

This was the 1970s, and the sound of social taboos being kicked underfoot rattled across the cobbled streets. Iconoclasm was the name of the game, and part of that was a great deal of opening up of relationships and sexual experimentation. I was an alien abroad. Indeed a broad who had brought to this city the most conventional ideas on sexual behaviour. But the thing that shook those conventions most thoroughly was seeing free and easy sexual behaviour, that seemed amiable and not very troublesome, if at times requiring complicated logistics. It primed me for choosing to be part of a threesome.

This was not what I had intended. When I became involved with Ron, a Dutch-Indonesian psychologist of considerable charisma, I believed he was single, and that was how I wanted it. Soon after our affair had begun, however, Ron let me know that there was another woman. Els was one of his students at Leiden University where he lectured.

He initiated a meeting between us in a way that was as I now see it, insensitive to a fine degree. He invited me to a concert with him and Els and it was when we all met up that I realised what was going on. Els, I later understood, had come to accept that a relationship with Ron meant she must be 'open' to it including others. I had not yet had this conversation.

Waking the next day, knowing that Els had spent the night with Ron, imagining… wondering…how had their intimacy compared to that which I had with Ron, turmoil took over. I was dazed, shocked, and it struck me that, as he had been unfaithful to me, I must give him the shove. Through my teens I had consumed a large diet of Valentine comic strips and women's magazines in which men who strayed from the path of fidelity and devotion to one woman only were rogues. From this I had drawn an unquestioning moral code. As well, my own parents were evidently (and I have no reason to doubt it was the case) entirely true to each other. Whether they had other yearnings I did not and do not know.

When I confronted Ron and explained that this kind of sexual openness was not what I thought I had signed up to in beginning an affair with him, he insisted with the force of his intelligence and charm, that we must talk and that he wanted me to understand his thoughts before making a definite decision.

So he introduced me to his philosophical belief – one that was very much a part of the thinking in Holland and similar Scandinavian countries at that time – that humans who are programmed to explore, experience and have a desire to taste as much of the best of life as they can, naturally want to extend this to the sexual sphere. If they are inhibited in this all-too-natural impulse by limiting conventions and religion, then the result is frequently a lot of lying and deceit, many broken relationships and a sum of human unhappiness that does not stack up. Wasn't it much better to acknowledge that sexual desires outside the monogamous are likely to occur, and to have a relationship that is strong, loving and understanding enough, to allow for this?

This libertarian argument has, of course, been a mainstay of various alternative lifestyles, and as discussed above is being resumed in a different context for the 21st century, but it was new to me and it convinced me it would be a profound failure to retreat into the conservative (although only with a small 'c') young woman that I was.

So I settled for being part of a threesome with Ron and Els, although we kept our individual homes. Els and I came to know and like each other and we acknowledged that, as we both loved Ron, being jointly involved with him was workable. It surprised us to find that, knowing there was no dark secret, and that we were both loved and secure in the relationship, enabled a camaraderie which did go some way towards mitigating against jealousy.

In due course I left Amsterdam and this relationship. It was a decision which came about in part because I realised I wanted a relationship with at least the possibility of it evolving and perhaps incorporating children. But that was not on the cards with my *ménage a trois*. I remember thinking before deciding to leave, that it was rather like Dorothy Parker's comment on a Katherine Hepburn performance – that she ran the gamut of emotions from A to B. There was no scope for Ron's and my relationship to progress so long as there had to be equally distributed time for both me and Els. Even a two-week holiday for the two of us on our own was out of the question. Nor was the idea of a polyamory set up with us living under one roof what any of us considered.

Without this experience, I would have been as convinced as anyone that monogamy is the bottom line for a relationship if you want equality, trust, respect and a life not ripped to smithereens with sexual jealousy. Instead I came to see how it might be possible to build a sustainable home with more than one sexual partner, in the way Megh, Matt and Dave have done, and later we will hear more of how they have fared since I first interviewed them.

It happens that the relationship I have with Olly came with the unspoken assumption that we would be faithful to each other, and yet there have been times during our years together when that has felt like a constraint too far – particularly so when things were not going well; when I felt the commitment I had signed up to was not bringing the things I wanted from a relationship.

I can see how I'm-the-centre-of-the-universe stuff was preoccupying me. True, Olly seemed to be taking me very much for granted, quite withdrawn emotionally, but then I was very absorbed in my separate life – work, friends and dreams of how much greener the grass in the other field might be. I may have been unhappy but I was certainly causing both Olly and myself considerable melancholy as well.

It was at this time, I wondered whether bringing in someone we both cared for very much might have brought to our nuclear unit new animation, a broader support system, a wider framework for loving friendship. I knew nothing of polyamory at the time, but I did ponder quite seriously whether, if the 'other woman' was Pauline, a dear friend with whom I had shared a flat during my early working life in Manchester, it might be a positive thing. We had a deeply bonded platonic friendship and I truly loved her.

Later when I was with Olly he too, grew extremely fond of Pauline. We socialised a great deal, went on holidays together, and in due course she moved into the basement flat of our home. After a while the man she was to marry came too. Olly and I became extremely fond of him as well.

Would I have been jealous if Olly had wanted to include Pauline, sexually, in our relationship? If she had wanted that too?

How would he have felt if I had come to want intimacy with Pauline? Or with Pauline's partner? I shall never know. But I have an inkling that it could have been good, a multi-faceted relationship laced through with such deep affection and friendship that it might, indeed, have built something extra into our collective relationship and prevented some of the times of difficulties, disappointments and stand-offs that have occurred between Olly and me through the years.

It is quite possible a broader relationship that had come about out of already long established caring for each other, rather than just an ideological idea – the downfall for many alternative home lives – could have shielded our children from being caught in the crossfire between the two of us. A third, a fourth, person might have been able to mediate or just help us see how damned unreasonable we were being.

Had this come to pass would the way I – we – lived have been judged immoral? Would we have been condemned as at best wacky at worst disgraceful no matter how happy we might have been? No matter that our way would not have harmed anyone else? No matter that we weren't propagandists looking for recruits to our way?

Ethics of Polyamory

Once you get into exploring promoters of new monogamies, you come across *The Ethical Slut: A Practical Guide to Polyamory, Open Relationships and Other Adventures* co-authored by Dossie Easton and Janet W. Hardy. It became an underground best seller during the 70s and when the book recently re-issued, it was interesting to see that whatever else we may think has progressed, attitudes towards freer sexuality have not. There was much prurient media attention.

Easton and her co-author offer practical guidance on how such long-term relationships are put into practice and how they work. What you learn comes directly from Easton's own experiences, she explains.

'The idea started way back in the communal era in 1969 when I was in Haight-Ashbury. I said, "if I want to change my world in terms of how relationships are, and be non-monogamous forever in my own personal life, it should be about warmth and affection." One of the very first things I learned was how to be affectionate towards many lovers. There was no precedent, but it worked; I could love them and care for them… and be loyal in a new way… We were the love generation and we were very new to sexual freedom. There was a lot of idealism.'

Easton's personal situation is, 'my life partner whom I live with, and a secondary lover, and some playmates. Essentially what you are creating is… an interconnected family. A community.' Equally essential, Easton stresses, is that the book refers to an *ethical* slut, 'you should behave in such a way that your actions don't cause harm.'

Reg and Sarah, both in their late 30s, with the looks of a couple of thoroughly nice home guys, who live in the ultra-conservative state of Virginia in the U.S, are well aware there would be plenty of disapproval of the sexually open lifestyle they have evolved.

The are not interested in bringing anyone new into their one-to-one married unit, but they do believe sexual variety is important to them. They, as Megh and Matt believe that finding a workable way of meeting their desires will help their marriage survive and give succour to Sarah's 10-year-old daughter by a previous husband, and the six-month-old baby she has with Reg.

Both have broken marriages behind them in which they lived by their marriage vows. But they came to see sexual problems, imbalance in desire, and lack of sexual communication were at least part of the reason these unions did not last. In their new marriage they have 'made a point of being very open and honest with each other about our need for sexual adventure. We have worked out a way to make it good for us both, while being absolutely clear that being together, and having our own family, is what we want. That we absolutely do not want anyone else becoming a part of that unit.'

Sarah married aged 23, partly she says, to get away from her severe military, Southern Baptist home where she was punished harshly and often for things she did not understand. She says, 'I had a dream of creating a perfect home life. The Cleaver Family. My husband and I stayed together 13 years and

I worked hard at it because we had a daughter.

'On the outside everything looked perfect. We had a lovely house in a rural village, with two acres, but it was a pretty prison. I felt absolutely stifled, very unhappy sexually because my husband refused to make love with me telling me I was ugly and unlovable. I began to feel I must do anything I could to please him if ever he did want sex. The whole thing was horribly tense.

'Then two years ago I felt I would die emotionally if I stayed so I left, swearing I would never have a serious relationship again. I did a lot of sexual adventuring before I met Reg. We found we had a great deal in common, we seemed to be able to say anything to each other. We began flirting and from there came sex and it was tremendous.'

Reg had left a home where he had a formal relationship with his deeply religious family and left when he was 19 feeling a surge of excitement at being free. But by age 22 he had married, 'Because I was horny and religious I had to get married. However I saw it as something for life, and I assumed we would be monogamous. We had a son but when he was five months my wife left.'

He met his next wife through a 'cult-like religious group' and she joined him living in a communal home with other couples, but all monogamous.

They had a child but his wife, he thinks, had grown to dislike the community and went, leaving Reg with their child

He says wryly, 'I found myself horny and religious once again. He met Kim doing strip acts in a club.

'I was very turned on but rationalised it as the noble impulse to save her.' They had a brief sexual liaison then got married and within two months Kim was pregnant. She stopped stripping, began going to church and Reg felt he had achieved a conversion.

Kim had a daughter and son from an earlier marriage. Reg recalls 'to all intents and purposes we were a happy family although it was a manic time, and Kim had roller-coaster moods. I remained convinced I should stay and that I must be monogamous. But Kim threw me out and I went home and got custody of my children.'

Reg then met Sarah in the local Unitarian church in Virginia, where both were singing in the choir and he echoes what she said, about them feeling that they had found in each other a person they could be truly open and bonded with.

Because they quickly established that they wanted sexual adventure as part of their lifestyle, Sarah initiated this at a festival. She found herself drawn to a young woman and, in the lingo used for this kind of thing, asked if she would 'like to play'? Sarah explains, 'I told her I had a 'fabulous stud' available and we went into this cage space in the middle of a dungeon area. We had a warming up period and then Reg had sex with her and I was the dominatrix telling her what to do. I found it a turn on, but it was important that afterwards Reg and I re-connected. He understood that and was very loving and reassuring that night.'

This was the beginning of a regular pattern of sexual adventures with restrictions. The person or people brought in 'to play' were told, very clearly that hers and Reg's emotional intimacy was exclusive.

Reg is clear that sharing this way of being in relationship with Sarah gives them a stronger bond than they would have in a conventional marriage. He says, 'Neither of us really feels wired for strict monogamy, so why not recognise it? We feel we are very strong together, that our hearts absolutely belong to each other.'

Sarah, who is nursing their small baby, nods, 'We are very much a married couple. We want home, family, and a life in that respect that is utterly ordinary. And so I am a stay-at-home Mum so far as the children are concerned, then like other kids they have babysitters when we go out together.'

At the same time they feel the need to strive for acceptance of their style of open relationship and, with what must have taken some *chutzpah*, they 'came out' to their Unitarian Church. Sarah tells how, 'in a discussion on family and faithfulness. I stood up and said there are many permutations of how families can be faithful and loving but without monogamy. It wasn't easy, and I did wonder how they would react, but the Unitarian church is a welcoming congregation and we wanted to be honest with them and gain their acceptance because we believe what we have found may help others who want something similar but need to dare to address what makes them work.'

The Roots of Monogamy

However glowingly people in unorthodox relationships describe their degree of happiness, it does not mean they necessarily achieve a greater degree of happiness than those who choose to have conventional relationships where they are on the whole, as one friend said to the other in Anthony Trollope's *The Warden*, 'all in all to each other'. Indeed I could equally fill this chapter with tales of entirely faithful couples who would not have it any other way, but my point is that we should question being censorious of people treading the unorthodox route.

Not that protesting monogamous marriage is new. Frederick Engels in 1884 in *The Monogamous Family*, gives a historic romp through the ways the institution has privileged men and quite intentionally compelled women to accept that this was an appropriate order of things so that, by and large, they assumed domestic labour, childbearing and providing sexual pleasure was their unpaid duty.

Tracing the evolution of marriage Engels notes, ironically, we may conclude, that matrimony was seen as a sign that civilisation was beginning. But, 'it (marriage) is not as the reconciliation of man and woman. Quite the contrary, monogamous marriage comes on the scene as the subjugation of the one sex by the other; it announces a struggle between the sexes unknown throughout the whole previous prehistoric period.'

Monogamy for women was an absolute rule of marriage intended to ensure that husbands knew the children born to them were their heirs, and because women were seen, by law as the property of men. When a woman did have sex with another man and her husband did not object, the situation was called 'wife loaning'. If it was the man who sought another partner, it was called 'male privilege.'

That marriage was problematic for women was one of the things nineteenth century feminists saw clearly, even though there were few alternatives for women if they wanted a sustainable way of life, provision for their children. Many spoke out boldly against what Cicely Hamilton described as an exchange on the part of the woman of her person for, 'the means of subsistence'. Flora Madonald Denison seeing how thoroughly woman's sexuality was part of the package, rather than a source of mutual pleasure, spoke furiously of, 'an institution which robs a woman of her individuality and reduces her to the level of a prostitute.' Frances Power Cobbe was wittier inveighing against marriage as, 'analogous to the relationship between two tarantulas in a bell jar. When one of these delightful creatures is placed under a glass with a companion of his own species, a little smaller than himself, he forthwith gobbles it up', but it was with clear intent.

If anyone is poster girl for avoiding marriage and recognising that open relationships should be permitted, it was glamorous, turbaned, chain-smoking Simone de Beauvoir who famously had a relationship with Jean Paul Sartre which, through the years, brought in a galaxy of lovers.

It was, however, Sartre, de Beauvoir's lover for 51-years, who asked that they have a sexually open relationship. She agreed even though there was to be considerable pain for her in the doing. The fact their relationship was open did not slay sexual jealousy for de Beauvoir.

Sartre and de Beauvoir were also, from time to time, involved in group liaisons. In 1932 de Beauvoir was transferred to Rouen to teach and here she began a relationship with 18-year-old Olga Kosakiewicz, one of her students. In due course Sartre became part of the relationship... De Beauvoir had envisaged this triad giving 'authenticity' to her relationship, but in fact the complexity overwhelmed it, she declared, and Olga came to represent a very real threat to de Beauvoir's relationship with Sartre.

Others, too, have found open relationships far harder than the new monogamists allow for as they embark on such a lifestyle. Yet that does not mean they would choose otherwise. For all her suffering, de Beauvoir stoutly described the open relationship she had with Sartre as the greatest achievement of her life.

Sexual freedom was written into the *modus vivendi* of the Bloomsbury set along with their modern attitudes towards feminism and pacifism. A group occupying itself with literature, the arts, criticism and economics – Virginia and Leonard Woolf, Carrington, Lytton Strachey, Clive and Vanessa Bell, E.M. Forster, John Maynard Keynes and so on – saw themselves as libertarians and progressives who were not concerned with conforming to the rules of society. They were described by Frances Partridge as 'living in squares but loving in triangles.'

The literary editor, novelist and memoirist Diana Athill shares the view that too much emphasis on sexual fidelity can damage rather than enrich relationships. Barry Rekord, the man she lived with for 40 years brought his young girlfriend, Sally Cary, to live with them, and Sally remains, Athill has insisted, one of her dearest friends.

'Fidelity in the sense of keeping one's word I respect, but I think it tiresome that it is tied so tightly in people's minds to the idea of sex. The idea that a wife owes absolute fidelity to her husband has deep and tangled roots, being based not only on a man's need to know himself to be the father of his wife's child, but also on the even deeper, darker feeling that man owns woman. God's having made her for his convenience. And woman's anxious clamour for her husband's fidelity springs from the same primitive root; she feels it to be necessary proof of her value.'

'Closing the Adultery Gap'

For women of my generation caught up in the new wave feminism of the early 1970s, relationships may have seemed more egalitarian than those of our earlier feminist sisters, but that was often a fragile veneer. There were still very clear ideas about how women and men should behave sexually. And on the subject of monogamy, there was a far greater indulgence of men's sexual freedom than of women's. I remember arriving in the office for my first national newspaper job and, within hours, I had been told that the secretary on the news desk was known as 'the office bicycle' because she had slept with a number of her male colleagues. The fact that they had sex with any female not bolted down won them brownie points not nasty names.

For all that women were, indeed, experimenting with

sexual freedom there was nevertheless a strong desire for many men to find a virginal woman when it came to marriage – look at the importance attached to Lady Di's purity when she became engaged to Prince Charles. It was seen as gaving added value to the vow of monogamy.

Along with a great many teenage girls at the end of the 50s, I had been willingly seduced by the idea of romantic love, the joy of being the home-based carer tending the needs of a man, honoured to claim his name, have his children, and be utterly faithful on the assumption he would do the same.

But of course at the heart of all this was a lie that in due course we would discover. Men felt entitled to take lovers because they could and it was assumed a wife would 'get over' this fall from grace, because that's how men are. Women did not get the same indulgence.

During the second half of the 20th century women, with increased opportunities for education, careers alongside men's and economic independence were getting the kind of opportunities for extra marital liaisons that men have traditionally had. They took them too, so that statistics on women's infidelity rose steadily. In the 1980s the British sociologist Annette Lawson carried out a large study forming the basis of her book *Adultery: An Analysis of Love and Betrayal* (Basic Books 1988), in which she said she had found that the rate of *increase* in infidelity was higher among women.

A trend taken up vigorously by younger women 'closing the adultery gap", according to the American online site HuffingtonPost in 2008.

'Younger women appear to be cheating on their spouses nearly as often as men.' Data gathered from the General Social Survey based at the University of Chicago, where a national representative sample had been used to track opinions and social behaviours of Americans since 1972, found an increase in both older women and men, as well as newly married couples being unfaithful.

An increase in female infidelity may not be the best guide to women's progress, but it does show how women will equal men with their determination to have their sexual and emotional desires met when this is not happening in their committed relationships.

The need for a feminist perspective on women's infidelity is the point of Dalma Heyn's book *The Erotic Silence of the Married Woman* (Bloomsbury), written at the beginning of the 1990s. She explores the history of women's sexuality and the problematic nature of female desire, the way women have been taught to suppress their own needs and desires in order to fit men's wishes, to be the 'good' and 'perfect' wife.

Given the changes that had taken place in two decades Heyn addressed a conventional wisdom whereby we had been 'lulled into thinking that women's extramarital sex is not an issue'.

But Heyn insisted it was indeed an issue.

'Most striking were the women who were in pain – overwhelmed by the craziness of their lives since the onset of their affairs – but who still felt their affairs had changed them, if not their lives, for the better. The believed they had restored their sexuality, or found it in new way that made them feel they had unearthed 'a capacity for pleasure'.

And for pain. But that is not a deterrent. Very clearly marriage vows do not make us feel responsible, guilty or frightened enough to avoid temptation. A reality of the 21st century is that we shall – are – seeing more of it with the growth of internet opportunities for making sexual contacts and indulging erotic behaviour.

Delighting in Secrecy

Dr Janet Reibstein avers that, 'Men and women… all too often feel the gap between the marriage they have and their 'ideal marriage'. Perhaps because of this gap and their sophistication over sex and intimacy, men and women have affairs. But they are not supposed to and they know it. They are letting down the marital idea to which they still hold. Their affairs, therefore, have to be secret.'

This secrecy as much as the physical coupling can be the thing that gives the affair its delight. As the author of an article in the US Psychology Today has it, 'affairs generally involve sex, at least enough sex to create a secret that seals the conspiratorial alliance of the affair, and makes the relationship tense, dangerous and thus exciting. Most affairs consist of a little sex and hours on telephone.'

Yet the secrecy also does the harm Reibstein says. If an affair is discovered it can be like an exocet exploding into a relationship that has been built on the understanding that both partners are committed to monogamy. Powerful feelings of betrayal, of trust shattered, of humiliation at being so cuckolded, fury, sexual jealousy, a desperate desire for revenge and retribution, are a familiar and corrosive run of emotions that often come to dominate the marriage.

The impact of unfaithfulness on the shared identity and protected space of an emotionally intimate relationship, explains Dr Reibstein, can leave the betrayed partner feeling violated. 'Infidelity can be identity threatening for both partners: one for violating the 'rules' of couples' commitment, the other for abiding by the rules and having been unaware of the deception,' she says.

Confusion may hit the betrayed person broadsides if they

see their marriage as a good one in which they and their partner truly love each other. But this, observes the Psychology Today author, is to miss the point, 'being in love does not protect people from lust.' And if there is one thing that seduces people into abandoning home and all it contains of their life, it is lust. The power of lust convinces us what we feel is a transcendental emotion, not to be denied. That to refuse its siren call is to abandon the possibility of an erotic love that comes so rarely in a lifetime. And so on. The script is familiar and trail of destruction it can leave equally so.

Moving Past Infidelity

The revelation of infidelity leaves partners with a crisis to confront which can be terrifying and seemingly insurmountable. Yet there are couples who, if they recognise that they do not want the affair to destroy the relationship and also what Bert talks of as 'the whole edifice on which we had built our existence together', may find a way to prevent the affair leading to the divorce courts.

Bert tells how he behaved when his wife Louisa admitted that she had a lover. 'I was furious, terribly upset, hurt, and I felt in acute danger. But once I had got over the utter chaos in my head, the pain at the idea of someone else with Louisa, I realised there weren't many choices. I had to find a way to save what I valued or walk out on her.'

Louisa had been seeing a man who worked in a bar near where she worked. This lover had told her over and over how she was the most important thing in his life, that he had never felt such passion before.

What happened has the ring of a TV soap. Bert learned all this after seeing a text message left on Louisa's phone. Then he overheard a conversation when the man rang Louisa begging her to see him.

'When I asked if she was having an affair she said yes, but she'd thought I wouldn't mind because I hadn't seemed that interested in sex recently. We've been together nearly thirty years, and I guess as happens our relationship sex had become workaday. I know I haven't bothered enough with making Louisa feel good, valued. As I began to think about this I felt that what had happened was partly my fault, and that perhaps if she would break off the affair, we could work together on making our marriage stronger.

'She told me she didn't want to lose me, or the life we have built, the house we've been in since we married and where our children were born. All this came pouring out and I believed her. But she said she didn't know how to get rid of the man. He had told her he was in love with her, couldn't live without her and she said she felt bad at what it would do to him if she told him they were finished.

'I decided then that I had to take action and make sure it stopped. I had to save our life together. I told Louisa that I was going to see the man and tell him it was finished. She didn't say anything. I drove over to the place where he worked, marched up to him and said, "This has to stop. You are to leave my wife alone. Don't ring her up, she is my wife, the mother of my children and she lives in our house. And that is how she wants it."'

He remembers, 'The man came on with "you can't stop me, I love her and she loves me". I just cut in and told him to shut up. After I had left I wondered what I had to do next because I realised that he had made Louisa feel very important and cared about and that the same hadn't been happening in our relationship. So I suggested we go together to counselling.'

He pauses, 'It's not a magic bullet but it was hugely helpful to us. We have not been good at talking when things get diffi-cult, but the counsellor asked very direct questions and wouldn't put up with evasive answers. And so we looked at all the good things in our relationship, the reasons we had chosen each other, and it was like a fresh start, because we were saying these positive things and feeling very warm towards each other and we have managed to keep talking.'

Bert is pensive then, 'But of course that hasn't completely wiped out the pain and hurt I feel at Louisa having been so intimate with someone else. Some days there is an explosive anger and real dislike of her, but I don't want that to take over so I just go off by myself on those occasions. I assume one day it won't worry me and I do feel confident it isn't going to happen again. For me monogamy is important.'

For both Bert and Louisa keeping the home together, and continuing to be caring and protective parents, was important enough that they resolved to get over the affair and make sure it did not happen again.

What happens to children when we believe we can make choices for ourselves is something that Jen had to confront.

She had convinced herself she could incorporate the affair she was having with a younger man, into her married life, in such a way that her three children need not be affected, and their home would remain physically intact.

She was 35, had been married 12 years and had three small children when she began the affair with Sean 15 years younger than she. Sean began doing odd jobs around the large, ramshackle house they had in Northamptonshire. Jim, Jen's husband was frequently away on business.

'It sounds absurd,' Jen says. 'I was well aware I was being a Scarlet Woman but I just fell in love with Sean. I felt powerless, I was so much in love with him, and it was such a contrast to my marriage where sex was not much of a feature. The affair lasted 18 years.'

Jen put to her husband the audacious suggestion that Sean

be a lodger in the house, and her husband agreed seeing it as sense for one of their spare rooms to be occupied. So Sean moved in and the children, Jen says, seemed to accept this as a normal lodger arrangement and to enjoy his company.

'I love my children to bits and they are the bottom line. If I'd thought they were being harmed I would have ended the relationship with Sean, although it would have been almost unbearably painful, but they seemed fine.

Sean and I shared a bed when Jim was not home, but I made sure he was never there when the children came to me in the mornings.'

Yet the subterfuge became increasingly uncomfortable and with what she now acknowledges as the selfishness of youth, Jen wanted to tell Jim in the hope that somehow her relationship with Sean could be open and accepted.

Jen explains, 'I had a very warm, gentle relationship with Jim, but it was not passionate. Yet I hated lying to him. So eventually I did tell him that I'd fallen in love with Sean. I expected him to be angry, to issue an ultimatum – perhaps I wanted it in a way – but his reaction was very calm. He just said 'these things happen'. It gave me the message that I had his permission. I think Jim didn't want me to be unhappy and the problems we had with sex made him feel guilty. Perhaps my having sex with Sean was a relief for him because I don't think it was important for Jim. But his children and a stable home were very important. I think he feared I might leave if he objected to Sean.

'In fact, Jim and Sean were perfectly pleasant to each other, and in due course we became something of a threesome mixing together in the house and going on holiday a couple of times. Often invitations would be sent to all three of us.'

She reflects: 'I had convinced myself the children knew nothing, and that they enjoyed Sean as the lodger. But I now know that isn't true. One of my daughters talks of the confusion, the sense that their family was not like others. A feeling of things not being right.'

In her late teens this daughter went on to have a nervous breakdown and Jen wonders how far this disturbance had its genesis in 'my determination to have what I wanted without thinking about consequences.'

Her youngest son, too, has talked to Jen about the situation, since being grown up, describing a sense of something furtive. He often felt ashamed of his family, although he couldn't have said why.

Jen continues, 'He says now he wishes I had talked to him about it. I think he blames me for not having been truthful because his own relationships have been difficult, and he is convinced that has something to do with growing up with secrets in the home.'

In the end Sean left to marry a younger woman and have a family, Jen tells.

'I was in bits I couldn't think, just stayed in bed. This was very upsetting for the children because they didn't know what was wrong. Fortunately they had adult lives of their own by this time, so they weren't living with me.

'Now, I am in my 80s, and I still feel a lot of guilt. In a way I wish Jim had taken a stand and forced me to stop the affair. I'd have had to grow up and be a more satisfactory parent for the children then, but of course I cannot blame him for how he was. I have to recognise it was my responsibility and if the children have issues it is down to me.'

The hurt and anger the artist Louise Bourgeois experienced when, as a child, the young woman Sadie who was brought into the family ostensibly to be her governess, but she was in fact her father's mistress, has been made graphic in her work. In *Child Abuse (Artforum,* Dec 1982) Bourgeois depicts from a child's standpoint just how powerless, yet powerfully betrayed, she felt by her father and Sadie, and in a different way by her mother. In her pictures and writings you are drawn into the child's inchoate realisation of how her emotional safety has been abandoned by the adult players caught up in their drama.

Bourgeois wrote, 'Now you will ask me, how is it that in a middle-class family a mistress was a standard piece of furniture? Well the reason is that my mother tolerated it and that is the mystery. Why did she? Sadie is supposed to be there in my home, for me, as my teacher and actually you, my mother, are using me to keep track of your husband. That is child abuse.'

So what of Tomos, the child of Megh and Matt who is being brought up in their poly family? If there is a criticism that is likely to be voiced forcefully it is that children may be confused and emotionally harmed by irregular family arrangements, and particularly sexual sharing, as Jen says her children were.

Those things are most likely to happen Megh says, very firmly, when affairs are the known-unknown secret that children sense but do not recognise what is making them feel uneasy. She and Matt were clear that Tomos should not have to engage with anything that would make him feel different to other children, while he is still too young for them to explain their philosophy to him. They do not, Tomos is not in on the sexual arrangement in their threesome.

'Tomos knows Dave is a good friend, and a loved part of our family, and in due course if he asks questions we will explain. But when I began the affair with Dave I always went to his place and Matt was at home looking after Tomos. If for some reason Tomos wanted me home badly, Matt would just ring and I could get there quickly. Now I go downstairs to see Dave, usually after Tomos is in bed or away, and Tomos will quite often go and visit Dave and play with him.'

Matt nods, 'the biggest change with us all living together is that I see Dave less and less as Megh's partner in any sort of competitive way, but he is just one of our family and we are a very solid unit.'

Loving Links

The pain that may be inflicted on children by illicit affairs can be dreadful, David Miller knows, and so he describes himself as a realist. You cannot escape the fact, he says, that there are married people who, for all sorts of reasons, feel the need to have sex outside their marriage. But they also very much want to protect their families and keep the home together, so their goal is the utmost discretion. With this in mind a decade and a half ago he set up Loving Links, a dating agency for married people.

Miller and I meet for morning coffee beneath the dancing gleam of chandeliers in the Palm Court at Central London's Langham Hotel. To guide me in recognising him, Miller describes himself as 'the poor man's Steven Spielberg'', although in reality he is handsomer, foxier and probably more flamboyant in his self-promotion. Witness the delighted grin as he relates that the *Daily Mail* once referred to him as 'a threat to every house in Britain'.

Not that he agrees. He says he is probably doing a great deal to keep marriages together. The men and women coming to him are usually not very unhappy in their marriages but there are flaw lines and dangerous dissatisfactions.

'Often the partners are good friends, love their kids and enjoy being parents. They have put a lot into creating a home which meets their needs. But then there is sex and if that is not going well, it can be a real problem. So it is a good thing that sex is one of the very few sections of a marriage that you can take out and deal with elegantly.'

Following this thinking Miller introduces clients – there are more women than men – who are looking for sex without complications and he prides himself on the discernment with which he does it.

'It may be that a client's partner has stopped wanting sex, that they no longer fancy each other, that the sex they have is simply not satisfying.'

He insists he steers away from potential clients he suspects are ready to ditch their marriages, 'my main concern is to keep the core relationship strong, the home intact. If I were to take on people looking to fall in love and find a partner, the whole thing would be harmful and unpleasant. My role is to remove the problem caused by whatever inadequacy there is around and leave the perhaps 80 per cent of the marriage that is good so then people can get on with that.'

He knows it is not just the *Daily Mail* that would regard him with opprobrium but is unabashed, 'I see what I do as relationship mentoring for a new millennium. I might not call it pure as the driven… but I do it with courtliness and I have a system that guarantees absolute discretion so that the partners of my clients rarely get hurt. If I thought it added up to more unhappiness than happiness I would stop.'

James is a client of Loving Links, and when we talk he tells, very earnestly that what it offers has 'undoubtedly' helped him achieve his goal of staying married and giving his children a stable home. Before he heard of Miller he was reaching a point of 'worrying restlessness'.

'My wife had lost interest in sex and I was finding that very hard. We sleep in the same bed and I lie there wondering if there might be the possibility of something happening. It never does. But lack of sex with my wife affects me very badly. I become moody, and feel we are very far apart. My wife too is aware that our marriage doesn't feel right.

'I am a product of the 60s where we believed we could be very open about sex yet it wasn't possible with my wife, and we reached the impasse I describe. So here I am embarked on doing something which is incredibly secret because it seems the only way to stop myself wanting to leave. I had a very stable home myself as a child and it matters to me hugely that my children have the same.

'Through Loving Links I have met ten women and slept with half of them. I have only once become more attached to a woman than I intended and it got to the point where I did contemplate leaving, but once I looked over the precipice I drew back. My daughter experienced the break up of a friend's parents and she said to me, "If you ever leave us I'll never speak to you again."'

James tells nobody what he is doing and is only talking to me because I do not know him. He says: 'I am well aware society would condemn me. But in fact my wife and I get on better now because I am not so tense and moody and she seems relieved I am not wanting sex. We have a strong bond around mutual respect and appreciation of what both of us do for the children. We have a nice house and we have put a lot into making it as we want. In fact I feel our home and our family within it represent the best of what we have done together.'

Amanda met her husband when she was 16. She is now 51 and they have two children aged 20 and 17.

She is a striking, vivacious woman describing her husband as, 'my best friend, and we understand each other very well'. Even so she follows this up with an outpouring of talk about how she spent her younger years being a good wife and mother, tending a husband whose demanding job meant he was ever more exhausted in the evenings and at weekends. She by contrast has had more zest and desire to be out in the world since her children have grown up

She tells, 'I had been wondering how it would be to use my sexuality in a vibrant way and at the same time I heard about what David was doing. He took me on and texted me names of people I could meet on a secret phone which is only used for Loving Links clients. It's all very discreet and careful.'

Amanda met a selection of men. 'Some I liked a lot, others were rum, some felt like care in the community.'

Amongst them, however, were men she enjoyed having sex with but she says she was very clear she did not want more. 'I have never regarded my liaisons as affairs because an affair is organic and will go somewhere. These encounters are going nowhere and I will not fall in love with the men.'

She hesitates when I ask if her husband suspects anything.

'I ask myself sometimes, but if he does I think he is just waiting for me to get over it. He is very wise and very generous but he is so weighed down with responsibility and work he finds it hard to relax. He is not the man I married. I think if I hadn't done this I would have gone potty. I'm not on anti-depressants as so many friends are.'

So where does all this leave us? And how does it relate to home and its meaning for us? Home is the place most of us position our key relationships, spend private time with our significant partners and work out the moral basis of our sexual relationship. And the overwhelming majority of people, as we have seen here, very much want a stable, secure home for family life.

The vow of monogamy suits plenty of couples well, enabling them to feel secure, safely intimate, two people locked into a private world and the sacrifice of sexual adventuring is agreed as worth it. For such people home has a particular meaning as a place where, whatever the outside world gets up to, they live by their own rules. Dossie Easton, for all that she has based her life on open relationships and makes the point that scientists, using DNA testing, have not found one species that is consistently monogamous, also agrees, 'clearly – there are people who would prefer to be homebodies, want a quiet life, want things serene – and that is just fine.'

Yet we also know that there are others, in substantial numbers, as we have seen, who break the monogamy pact with all too often the destruction of all they have built up in their home lives.

My point in this chapter has been to look at what kind of relationships may help to hold together home, provided of course it is a home worth preserving, with relationships that are not destructive or abusive. And to acknowledge how difficult it may be to find a way to maintain the bonds we have created, usually with optimism and faith, with other people, and what might help.

Finding out what makes couples work is the task of *Enduring Love? Couple Relationships in the 21st Century*, a research project being conducted by Dr Jacqui Gabb, Senior Lecturer in Social Policy at the Open University, and colleagues. They have been given half a million pounds and the idea is that they will have a dialogue with government about how to work with couples to sustain relationships.

Gabb and her team are also working with Relate and One Plus One, the relationship research organisation, but as the work is still in the early stages, what Gabb has to say is based on earlier work she did on relationships for a report *Behind Closed Doors*.

'I don't think one model fits all. What is interesting is that relationships are not necessarily structured around two people, and successful relationships may be open to an array of intimacies; some may be glued-together by having significant others around as friends for example. Others may be open to non-monogamy, to casual sexual partners but who then wonder how it should be when children come along. People need to find what works for them and the rules need to be constantly re-negotiated.'

If relationships are to be supported it is important not to be prescriptive, Gabb says very clearly. 'The important thing is horses for courses so if someone doesn't want sex for instance they may be happy for partner to get it elsewhere and so on.'

If similar ideas are compounded and brought to the government dialogue it should be interesting. For so far past and present governments, while stressing their interest in supporting families and the children the have, have certainly not included in the definition of family values the kind of radical coupling discussed in this chapter.

But that might be the most constructive thing they could do. It seems to me that Gabb is absolutely right: in order to help couples, intimate relationships, children's well-being and home life to be the best they can, we need to be open-minded and not condemnatory. We need to see whether Megh, Matt and Dave or people involved in the Loving Links' liaisons, for instance, really are putting their families more at risk than does the couple who resolutely sit, stony-faced evening after evening, suppressing troublesome desires for something more life-enhancing than they have.

The only moral stand I have is in believing whatever we do should cause as little harm and pain to others, as possible. That given it seems to me that we stand a far better chance of seeing significant relationships and especially those with children, remaining intact if, as a society, we loosen up on ideas of what is and isn't acceptable sexually and let individuals work out their own morality, its parameters, its flexibility according to their own desires.

IN THE BEST INTERESTS

I wrote, grandiloquently in my diary, 24 hours after the birth of my first son, 'I will never not be vulnerable again. I had no idea how stunningly true this would be.

Then later, in a magazine article that I unearthed, were my words, 'The beginning was for me, pure unadulterated love. All those silly, sentimental clichés rolled into one, as I gazed in amazement at the tiny person cradled in my arms, flesh of my flesh, the stunning answer to nine months of unanswerable questions'.

We – men and women – fall in love with our children when they are born. Look anywhere in the world and you find celebration, the singing of songs, philosophising. In all kinds of circumstances children are greeted with a visceral, exalted gladdening of parents' hearts. In every kind of circumstance parents make the greatest sacrifices, put their own lives on the line for love of their young.

It may begin with alterations to the home; fixing things that could be a risk; papering a nursery with flying stalks; spending too much on a frilled cradle to take pride of place. Re-organising the way space is used. But the seismic shift in our lives, the momentousness of what a child will mean in our lives, takes place in the emotional domain.

For me it happened just about as soon as we arrived home from hospital where I had had a few days being very well looked after, being given all the help I needed with feeding, bathing, holding my child. But stepping into the house which already felt altered in its mood, I realised that from now on every single thing that happened to Zek, all that was done to him, was down to Olly and me. My parents were dead, and Olly's mother, the only remaining grandparent, lived in Holland. I took our precious bundle of life from his basket and sat, nursing him on the chaise longue in our sitting room. It was so familiar as a place we would crack a bottle of wine with friends, spend evenings pinning antique garments bought in the Portobello Rd on the walls, painting some piece of furniture, invite my Dad in for a makeshift meal. My accountant threw in his 'abiding memory' of me sitting cross legged on he floor, eating figs from a large jar. I was more child than adult and my home with Olly had been my playground.

It felt so unfamiliar as a place to bring up my own child.

Olly and I sat looking at Zek, then, frantically at each other. Did we actually have any knowledge, any skills, with which to care for this so-fragile-seeming little person? We'd skimmed through books and gone to ante natal classes that had appeared to be talking about life in an alien world. Besides, unintentionally, I had worked until the day before I gave birth. I'd planned to take my maternity leave from the *Guardian* leaving a free week to have a leisurely coffee with a friend or two, maybe see a film, and prepare myself and the house for this unknown being who would be joining us.

It didn't happen. The evening I left work, they held a champagne party for me, and I happily drank far more than a pregnant woman should. Olly, alongside me knocked back the glasses, too. Then about the time an early morning autumn sun was spilling palely across the sky, I woke in my bed realising I was dripping wet. My waters had broken.

'Wake up' I shook Olly 'my waters have broken. I'm having a baby.'

'You can't be. I have a hangover' he grunted from his sleepy world. But I was and 13-yours later our son was delivered. Any notion of hanging-out time could be forgotten. Big time.

To return now to the feelings invoked by a new child, and particularly the first, what I am describing is, of course, the most universal of experiences. While also being the most unique for each of us. It sends many of us slightly dotty, catapulting us into the desire to let every single person know how transformed we are by becoming parents. New parents write music, create films, put art and words on paper, re-make contact with neglected friends and relatives, or just talk, talk, talk trying to describe the very particular rapture of the experience.

Listen to what the writer Anne Roiphe had to tell of how it was for her, 'I was in love with my child, not sanely, not calmly, not rationally but wholly and completely, the way people get on an airplane and give control to the pilot, to the currents of wind, and let themselves be lifted up, taken away'.

You hear a similar sense of being stunned by the extraordinary strength of feeling in the words of Jonathan Self in his memoir *Self Abuse*, 'I can access the powerful emotions I experienced when each of my boys was born with incredible ease: the wonder, joy and fulfilment of becoming a father. It brings tears to my eyes, a lump to my throat, just to think of the first time I clasped them in my arms.'

My partner Olly did not articulate his feelings quite so elo-
quently. But there in the delivery room he was handed our tiny
son Zek, wrapped in a honeycomb blue blanket his fierce eyes
dominating a face crinkled like tissue paper, his mouth already
forming a protesting howl at the indignity of all he had just
been through. I watched stunned delight fill Olly's face, and his
gaze of wonderment was the beginning of a love affair, the
reason he could now see that he had been compelled to spend
evening after evening in our sitting room, painting designs on
a wooden cradle he had made during my pregnancy. That wonderment continues to this day and with our second son Cato,
too, although now Olly must peer upwards at the six foot two
inch young men they have become.

At which point lets take pause for a moment from the celebration this new stage in life will bring if we are fortunate –
fortunate indeed for it is a valuable launch pad for the testing
24-hour role that is parenting. Let's pause and remember that
the beginning does not feel this way for everyone. An unwanted pregnancy, a birth that comes about in a savagely unhappy
relationship, post-natal depression, blind fear, a sense of displacement so acute the parent can see only loss not gain, fear
of how to cope materially, may all mean a new child is not welcomed into the family home with unbounded joy and optimism.

Parents who yearn to feel as they have heard others describe
are so often painfully aware that they cannot summon the feelings that are expected of them. They may be trapped with guilt
like a dirty secret. The sheer exhaustion of a demanding baby
which deadens every bit of animation, can leave us joyless. The
home, then, can all too easily feel like a taunting prison where
we are trapped with a profound sense of inadequacy. It is in
this case a place that cannot support us or offer us anything in

the way we need. If this is how it is compassion and under-standing are much needed.

Whatever the experience we have of birth and the after-math, home will almost certainly be the place in which we involve ourselves in our children's growing lives, most fully, and where they have a hub for their most formative experiences. So in this chapter my perspective is how home is experienced by children, how do the ways we as adults organise their home lives, impact on them.

Within Our Four Walls

That impact is there from the very beginning in the experience of a baby bonding, of feeling secure in their private world and it goes on until children feel independent enough to step outside the home into their own lives.

Like most people I can reflect on the good, the bad and the ugly that have all occurred within our four walls, and I can see how at best the way home life was played out quite definitely created security and happiness for our children. Just as I can see how the thunder of our uncontrolled rows, the anxiety which our children could not comprehend when the atmos-phere was grim, had a very real effect. An effect that was in our power to make or break.

We sent our elder son to weekly boarding school aged ten, and although he returned every weekend and we assured him if he were unhappy he did not have to stay, I can see now that for him, although he was happy enough with the school and friends made there, it was a loss of home that did not feel good.

And we missed him bitterly. If time could be wound back we would not do that again, emptying home of his exuberant presence, and leaving his brother uncomprehendingly lonely.

From our point of view, as we have often discussed, it feels as though there are vital frames missing in the story of our son's growing years when he was simply absent from the picture. We talk with Zek about it sometimes, and he is clear that he would not send his own children away from home to school.

Lionel Shriver, in *A Perfectly Good Family*, an affecting portrait of a childhood home rattling with unexpressed feelings and resentments, wrapped into the performance of a happy family, leads us through the pleasure a physically lovely house and expansive land around can bring, yet the thrust of Shriver's tale is how much it is the emotional life inside the home that matters.

'In my experience, a house is never a mere building. According to standard Jungian interpretation, in dreams a house is a stand-in for the self. The house where you grew up must have more power to evoke that house-self formula than any other.'

Just before I sat to write this, my dear friend Caroline, whom I have known since we were both five, called and as we talked around the subject of home it was she who led my focus to how much the house I grew up in and what occurred there, had laid a foundation for the way I viewed childhood.

Until we reached puberty, Caroline would visit my home a great deal. We were devoted school best friends and she was much adored by my mother. She started telling me how just a few days earlier she had been relating stories of life in my home to her own thirty-something daughter, and how it had contrasted with her own more tightly-reined home.

She was re-living it with me: how we had ridden on the running board of my father's battered Armstrong Siddley car shrieking with laughter; the dances she and I staged for the two of us, in our parquet-floored sitting room. We dolled-up in lashings of organza, taffeta, cotton, silk trim from the dressing-up box and my father would obligingly put on some faintly smart garment, my mother her best dress, and they would twirl around the floor with us.

My mother would deliver lunch on the days during our 'religious phase", raising her eyebrows wryly at the sight of us kneeling in front of a cross we had made, in my darkened bedroom, praying interminably.

My mother would sit us around the tea table and tell us 'out of school' tales about my father to make us laugh. The occasion he arrived home in terrible paddy because the AA had been very rude. It emerged he had called them out three times and on each occasion because he ran out of petrol. How so? The journey home was not so long, but my Dad only brought half a gallon at a time in case it might be cheaper at the next petrol station.

How – another act of parsimony – he would fill the bath he was taking with detergent and have the sheets in with him declaring, 'can't waste good hot water'.

As Caroline reminisced further about the guinea pigs with backward curls, the dog Archibald who slept all over the furniture, the lop-sided cakes and misshapen scones my mother made I was swept over with aching nostalgia for those days. The essence of my childhood experience of home, I realised, was the sense that my brother and I and our happiness were the centre point around which my parents shaped their existence. They always gave the impression of enjoying me and my brother, whether we were being sweet or a pain, although they certainly downed tools and made us stop when we got out of hand.

Caroline said, wistfully, of her own more conventional home life, 'I couldn't have been as you were in my home'. I felt a gratitude that caught in my chest, for my parents whose own backgrounds had not obviously given them such uncomplicatedly loving skills.

I believe my upbringing in a home bounded with palpable warmth and love has much to do with a fundamental belief that the world is as much a good place as the grim place we are forced to recognise it can also be. I hear, too, that assimilated sense of feeling the world is there for her in what my smart, sassy friend Janet Reibstein recollects. She described, in her memoir *Staying Alive* (Bloomsbury), what joy her mother took in spending time with her, and in her exploits.

'Normally my mother was cheerful, proud of me. She screamed with laughter at my made-up songs and ballets performed to a Little Golden record accompaniment. She encouraged me to perform at family get-togethers, which I did with no hesitation... and she applauded me with love.'

The Children's Society commissioned child development expert Judy Dunn and Richard Layard, known for his in depth work on happiness, to write *A Good Childhood* (Penguin). And in this exploration of the things that help and hinder children to grow well, they were clear that the home, where family and children are most likely to be engaged, is a place where children can count on unconditional love, as well as understanding disapproval of their behaviour within that orbit.

Which takes us back to the beginning of our children's lives and the way we can create a secure, loving bond that acts as a kind of trampoline for life ahead. Our children can bounce ever further, with confidence, in their independence, knowing that if they need they can land safely back.

Which sounds all very well, but what does it take to give our children that attachment? What skills do we need? How to translate the arrival home with a new baby and, very possibly, a fat load of trepidation, into a way of childcare that gives secure attachment. There are of course manuals and child rearing programmes galore and more of that later. Before we introduce some unknown expert into our home, it is worth hearing what Lloyd de Mause, director of the Institute for Psychohistory and author of books, but not child-rearing guidance, including of *A History of Childhood,* has observed

'The bonding through skin and eye contact between mother and baby after birth, stimulates in both of them the feeling that they belong together, a feeling of oneness that ideally has been growing from the time of conception'. That is no less true for fathers, I would add, even though they cannot breastfeed. I watch the way my baby granddaughter, who has been held, changed, bathed and adored by my son since birth, nestles against his chest, making little bird noises of contentment. Then when she looks up he is gazing into her face his smile overflowing with delight so that she gives him one of her big toothless smiles.

The ecstasy a child may take in such sensual intimacy at home is arrestingly there in the words of writer and poet Laurie Lee. 'I was still young enough to be sleeping with my Mother, which to me seemed life's whole purpose... I was her chosen dream companion, chosen from all for her extra love... The presence for whom one had moaned and hungered was found not to have fled after all.'

What you hear in that is an adult still able to recall the perfect bliss of knowing he was safely bonded to a mother and could trust her love for him absolutely.

The actress Eileen Atkins who grew up with few privileges and in a loveless marriage where, she says, her father only married her mother after being widowed because he needed a woman to look after the child he had, recollects how motherly love filled her home.

Now in her 70s, she says emphatically, 'I was a very confident, social child because I was so adored by my mother.'

De Mause, has much more of humane good sense to say,

but importantly he urges that the home should be a place where we can put aside the fears of not knowing how to parent and follow instincts, give ourselves free rein to be as close to, as responsive to, our new infant as possible.

This kind of talk is often read as suggesting parents – or more particularly mothers – should not work when their children are small. For quite a lot of us this is not an option. For whatever reason we have to work and others are, understandably, reluctant to sacrifice a hard-won career.

But most jobs give several months maternity leave these days, and often with the option of longer. So spending that early time when our children are utterly dependent, giving ourselves up to their needs, seems a reasonable, indeed important, thing to do if we are convinced by the likes of Bowlby's attachment theory, and de Mause.

So I am frankly shocked when I hear of mothers, given that they are the ones who have gestated, provided a nine-month womb-home for their babies, talk of how they have returned to work within days of giving birth. And I am not talking about people in such insecure jobs, so in need of income, that they do this because they have to. I am talking about the high-powered careerists who boast about how little time they have been away from the office after giving birth, and have handed baby over to a highly-paid nanny at home. The father is, very likely, also back at work after a couple of days paternity leave. Unless it is utterly unavoidable, and most high-level careers are supported with a team of people to hold the fort efficiently, this strikes me as remarkably cruel.

Physical Contact

I met Karren Brady early on in her stellar career – she is now a sporting executive, television broadcaster, newspaper columnist, author and novelist, and vice-chairman of West Ham United having been managing director of Birmingham City Football Club. She was abuzz with excitement at seeing how far she could take her considerable talents, by being single-mindedly ambitious. She did not have children at the time, but went on to have a daughter. Last year she spoke out about how she regretted taking only three days' maternity leave when she had her daughter 15 years ago.

'Back then phrases such as work-life balance and flexible working hours didn't exist and I put pressure on myself to carry on as normal. So if I could go back and tell my younger self something, it's that a career lasts a lifetime. Taking time off is not the end of the world.'

You can't help thinking we should try to empathise with a child who has been delivered into our world, programmed with the reasonable expectation that it is wanted and welcomed. That at least one of the parents responsible for its existence will actually want to be upfront and personal.

Professor John Gottman is an award-winning psychologist and specialises in child development at his Foundation in Seattle. He sees children when things have become jarred or impossibly difficult with the home relationships. He has seen parents a-plenty worried about whether they are getting their parenting right, and no surprise in his view, 'so much of today's popular advice to parents ignores the world of emotion. Instead, it homes in on child-rearing theories that address children's behaviour, and particularly misbehaviour and get caught up in huge anxiety over achieving an obedient and compliant child.'

Trusting Your Instincts

It is understandable that, with the packed-tight lives so many of

us live, and in an age when problem-solving has a high curren-
cy, we find the idea of certainties being imparted by the
nouveau baby and child-rearing gurus, having their books and
TV programmes on hand when we are parenting at home,
comforting. You have Gina Ford, Super Nanny and others at
least professionally qualified, then there are the celebs. who, by
dint of being parents, have their ideas on bringing up kids successfully, set before us Take Goldie Hawn's just published: *10
Mindful Minutes: Giving Our Children – and Ourselves – the Social and
Emotional Skills to Reduce Stress and Anxiety for Healthier, Happy
Lives.* The title alone would give most kids indigestion.

The qualified experts may well be helpful when we need a
word of guidance on a particularly thorny issue, but isn't there
a risk these people who don't know our children but whom we
are encouraged to turn to, actually undermine the idea that we
can trust our own instincts? That without them holding our
hands, we risk having a ghastly time of parenting, so that
within the home the pleasures we hoped to take in being a
parent will be up-ended as Gottman suggests?

After all these purveyors of wisdom may be doing it out of
concern for a nation struggling to bring up its young, but you
can't help thinking that the big bucks this currently trendy spe-
cialism offers have at least as much to do with it.

The idea of a programme which will basically give you an
A–Z of what to do in any situation, and you don't deviate from
following, may be tempting. But it is instructive to remember
Dr Truby King who, with considerably less promotion, had his
child-rearing methods taken up in the immediate post-war
years. In *Our Babies* which he wrote with his wife Isabella, King
insisted on four hourly feeding and if your child wanted more
then put them somewhere you could not hear the howls and
they would soon learn it was no good making such a fuss.
Likewise regular sleeping was a must, and leaving a baby to cry

in vain for attention if she or he couldn't or wouldn't sleep was the solution. Strictness over toilet training was the rule of law. Indeed in every way King insisted on a strict regimen which avoided cuddling and other attention as a way of building strong character.

It is not hard to imagine how far we would have to push away empathy with our children's feelings if we followed a way that ignored their distress so dedicatedly. Our imagination is given substance in Doris Lessing's account of how her mother 'leaned on' the methods of Dr Truby King.

'What I remember is hard bundling hands, impatient arms. Truby King was the continuation of the cold and harsh discipline of my mother's childhood and my father's childhood. The baby must learn what's what and who is the boss right from the start, and this essential instruction must be imparted while the infant is lying alone in a cot, in its own room, never in the parents' bedroom. He, she, must learn its place'.

Lessing is not alone in seeing how King's strictures shaped her home life. There is an American website described as for survivor's of King's methods, and here is what one has to says: 'I am now aged 49 and still having counselling for the effects of being denied love by my mother. It's possible to stop babies crying in the short term, but in the long term – well, I'm still crying now, with a string of blighted relationships behind me. Routine is one thing, but cruelty and the denial of love is quite another.'

You could have taken the words from the mouth of John Bowlby, who brought controversy and fame with his theory of attachment and maternal deprivation. But the passionate conviction he had came from his own experience of profound loss as a small child. He was born into an upper middle-class family where he and his siblings were raised by a nanny with just teatime visits to his mother and he saw his father briefly at the weekend. When Bowlby was four the nanny left and he remembered throughout his life how traumatic that was, describing it as feeling like the loss of a mother.

Aged seven he was sent to boarding school, so even the afternoon visits to his own mother, in his own home, were gone.

The experience of feeling he could not be important enough to his parents, also marked the young life of Burgo Partridge. His parents writer Frances and Ralph were vibrant members of the Bloomsbury set, uninhibited, and, in Frances' words, 'quite uninterested in conventions, but passionately in ideas'. Conversations around ideas defined the frequent social gatherings at the Partridges' family home Ham Spray, but there was not much place for a small child – 'he had grown up in a household where not many concessions were made to childishness' records Anne Chisholm in her biography of Frances Partridge.

Burgo was brought up by a succession of nannies with his beloved grandmother visiting regularly. His parents went away often without him and he was tearful and desperately unhappy at having to go to school, because he did not want to be away from home.

Then, like Bowlby, he was sent to boarding school and, Chisholm records, 'There now began a time of wretched unhappiness for Burgo. Away form home (he) began to be tormented by the thought that in his absence his parents might have died.' He would run away home and be promptly returned. He was moved to Millfield, but a temporary respite from his unhappiness soon ended and he wrote a harrowing letter home about his fears of his parents dying and equally strong fears that Frances and Ralph were not, in fact, his parents at all.

The memory of how traumatized he had been by the loss of Nanny. the one person he had felt he could rely on to be there for him, as a child, led Bowlby to study child development, psychology and psychoanalysis. He won awards for his work and considerable fame for what he had to say in his seminal trilogy *Attachment and Loss*. The essence of his theory was that the success of all relationships or 'attachments' in life is dependent on the success of the first one – of the bond between the infant or small child and his or her mother or primary caregiver.

It was a theory that went out of fashion, but is now talked about a good deal by those involved in children's mental well-being. At the same time we've seen neuro-science marching forward with an ever growing body of research demonstrating how differently the brains of children who have had good attachment and those who have not, develop.

This was starkly demonstrated me at a conference I was attending where we were shown photographs of a three-year-old who had been well nurtured emotionally. The brain was a gently-formed plump sphere. The other came from a child of the same age reared in an Eastern European orphanage where the babies were rarely held, gazed at or spoken to affectionately. In this case the brain resembled a tiny wizened boxing glove. These are, of course, extremes but plenty of studies have demonstrated how the brains of children brought up without the security of reliable nurture and emotional care may be distorted, sometimes with very serious consequences.

Phoebe Cates, actor wife of Kevin Kline with a sensitivity not always apparent in Hollywood parents: 'It's really the mother who the baby wants the first few years, and it's important that the mother be constant.'

A Self-Interested Act

Our children don't ask to be born so surely they have a right to assume we will be available to them when they come along. We have children, presumably, because we want them as additions to our lives; they represent what family and home are about for many of us. Yet how many of us can also, honestly say hand on heart, that we had children for their own sakes? It seems to me it is an inherently self-interested act unless either it was unintended, or you see yourself as selflessly furthering the human race for the good of the species.

Had I been more in tune with such an idea I might not have scampered off just two weeks after Zek was born, and I was breastfeeding him on demand – which meant often – to have a boozy lunch with the work colleagues I would not be among until my maternity leave was over. I went without a thought except for the anticipated pleasure of this outing, leaving our baby with his Dad – after all good feminists had learned that it was essential fathers should share childcare – and a small amount of expressed milk.

That lunch reminded me how much I enjoy a freewheeling social life and although the odd tweak of conscience reminded me that my tiny son might need me, I was able to push such thoughts aside with another swig of wine. When some three hours later I arrived home both Olly and Zek were frantic with exasperation. Olly wasn't howling as Zek was but he was angry with me.

'I've tried everything but it's not me he wants. I can't be a mother substitute when he is so young.' He had tried to feed his son, but Zek hadn't wanted milk out of a sterile bottle, and the result had been a couple of hours of non-stop crying which no amount of cuddling, walking, and cradling by Olly had helped. I cannot have felt very reliably constant to my uncomprehending newborn.

By the time I brought my second newborn son, Cato, home I had read and Alice Miller, eminent psychoanalyst and author

of many books about the cause of damage in childhood experiences. I was sitting in the kitchen of our apartment at a long
pine table by the window. Spring sunshine spread itself across
the surface and our cat curled luxuriantly into satisfied sleep.
Cato was lying in a checked cotton bouncy baby chair. I was
reading with one eye on him, to a symphony of grunts and
gurgles, the unarticulated way newborns forbid you to forget
their presence. In due course the sounds would build up to
hungry howls, my baby only placated when I tucked his soft-
ening body against my torso, as he fed, sucking deeply, with
what always sounded like a sigh of pleasure. Miller's words
came to me, 'the newborn baby or small child is completely
dependent on his parents, and since their caring is essential for
his existence, he does all he can to avoid losing them. From the
very first day onward, he will muster all his resources to this
end like a small plant that turns toward the sun in order to
survive.'

So that's it, I thought, he is using his resources to get what
he needs from me. And by simply responding spontaneously
and meeting his needs I can make his new home a place of
reassurance and pleasure.

Yet when it came to doing as we wanted, Olly and I did not
pause to consider how it would feel for our youngest son Cato,
a child who had never known us away from home for so much
as a night, when we interrupted the secure rhythm of his life
abruptly. He was used to going to the child-minder he adored,
during the daytime while we were working. He was collected at
tea-time so that we had a couple of play and bath hours before
bed-time when we sat with him until he fell asleep, eyelashes
dropping like the curtain on a theatre set.

Olly and I decided we would go to America for my brother's
wedding and make a ten-day holiday of it. I pushed aside the
uneasy voice at the back of my head 'suggesting' it might be

too long, that we could not explain to Cato in any way that would make rational sense that we would definitely be back, that ten days was not really long.

When we phoned from the US, the childminder assured us Cato was fine, and so he probably seemed. But when we arrived to collect him he was very different to the rumbustious, spontaneous chap who would leap up for a big hug with hoots of delight, as a rule, when we collected him. This time he greeted us in a restrained, almost polite way. At home he was eerily quiet. We cuddled him, held him a lot, told him how much we had missed him, gave presents he took indifferently. The distanced behaviour went on for several days during which he treated us with extreme wariness as though we might desert him at any moment. He was clingy and anxious – so different to his familiar easy-come easy-go way of being. He had lost his confident cheeriness and immediate willingness to go when friends invited him on an outing.

Nor did he want to go to the childminder who had treated him with extreme kindness, as had her family of teenage children, while we were gone. He cried frantically when we reached the door and dragged away from me or Olly. So I took time off work and stayed at home with him. His father alternated my days, and slowly we watched Cato seem to regain trust in us.

Enlightenment as to what had probably happened with Cato came some time later when I was researching an article on childcare. The psychologist I was interviewing explained that young children cope with a certain amount of absence of the person they have cleaved to as the main carer, but they need to be able to hold in mind a sense that this person is reliably there for them. This they can do for a certain number of hours usually. The psychologist explained, 'we call it assimilation and so long as the child has the feeling of the parent or caregiver being there for him or her, things are all right. But when say the child gets tired, doesn't feel well, is frightened, they may lose the sense of that significant person being available to them, home may feel unsade, and at that point they feel frightened. If the situation goes on too long fear turns to a sense of abandonment.

'Children are resilient and they can cope with this once in a while, but if it happens often, if the child stops feeling able to 'hold' the loved person in mind, they will probably display grief, cry, be fretful. Then if none of this has the desired effect of bringing the person they need, children feel helpless and have a way of shutting down emotions and possibly becoming depressed.'

She paused, 'if you don't understand what is happening it is easy to mistake the withdrawn behaviour as your child having 'quietened down', a sign he or she is maturing. And children who do not feel safe with their parent or caregiver, who, without articulating it, fear their parents will abandon them, are often very biddable and people may remark on what a 'good' child you have.'

During the years I have written about and edited a magazine concerned with young people's mental health, I have seen too many damaged young people, across the social and economic scale, of various creeds and religions, for whom secure attachment is a sick joke.

Surely if we choose to have children, we should be very clear that we want to incorporate them into our lives, and what that may mean.

Resenting Motherhood

It is a thought brought sharply into focus by the recent publication of Rebecca Asher's *Shattered: Modern Motherhood and the Illusion of Equality* (Harvill Secker). The decision she and her husband made to have a child seems hardly the impulse of two people who very much want a child for its own sake. She describes the ambivalence in 'wrestling' with the shall-we-shan't-we question and then how, as she 'hurtled 'towards the end of her 30s she and her partner 'took the plunge and hoped for the best.'

Asher is very clear she loves her child, but there seems little pleasure in what she has to say of the experience of motherhood. She describes in her book, dismissed by Eleanor Mills, in the *Sunday Times* as 'a 270-page mega-whinge' how, after the two weeks following her son's birth, during which her husband was on paternity leave and they lived a 'jet-lagged haze of exhilaration and adoration' for their son, things changed. Her husband had gone back to work and the feelings that preoccupied her were 'loss of autonomy and self-abnegation... gruelling, unacknowledged servitude. The certainty I felt about having a child vanished – I loved my son but... despite this love I came to resent motherhood itself.'

With this level of self-pitying maternal self-absorption, you cannot help wondering how home life is for the 'loved son' in this ambivalent environment he has been brought into.

When Asher's book was published it brought out fiercely opposing, passionately argued views which took me back to the days when motherhood was a major subject for new wave feminism and the joy of being a mother was vigorously challenged. It seemed resentment topped any possibility of simple pleasure at having a child. Virginia Held wrote an essay: *Who Is To look After The Children?*

'Over and over one encounters the argument that if a woman chooses to become a mother, she must accept a recognised set of responsibilities and obligations that are quite different from the responsibilities of being a father... A mother is expected to care for her child and to take full care of the child – cheerfully and contentedly – And if it is thought the child will develop problems due to early separation from a parent, it is the mother who is thought responsible for preventing them.'

Judy Slift writing in Mothering – *Essays in Feminist Theory* (Rowman and Allenheld) talked of, 'the drudgery, the monotonous labor, and other disagreeable features of childrearing'. While on the other hand 'the joys and compensations of motherhood are magnified.'

I was among plenty of women who understood that the inequality in childcare, the beliefs about whose work it was to make sacrifices for a child were the legacy of a male ordered society. The need to battle for structural changes was clear. Yet that was different to what was also being said, and is echoed in the quotations above, that having a child was an imposition igniting hostility more than pleasure in quite a few mothers.

The curiously unpalatable aspect of such sentiments is that the child becomes unimportant, a hostage to political ideology. There is no place in such self-important discourse for the internal experience of the child created, and whose feelings about being viewed with such negativity, appear to be nowhere of concern.

What a contrast to a young woman friend whose partner had given birth to a baby, conceived with donor insemination, a month before. She was holding this bundle of a life, he dozing on her shoulder. She wore a smile fit to break her soft skinned face even as she told how the baby scarcely slept, took a long while to eat and was often fractious so that she had been functioning on just an hour or so of snatched sleep. Her partner who worked freelance was already having to go back to work although she did all she could to be home early to share childcare. I suggested to this mother that she might be able to get someone to come to the house and take the baby for a few hours while she and her girl-friend slept. But she shook her head vigorously.

'I wouldn't want that. I'm so thrilled with the baby I want to be with him. I want him to know I love being with him.'

As do a great many parents it is important to remember. It is easier to understand resentment and anger in the case of women who have their children unwillingly or unwittingly, but what of we who have chosen to get pregnant? This is, after all, one place where women have control in their lives, over whether a child is born or not, and possibly how close the father is allowed to get.

Biological Privilege

On the one hand you can say women are oppressed because the expectation is that we, particularly in the earliest days, are likely to do the larger part of child care and particularly of course if we are breastfeeding. Or, at the other end of the spectrum, if you have a domineering or coercive partner who makes you feel there is no alternative but to do all that is required for the children.

Or you could say that as women we are best created to give a small baby what she or he needs, and that men can never be emancipated to have this frontline responsibility and control. That we are fortunate our patriarchal society has accepted we need to be home with our new babies and has traditionally given us longer paid leave than men. The supremacy of mothers in children's lives is something that the courts, too, have taken as a reason mothers have over the years been most often awarded custody.

You could say, as I do, that we women are mighty fortunate to have what I call biological privilege.

A Lack of Empathy

A thing that puzzles me is people who produce children but seem not too keen on them once they are there. Is it a vain urge to prove that they can have the perfect family (very possibly on top of other conspicuous achievements) as part of the image? The reality is then, apparently, an irritation, a mortal risk to the luxurious sofas, the carpets flown in from distant lands, the immaculately painted walls. And of course all that free time there was before.

To follow my point listen in to the conversation journalist Dylan Jones describes hearing at a social event he attended – and I too have heard such sentiments expressed. At a party he was attending, Jones talked of parents who 'seem to be every-where, saying they can't wait to get rid of their children for the summer... how they organise for their children to be picked up from boarding school and taken straight to summer camp'.

One mother Jones recollects brayed, 'with any luck I won't have to see them at all.'

So not much bonding *en famille* for them then, even if home is impressively styled and adorned when they are permitted to be there.

A contrast with the effort Sigourney Weaver makes, even when working arduous hours, to let her children know she will be home and will be there for them.

'Last night, I went home after forty TV interviews, I had to construct a long story for my daughter. I thought "This is the important part of the day and I MUST find the energy to do this". She's my first priority... That's the hardest part for me as an actor now, making sure that I can really do my work and at the same time maintain a proper presence as a parent.'

The contrast with what a teenage girl I interviewed for a

book on young people's mental health problems told, was heartbreaking. She and her brother had been brought up by a succession of nannies while both parents worked long hours and socialised away from home most evenings, explaining it was necessary for their work.

When she was ten, the girl told me, she had written her mother a note asking if she could, please, be there just one day when she came home from school.

'My mother was furious and shouted at me, saying I was selfish and didn't I realise she was working so hard to give me the wonderful standard of living we had. That meant private schools, smart holidays, spending a lot on clothes, but it wasn't what I wanted.'

As we talked on she told me of her eating disorder which had become very bad, of being thrown out of several schools for 'bad behaviour' and then for drug use. She didn't make friends easily. It was she who suggested that never having had 'parental guidance' might have had something to do with her troubles.

That is something that psychologist and author of the best selling *Emotional Intelligence* (Bloomsbury), Daniel Goleman would agree.

'In the long spread of human history, the way children have learned basic emotional and social skills has been from parents... These are hard times for children... There has been a sea change in the nature of childhood over the last decade or two, one that makes it harder for children to learn the basic lessons of the human heart and one that ups the ante for parents who used to pass these lessons on to the children they love... The failing to learn the basics of emotional intelligence are increasingly dire.'

What lesson about the importance of emotions will the son of a couple I met some years ago have learnt I find myself wondering even now. I knew these parents through work and met them at a launch party for a magazine. Their son had started at secondary school that day and had rung his parents at four pm when he got home expecting to see at least one of them. He wanted to know if they would be home soon so he could tell them about his day.

This was seven pm and the mother gave a guilty giggle as she turned to her husband and said, 'you know we really should get home to see George before he goes to bed.'

At eight-thirty pm the parents were still there, accepting another drink and working the room. At 10p.m. as the event closed they departed with the rest of us.

How much could George value himself, I wondered, if something as momentous as a first day at secondary school was apparently not an urgent call on his parents' time?

The Legacy of Suffering

This is not as conspicuously cruel as the sustained mental and physical cruelty Ingmar Bergman's father saw fit to inflict on his son, leaving the boy then man marked with a painful psychological legacy. In his film *Fanny and Alexander*, regarded as very largely autobiographical, Bergman takes us into the place of fear and loathing that the home can become. His father was a Lutheran minister and during a television interview Bergman talked with anguish of a childhood that was a long story of humiliation during which, for instance, if he wet his pants he had to wear a red dress all day so everyone would know.

The Bergman children were beaten until they bled and the mother Ingmar adored would dab the wounds afterwards. That she stood by then dealt with her husband's sadism must have been conflicting enough for the child. Then there was the confusion of his father orchestrating 'good humour, plays, songs, music, poetry reading' alongside the 'austerity moralising, denial, rigidity, brutality' as Bergman described it

Has this suffering played its part in Bergman going on to produce acclaimed films which critics have described as dealing with recurring themes of repression, guilt and punishment? There was, he has said, a voice in his head, endlessly demanding to know why he hadn't done better. If so I would conclude the price of his home upbringing, in human terms – he did not succeed in sustaining relationships, including five marriages and many lovers – has been appallingly high.

The artist Evelyn Williams, 82, offers tea in the sitting room of her home, a room hung with the intense pictures she has built her career painting. Almost all feature mothers and children and the space between them. Babies and young children reach out trying to make contact with a mother who is often turned away, or moving away. The pictures are often large, pale and urgent.

Her mother's emotional absence has been felt as psychological cruelty: 'My mother had very much wanted me to be a boy because she had already had a daughter, and I never stopped 'knowing' I was a disappointment and not good enough. The irony was she had wanted to please my father by having a son, but he adored my sister and me.'

The feeling of not being wanted was compounded when she was sent away from home to join her elder sister Branwen at a progressive boarding school.

She has few memories of those early years, but those that come now are of hanging on to the banisters of the big stairs in the front hall crying and feeling immeasurably desolate. Of rain slashing down on to the bleakness of the East Anglian landscape, the East winds howling across the flat ground.

'I know the staff were kind to me and did their best to care for me, and I enjoyed things like Saturday night dances and had friends. But a small child needs home and the care of loving parents I believe. I see that with my daughter and her children. She is so close and caring. I'm glad of it of course but it leaves me with a painful sense of yearning.

'Yet it didn't help when I was home because my parents had such an intense relationship that my sister and I always felt there wasn't really space for us, so we saw ourselves as outsiders. Home was full of emptiness and I really don't believe my mother knew how to love. She put on displays of affection for me but they were always like a performance for herself.'

She sees no reason to be forgiving of her mother, but as an adult she came to understand that what she went through was, in some way, a continuum of her mother's own emotionally deprived experience in the home.

'Her own mother adored the elder brother and showed very little affection towards my mother who was gangly and not pretty then. In fact she grew to become a beautiful woman.'

'I think of my mother occasionally and I am still quite antagonistic. As an old lady she would be overcome with grief and talk about dreams of me lost in the snow. And she would say things like it having broken her heart when I was 'taken' away to school and that she should never have agreed. But I was away for years and she could have had me home.'

For Evelyn comfort and a sense of her own worth have come through forging a successful career as an artist in which the haunting pictures depicting the despair of being unable to reach the mother either physically or psychically ache with Evelyn's own sense of being too 'wrong' to merit emotional maternal closeness.

Abandonment

What you grasp reading Adam Nicolson's childhood memories

as he relates them, is the confusion of the growing boy, trying to understand why his father seemingly takes pleasure when he engages his son in activities or intellectual pursuits, but cannot offer closeness.

Father and son went on canoeing expeditions and there were summer mornings at the breakfast table when father and son pored over a two-and-a-half-inch map of the Kent Weald exploring gridlines, contours, the stipple of scattered farms. Nigel Nicolson would suggest places for Adam to go exploring, and he would set off spending hours and days 'looking for these places he had made precious and important to me.'

Yet it was within the walls of their imposing home that he experienced his father's emotional barrenness when it came the desire for uncomplicated love was experienced.

Once his mother had left the home, escaping what Nicolson describes as 'the distant, unisexual and reproachful supervision that was all my father could offer', he was sent to boarding school.

Nicolson describes how, when he was sent away his father wrote tantalizing letters which made the youthful Adam weep with longing for home. Indeed his headmaster wrote a letter to Nigel Nicolson describing Adam as 'the most neglected boy the school had ever had'.

As a young man Nicolson observed once to his father that 'he treated his books and everything he wrote in the way that most people treated their children, with endless, careful nurture.'

It is possible that the two sons to whom Julie Burchill gave birth might have preferred even a mother emotionally crippled but nevertheless there, to being abandoned one after the other by Burchill who went on to make them conspicuous by their absence in the vainglorious memoir *I Knew I Was Right* (Arrow) she published in 1998, in her late thirties.

The first son is Robert, the child she had in a very young marriage to Tony Parsons, writer and broadcaster. Burchill left home when he was five-years-old, without warning. She told the *Independent* newspaper: 'I felt a bit weepy at the station but then I thought 'this is pathetic''. So you put on more lipstick and walk into the sunset.'

Cosmo Landesman, the father of her second son, describes how one day in April 1995 his wife Julie Burchill, who was 'brilliant with their son, decided to take a walk on the wild side.'

The anger he felt is evident when he describes how Burchill, author of media columns, excoriating all kinds of behaviour, harmful to others, departed.

'Overnight I went from happily married husband to home-alone dad with our eight-year-old son Jack to look after'. He could not love away Jack's grief however hard he tried.

'Within two weeks of her departure Jack's brave little face began to show signs of the strain. He acquired a series of nervous tics and twitches. He would gnaw on his lips and sigh. Eventually he said "Dad I don't like this new life of ours."'

If you pause to consider how these boys must have felt you understand how devastating this abrupt deeply narcissistic act by their mother must have been. How just like that her sons' homes became a place of loss, leaving them impotent in the face of abandonment.

It puzzles me what can have happened to so distort a woman that she gives birth to two children, creates a home for them in which they are led to believe they can feel secure, then ups and deserts once they are, seemingly, surplus to requirements.

On the other hand I am greatly impressed by how many women will sacrifice any semblance of happiness in their own lives in order not to leave children; women who will hunker down in refuges and create the best home they can, will spend every penny they have fighting for custody, because the idea of not being there to care for their children and give them a loving home life, is unbearable.

Fathers, of course, walk out on their children in greater numbers than do mothers. This is also worthy of much condemnation. Children are, too, often bitterly hurt by the father who separates from their mother and creates a new family, then seems to slough them off, making it plain they are barely welcome in the new home.

This may be partly a product of men, for all sorts of reasons, some reasonable some not, having seen themselves as less significant than mothers. Which makes it important that fathers understand just how much they matter. There's enough written about it these days for them to have little excuse for ignorance.

Something of a sea change can be seen in figures showing that in the UK fathers of under-fives are doing one-third of parental childcare according to the Equal Opportunities Commission.

Stay at Home Dads

HomeDad.org.uk is a UK support group dedicated to helping stay at home dads. Recent research by them suggests that 155,000 men look after the family and home full time. And the number of men working part-time has trebled to one million in the past decade and a half.

Nick Cavender's wife Kristin wanted to carry on working when their daughter was born, but they were concerned about getting good enough childcare or leaving so young a child with someone else. So after six months Kristin returned to her job which could support them both, and Nick agreed to stay home. Five years later he is still there from choice.

How nice for fathers to earn the kind of appreciation Clarence Buddington Kelland felt towards his father.

'He didn't tell me how to live; he lived, and let me watch him do it.'

You hear the regret in the voice of Nancy Regan along with the sons of Ronald Regan, at what was missing in the paternal relationship.

Nancy has said of Ronald, 'His relationships with his four children could be distant to the point of estrangement'. While Michael Regan, adopted by Regan and his first wife Jane Wyman, has criticised his father's absentee parenting. Ron Regan wrote in his recently published book *My Father at 100* of his search for paternal approval, 'Like all my siblings, I loved my father deeply, at times longingly. He was easy to love but hard to know.'

For fathers like actor Matthew Modine the realisation may come when children are still young enough that harm from their absence can be repaired or mitigated. Even so he says, 'I was gone out the country for six months filming… I've got a couple of kids. Six months is a long time to be away from a five and ten-year-old. I've been playing catch-up, but you can never make up the time that you're away. It's gone – and gone forever.'

Or, like actor Gene Hackman, recognising it late on as he admits.

'You don't realise until years and years later how selfish a job this is – you have to commit and in order to commit, you leave family outside of it… Years down the line you realise what you've done to people who you care a great deal about.'

Children and parents united, happily embroiled in the business of life, on the same wavelength, is one of the things that can make home a place that feels happy and gratifying.

Pushy Parents

But how does home feel when it is a place where children flop-ping, letting go at the end of a day of school, having friends around for unstructured play and relaxation, is regarded by parents as a place that constructive learning and a quest for measurable success should happen? A place where love may seem to be forever conditional on children matching parental aspirations and expectations.

As I began this chapter Amy Chua, high priestess of ambi-tious parents, hit the headlines with her provocative 'memoir' *Battle Hymn of the Tiger Mother* in which she described the intensely pressurised, and frequently confrontational 'Chinese mothering' she used to make sure her daughters Sophia and Lulu dedicated themselves to fulfilling her ambitions for them to be the best of the best in everything they did.

Home was not intended to be a place of leisure but rather the place where, once school was over – and the Chua girls were expected to get straight As in their exams or be lashed with maternal opprobrium – they spent hour after hour prac-tising violin and piano on top of any homework there might be. Failure to match Chua's demands was harsh: she once threatened to burn her daughter's stuffed animals if she did not play a piano composition perfectly, called the other 'garbage' when she did not match up in an exam. She threw back a birth-day card her four and seven-year-old girls had made for her saying she expected something that had taken more effort.

Nor does Chua pretend that home life was fun with this regime – having friends around or sleepovers were absolutely not allowed. While Chua, a Yale law professor married to lawyer and novelist Jed Rubenfeld, cites as evidence that her efforts were entirely for her daughters' good.

'My main evidence is that so much of what I do with Sophia and Lulu is miserable, exhausting and not remotely fun.' Nor apparently for them. Lulu as she reached her teens rebelled angrily, loudly, and defiantly against her mother's demands, and accused her of wrecking her life.

Chua may be extreme, particularly in being so upfront about her hothouse parenting and her book attracted great controversy, even death threats by those outraged by her methods. But it is easy to see how a child may feel there is nowhere to run when home is as heavy with expectations and conditional approval as this.

Western parents might not be as upfront as Chua about admitting that their children's autonomy is not a concern. Yet the pushy parent, the helicopter parent, the parent who plots their child's education in the most academic schools, from birth if not earlier, have grown steadily in number the past three decades. Their offspring are the children of the new millennium era in which so much of our worth is measured by work status and our earnings.

A time when, as Anastasia de Waal at the Future Foundation observed in 2010, 'Parenting and childhood are becoming less and less organic and more and more choreographed. Within all this optimum-parenting pressure has been a sort of commodification of children. Your child is potentially the ultimate accessory of success.'

That was what Andree Aelion Brooks found some years earlier, when she conducted her fascinating study *The Children of Fast-Tack Parents*. She interviewed families and children of highly successful professionals, and parents in their 30s still climbing the 'ladder of success' and 'many saw themselves living in a world where keeping up with the chairman of the board has replaced keeping up with the Joneses. So not only were their children expected to achieve similarly in the world of work, Brooks found, but there was the added role model of parents who lived 'a value system that equates net worth with self-worth and these parents are typically "beautiful people" – ultra-thin, physically appealing and with an innate sense of elegance and style.'

Brooks' starting point had been a conference with a gathering of people concerned with young people's mental health problems. She found a disproportionate number in the 'upper enclaves' where in most cases both parents needed to devote far more than forty-two hours a week to their jobs.

'Such parents frequently place as much pressure on their children to achieve as they have placed upon themselves. Second-rate doesn't rate in the vast majority of these households. It is absolutely, positively unacceptable.'

Brooks' work was published at the end of the 1980s, but her book taps in to the anxiety *de nos jours*, where not a minute of a child's life must be aimless or 'wasted' in play and activities that do not have a demonstrable role in helping them become a super-kid.

It brings to mind the words of the father in Harmony Korine's film *Julien Donkey Boy*. We see Werner Herzog as the father, terrorising his son into running on elbows up and down the stairs, he hoses the lad with freezing water and orders him not to shiver like a weakling and so on, all the time screaming 'you have to be a winner'.

It's easy to laugh at the neurotic excess in this portrayal, but is the message to the boy child essentially very different to the message that resonates throughout the homes of parents who have the greatest ambitions for their children?

Not in the view of Alfie Kohn, author of books on education and human behaviour, 'Many parents push their kids with the best of intentions, but some are so busy basking in the reflected glory of their children's accomplishments they overlook the damage being done by the pressure to live up to their expectations.'

Patricia DiBartolo, lead researcher on a US study is one of many professionals now emphasising that the problem is that children are daunted from a very young age by the belief that their parents won't love and respect them if they don't get to the top.

DiBartolo explains, 'these children cannot accept the mistakes they make in the course of learning.

'Perfectionist kids get caught in a vicious cycle. When approaching a task or project they feel less able to succeed, get anxious and then evaluate their task more negatively than their non-perfectionist peers.'

Alice Miller believed we put over-pressured children at very real risk of developing the 'as-if' personality. She explains in *The Drama of the Gifted Child.*

'Accommodation to parental needs often (but not always) leads to the as-if personality. This person develops in such a way that he reveals only what is expected of him... is admired everywhere and needs this admiration; indeed he cannot live without it. He must excel brilliantly in everything he undertakes... He too admires himself for his qualities – his beauty, cleverness, talents – and for his success and achievements. Beware if one of these fails him, for then the catastrophe of a severe depression is imminent.'

The internationally acclaimed violinist Vanessa Mae acknowledges that without her mother overseeing her hot-housed childhood she would not be the success she is today. But such has been her mother's single-minded ambition that Mae chose to break with her mother and says now that there is no chance of a reconciliation, 'My mother's love was always conditional on my performance as a musician.'

Which brings me back to how home feels at best when it is

embracing, supportive, a structure that makes a child feel worthwhile. This is how it was for Eudora Welty who talks, in her writings, about the loving family she was born into and the significance of her happy home life in Jackson, Mississippi.

When her elderly mother was ill Welty, aged 52, returned home to look after the her and her two brothers. Six years later all were gone, yet even so Welty continued to live in the family home until her own death.

In the Pulitzer Prize winning novel *The Optimist's Daughter*, the most autobiographical of Welty's novels, the heroine returns to the house of her childhood to recognise truths about her family life and suggests poignantly that home, 'bestows on us our original awareness… the home tie is the blood tie.'

Meghan O'Rourke wanted to honour the memory of her mother, after her death, by recalling the joyous childhood her mother had given.

'She loved being with kids. She had a vivid sense of what makes children feel safe, and she believed in a child's experience of the world. She spent hours with my brothers and me, making gingerbread houses or sledding or cutting out paper snowflakes. She taught us all to make apple pie and read *The Black Stallion* out loud to us.'

There are many reasons home life can be challenging, difficult, painful for children, and as parents can't we all think, cringing, of the things we have inflicted on our kids out of selfishness, stressed irritation, antipathy if they have been driving us crazy, hostility if they seem to be aggravating difficulties in our relationships?

But ultimately what we need is a caring compass, an internal mechanism that adjusts back to the default position of recognising we are responsible for our children's young lives, and that we have a moral duty to do all we can to make it a time in which they know we are on message with them, wanting them to feel good, be happy and for their domestic world to seem a harmonious place.

At which point I shall give the last word to the wise Donald Winnicott who, sums up beautifully.

'The parents' job of seeing their children through, is a job worth doing; and, in fact, it provides the only real basis for society... But the home is the parents' not the child's responsibility.'

8

A HOUSE IS NOT A HOME

A broken home is the most graphic of images. You can just see it: bricks and mortar crashing to the ground; a bulldozer ripping its way through the fabric of the building. Or perhaps a home where the pleasure once taken in it has turned sour. About this home, unable to provide security and succour any longer, there is a palpable sense of its soul atrophying.

You hear it in the abiding anguish of Michael Regan, son of actors Ronald Regan and Jane Wyman: 'Divorce is where two adults take everything that matters to a child – the child's home, family, security, and sense of being loved and protected – and they smash it all up, leave it in ruins on the floor, then walk out and leave the child to clean up the mess.'

Sally was in her late teens when she learnt that her parents were divorcing. The sense of the place that had been her stability wrecked beyond redemption remains, even though she is now well established in a young adult life of her own.

'It's like Humpty Dumpty when he falls off the wall and breaks into so many bits he can't be put together again. That's how it was when my parents fought. The love that had once been there was turned into hideous recriminations, I began to dread going through the front door because everything felt so insecure, as though the whole structure was struggling to hold together. Then they parted and although I stayed in the house with my mother, it was no longer the caring home I had known in earlier times. It could never be put together again.'

Home is where the drama of a marriage in decline and then the death throes will almost always be acted out. A home of splintered love where partners who had been happy to act as one in exchanging love and caring, united in safeguarding their children's souls, are lost in their individual striving to reach the best endgame possible.

So, before the terminal breakdown of the adult relationships, children will sense that everything feels wrong, but without comprehending what. Rituals that had symbolized the holding together of home life, are too painful to be sustained – mealtimes, for instance, may be such an endurance test that appetites die or people choose to eat separately. And the making of food, once a pleasurable offering, is reduced to a dutiful preparation of sustenance. A cherished garden, once a place for cheery family gathering, loses its sense of purpose and allure. Who cares if the plants wither from lack of tending?

The writer Will Self expresses the scale of what it meant when his parents separated in terms of home as a place of safety for him, 'When I was nine my father left the home... essentially my idea of home was irretrievably damaged at that point.'

Selling Up

There can be a particularly despairing sense of finality when it comes to bitter battles over who gets what. Where will pictures bought as a couple end up? What of lovingly gathered objects that have given home its individual aura? For a partner leaving, having a share of the spoils can become overwhelmingly important. It might be something as small but meaningful as CDs chosen in high spirits, something as drastic as the ripping out of built in furniture and fittings. Although I have yet to hear a more dramatic tale than that of the Cambodian family who cut their home in half when they separated.

You might not immediately think the taking of material goods could rate so highly when the demolition of a relationship and home base is taking place. In fact the taking of goods can feel like an abusive act explains psychotherapist Janet Reibstein.

'The taking of things chosen together, objects that add up to the life shared, can leave the home feeling empty, stripped of life, oppressively symbolic of the lost relationship. And, of course, it is perfectly possible that the person doing the taking wishes to make their mark in just this way.'

The gaps where certain chairs had been, the dirty marks on the wall where pictures once hung, the dusty gaps on bookshelves, half the home's curtains gone and so on, can be singularly upsetting for a child who may feel home is unravelling around them, even if they know they will remain in the building.

All too easily you see how parental loathing, symbolic of the bricks and mortar being lost, imprints itself on the children's mental state, confusing and conflicting.

It is something seen, through the media, and acted out in courts around the country on a daily basis with estranged couples fighting their corner in the divorce courts

In extreme cases the children's needs are spectacularly disregarded. Take the case of Larry v Catherine in southern

Ontario. Their behaviour so appalled the judge who dealt with them in the divorce court that he described the mother as 'brainwashing the children to loathe their father'. He gave as example her texting the daughter for information about her father's whereabouts, 'is Dickhead there?''

'The husband, the judge talked of as 'an empty tool box when it came to parenting'. What must home have been for children where, in the judge's view their parents were with no attempt at discretion 'marinating in mutual hatred so intense as to surely amount to a personality disorder.'

The tragedy of love turning to loathing, urgent desire to antipathy, is the way it brings out the worst, so that people who may have been very capable of rational, co-operative dealings before, have no such skills remaining in their quivers. Is anyone realising, as Mike McManus discussing divorce in a Virginia, US newspaper puts it, 'every divorce is the destruction of a small civilisation' for children?

The top model Heidi Klum, known for her professional demeanour as a cool blonde with bags of *sang-froid*, said of the end of marriage, with four children, to the singer Seal, 'it is like being in the eye of a tornado… Sometimes in life a curveball comes at you'.

I have not been through a divorce but when Olly and I were getting on badly enough to contemplate separating, I had a sense of what it was to realise that a home lovingly evolved as a place to enjoy being family could become emotionally cold, where all the things that have been fun to do together, turned into a raw sense of impending loss.

Caught in the Middle

By far the majority of parents care deeply about their children yet the enormity of their home breaking up can make it difficult to do as they would wish. As Penny Mansfield, director of One Plus One the relationship research organisation explains, parents who are myopically consumed with getting justice and not being left in a desperate situation, may be enormously distracted, and far less attuned to their children's needs than usual.

Branwen Lucas has seen this acted out. She spent several decades as a social worker involved with children and families. She is one of the most compassionate and wise women I know, but it is dispirited frustration that takes over as she describes how, time and again, she would be in a clinic with parents and children and it was clear they were 'too caught up in their own battle to see the needs of their children.' She recalls the time a child was playing with a mother and father doll and the child doll was alone outside. 'I asked the mother and father what they thought was going on with their child, but they didn't see that it had any meaning. On other occasions parents did understand, and they might ask then what they could do to help their child. But it was very saddening work because I saw so clearly how children "lost" their parents during separation. Just as I saw the children acting out their distress very clearly and you wanted to say stop being two angry people, be parents, take your child home and help him or her to feel it is a safe place again.'

We should not forget, however, says Fiona Williams working on changing family lives and family relationships, for the Economic and Social Research Council *Rethinking Families* (Calouste Gulbenkian Foundation, 2004) how many parents – she interviewed plenty – saw their children as a lifelong commitment and talked of profound emotional investment in them, even if their relationship with the other parent did not last

Indeed most of us will know parents who agonise over how painful their separation with its consequences will, inevitably, be for their young. Parents who do all they can to minimise the suffering. Melissa recollects only knowing her parents were divorcing because together they sat with her and explained in calm voices, referring to each other throughout, and assuring her that they would certainly remain friends.

'When I compare it to the stories I hear from friends of parents forever screaming at each other, refusing to be in the same room, so that everyone is treating the house like a poisoned zone. I feel pretty lucky. It was still a shock, when they told me, and not what I wanted but they helped me and my brother understand that although they couldn't manage to go on living together, they intended to go on co-parenting us just the same. On the morning my Dad was going they produced a diary and wrote in the dates when he would be coming to see us.

'My mother explained she would go out for the times when he would come and be with us in the house, and once he was settled in his new home we could stay with him. They also agreed we would still sometimes have family meals, and dates for those meals were written into the diary. Before Dad left we had a big family hug.'

Children are not, of course, the only ones to suffer or to feel the security and comfort of home evaporating as the structure of life is disintegrating. Adults suffer – of course they do – when partnerships built on caring, hope and faith, are ending, even if it is not a tearing limb from limb job. As I was writing this chapter the discovery of Arnold Schwarzenegger's child by the woman who had been his family's housekeeper for 20 years, came to light. The pain his wife Maria Schriver was etched into every corner of her face. The house where she, her husband, and the trusted housekeeper had lived, Brentwood Mansion in Los Angeles, has been described as 'a cherished home which had been Maria's sanctuary from the ever present rumours about her husband's infidelity'.

Then there is the desperation in the words of this man whose wife wants to leave him and who sees the reassuring pattern of home life, under threat. 'My wife and I have two young children but she tells me she doesn't love me any longer. I feel so scared and alone. I didn't even see this coming. I have been a jerk to her due to my own personal stresses. I am very overweight, work a very dangerous job that doesn't allow much sleep. I can't lose my family... I can't imagine my wife in the future with another man and another man holding and kissing my children. This all makes me so sick to my stomach. I am hurting so bad. I have expressed to her how much I love her and my longing for her to not leave and try to stay and work it out. She is very resistant. She already seems to have plans in place to be able to leave. I can't imagine not waking up to see my children or coming home to my wife. I am destroyed. I hate that I have been letting her hurt for so long. I feel like I have lost a fight I never had the chance to be part of.'

Parents male and female go through agonies at the idea of not living in a normal, day-to-day way with their children. Lewis whose marriage broke up when his sons were at primary school, saw a good deal of them, but he has never stopped feeling the deprivation in his life, 'My wife got custody, lived close by and was happy for me to have the boys over frequently, but the way they and I were together changed and became more strained. I think I was kind of pleadingly eager for everything to be right for them on their visits. It is very different when your children are visitors to when they are just there getting on with their lives. I regard this as the greatest sadness of my life.'

Yet however distraught the adults may be in a relationship that will no longer hold together, with one or both sides wanting out, the shattering of home life has a particular brutality for children because adults are in charge, making the decision to separate with all that implies. And even when parents talk with children and try to help them feel they are part of the process of planning a future, the fact is they are, ultimately, almost always powerless. Hostages to whatever fortune their parents and lawyers hash out for them, only able to speculate on what their home or home life will be in the future.

The Breaking Point

But marriages will go on not lasting, however high the price, and children will continue to be caught in the decisions adults make about calling it a day. It is unlikely that any amount of government pleading, coercing, will prevent that. Not even if, as David Brooks says in his book *Social Animals*, a stable marriage has 'psychic benefit' worth £65,000 a year. There are many reasons why people will break up the home when they have reached a point of misery or lack of happiness although the threshold for deciding it is intolerable varies greatly.

I have not forgotten a man I interviewed who had chosen a classic 'mid-life crisis' reason for wanting to leave home. He told me he had fallen in love with someone else after 20 years marriage to his wife. His analysis of why he had to go may have been melodramatic but he saw it as insurmountable, 'I thought I would die if I couldn't be with this new woman'. So he told his wife, describing with a shudder how she had been standing in the bedroom brushing her hair, facing the mirror.

'She swung round and hit me and hit me with the brush. She was sobbing. It was terrible. And my teenage daughters were furious, they wouldn't speak to me for two years. I made regular visits to the house but it was very evident I was not part of the way they had re-shaped life there.' Nor did it all add up to the rewarding ending he had envisaged. This was eighteen months after his divorce and, as the man talked there were tears in his eyes which he did not disguise.

'The sense that I had followed my destiny and was with the person I truly loved lasted a very short time. I realised how impossible it was to be happy having made the family I had created and been with for two decades, so very unhappy. I missed them dreadfully. The new woman and I split up and now I am on my own. My dearest wish is that I could be walking up the front path coming home to my family, to chat and laughter over the supper table, at the end of the day, just as it used to be.'

In Jenny's case it was very different and although she struggled hard against ending a marriage to a man she loved deeply and passionately, and with whom she worked. Yet she came to the point of feeling so psychologically exhausted she feared not being able to go on coping.

'I believe he loved me as I did him but it became increasingly hard to live harmoniously together. He was older than I and had old-fashioned ideas about who looked after the home. It bugged me but it seemed ridiculous to say "I am going to leave the great love of my life because he doesn't do his share of cleaning the kitchen or the lavatory." I got into the habit of telling myself it wasn't so important.

'When our daughter was born things were fine for a while, but then he seemed to become very upset with me over small things around the home, there was bad temper and shouting. He had had a very difficult childhood and I had hoped that having a home and child of his own would be healing, but it wasn't.

'We broke up when our daughter was 16. It was a very tough time for her but she says now being free of the bad atmosphere felt better. It was liberation for me. I realised that I could have my own ideas, I could have friends over for dinner and go to them – my husband never wanted to see my friends. Most cathartic of all I re-styled the home which I kept, including putting in a carpet I really liked and which he had hated. More importantly, I think, I tried to involve our daughter in making home feel good, for her.'

A Bonfire of the Nuptials

That is different to what I call the cult of narcissistic divorce which seems to be the style *de nos jours*. We have become steadily more used to the idea that discarding a relationship which no longer seems blissfully fit for purpose, is just fine, kids or no.

Which brings us again to the ubiquitous role models of the day – people in the public eye, performers, celebrities – who are recorded separating and divorcing as though it were a TV game show in which they compete to notch up a record figure.

There may be a lot of hand-wringing and sentimental schmaltz, talk of deep regret dished up for the media, but nevertheless off they go. Then there they are once again being photographed all loved-up and telling the world how they are marrying the man or woman who makes them happier than anyone ever has before. At least until that marriage hits the divorce courts.

Larry King with his eight marriages comes to mind, alongside Mickey Rooney with nine marriages, Elizabeth Taylor and Zsa Zsa Gabor who are poster girls for serial marriage in the high numbers, even though Gabor is on record declaring, 'Divorcing a man because you don't love him is almost as foolish as getting married just because you do'. James Cameron, creator of Terminator, Titanic, Avatar has tied the knot five times and is still a relatively young man. Billy Bob Thornton has five marriages under his belt; Patsy Kensit numbers four, with Tom Cruise trailing at a mere three.

Singer Tammy Wynette, five times wed, makes you wonder to whom she dedicated her chart-busting song *Stand By Your Man*. The sum total of all this is a bonfire of the nuptials when these relationships so demonstrably not about sticking with the tough bits, hit the divorce courts and often with their highly-priced piles – homes for children who usually get scant mention in all the emotional brouhaha around how the divorcees are feeling. There again, whether we like it or not the goal posts have changed steadily over past decades. Sufficiently so that we have a divorcee married to royalty and nobody suggested our possible future king should abdicate. Indeed after an initial flurry of newspaper columns containing a bit of tutting, Camilla was greeted with smiles and affection, even though she and Charles had been complicit in a peculiar emotional cruelty towards Diana, his naive young first wife.

Indeed the Royal Family is now littered with divorces, in company with the upper echelons of society, politicians, philosophers, leaders in the arts, the sciences and so on and so forth.

So now we have almost half of all married homes pervaded with a toxic atmosphere, sullen silences, coded speech, outright accusations, screaming and crying, before divorce.

That or the silence of unsaid thoughts which can be every bit as troubling as rows out loud. Children may be confusingly privy to the known unknowns, the sense that something cataclysmic threatens their security, while remaining in ignorance.

The author Judy Blume, twice divorced, has described this experience in her children's book *It's Not the End of the World* (Macmillan). Karen, a child in the fictional family, realises her father is less and less around, no longer reliably there for family weekends, while her mother comes up with unconvincing explanations. When finally her mother admits divorce is on the cards Karen's pent-up emotions are unleashed at the recognition that the things she hadn't even realised she was so fearing are happening – unstoppably.

It may be shocking to suggest that many people would divorce frivolously, yet a recent report from America suggests that, lemming like, we may be more inclined to divorce when family and friends do so. Sociologists and psychologists from three North American universities examined statistics from a group of individuals over a 32-year period and have tagged what they found 'divorce clustering'', in their report *Breaking Up Is Hard To Do Unless Everyone Else Is Doing It Too.*

They looked at the effect of divorce among peer groups on an individual's own risk of divorce and found a clear process of what the scientists called 'social contagion.' When it happens to immediate friends, this increases your own chance of getting divorced by 75 per cent. The effect drops to 33 per cent if the divorce is between friends of a friend, in what the researchers call two degrees of separation, then disappears almost completely at three degrees of separation. The state of the marriage of siblings and colleagues also has a significant effect on how long your own marriage might last.

At least here children help, 'We do not find that the presence of children influences the likelihood of divorce, but we do find that each child reduces the susceptibility to being influenced by peers who get divorced.'

The meaning of a broken home begins with the marriage and when and why relationships go so wrong that partners choose to go through the traumatic process of divorce with the often emotional as well as material loss afterwards. An experience of which author Margaret Atwood said, 'A divorce is like an amputation, you survive it but there's less of you'. While actor Robin Williams uses humour to express the festering anger that is so often a residual part of the process, 'Ah, yes, divorce… from the Latin word meaning to rip out a man's genitals through his wallet.'

Tommy Manville, presumably not a bit amused, also let it be known with a sour jest, 'She cried, and the judge wiped her tears with my check book.'

The Fairytale Wedding

Are the seeds of destruction sown early, when there is there a link between breakdown of marriage and the call to consumerism, to spend, spend, spend in order to make a wedding day just perfect? It's hard to avoid believing so. Glossy magazines, newspapers and TV shows dedicated to guiding us through the business of marriage, depend on advertising for their survival, and that means instilling in us the must-have feeling. As we embark on the pretty serious business of creating a life with our chosen partner, a time when you might think recognising that it's not about a single day is an important reality check, we are bombarded with the idea that this should be The Best Day Of Your Life, The Happiest Day Of Your Life. One on which we become convinced it is essential to have a very special dress and trimmings, a venue and catering to impress. What could better make the day super-special than the knowledge you have the best of everything. And to hell with the cost.

The trouble is it is not to hell with the cost. Partly because starting married life in debt from wedding over-spend as plenty of couples do, can cast a very real shadow over what might be a carefree time.

We do better to have the outfits we can afford comfortably, even if it takes more inventiveness than cash, and to have our sights focused on the prospect of getting to know our partner in a new way, as spouse. Being prepared for the imperfect as well as the infinitely loveable, understanding that familiarity will likely mediate the heightened chemistry of early sex, and so on.

There are, of course, plenty of exceptions to what I describe here – lovely, low key weddings in churches, halls, in registry offices, beaches and fields, which do not involve excessive consumption and which are centred on the idea of the wedding being part of a continuum stretching into a future of sharing life and building an enduring home. But my point here has been to contemplate what easy prey couples tying the knot may be for the great machine of capitalism that so relies on us desiring something that will pick us out from the crowd, provide the material trappings for our fantasies.

A Culture of Perfectionism

One of the saddest things in today's Western world, is how fragile relationships seem to be once they are settling into the familiar pattern of life. Malcolm Brynin, co-author of *Changing Relationships*, a new book based on five years of research into family life published by the Economic and Social Research Council found eleven years is the average time couples stayed together before their marriages ended in divorce. McManus tells us that In America after five years, 23 percent of Americans have divorced. He cites the cult of self interest, 'The costs and benefits of a relationship are more fluid than in the past. People come together and stay together only when this is to their individual advantage.'

In a poll of 5,000 couples who had been married for over a decade. More than half felt undervalued. The average couple, it was found, gives up on romance just two years, six months and 25 days into a marriage. By the third wedding anniversary, 83 per cent of those surveyed said they couldn't even be bothered to continue celebrating the date they tied the knot. And as relationships begin to seem stale, the rewards not good enough for all the hopes and dreams that you invested in getting married, setting up home together and having a family, what gets lost? Williams takes the view that 'caring activities' are no longer prioritised in lives that are often too time pressed, too concerned with personal happiness, with getting what you are worth out of a relationship. She talks of an atrophying of the 'important dimensions of day to day activities which are so central to the sustaining of family lives and personal relationships – helping, tending, looking out for, talking, sharing and offering a shoulder to cry on.'

This walks us directly through the entrance to home, for most of these activities are, at best, a part of what home life embodies. America has the highest divorce rate in the developed world. Lawrence Kurdek for his report 'Predicting The Seven-Year Itch', charts the decline in the marriages of more than 500 Midwestern couples, over the last 10 years. Kurdek says that married couples' assessment of their marriage starts to decline fairly quickly after they have tied the knot and goes downward throughout the first four years. If they stay the course, it plateaus during eight, nine, ten years. Most chilling in Kurdek's findings is his conclusion that children are a considerable stress on marriage; having children prevented married couples from maintaining 'positive illusions about their relationship'.

So the modern yearning to cling on to fairytale illusions about romance overwhelms the possibility of children. For all the strains they put on a relationship, they are a love-expanding addition to our committed relationships, and a reason to make a big effort to keep home secure and intact. I look around my friends who have dipped and dived through a few decades of keeping family and home together, and realise that a defining quality is a kind of earthy practicality. For sure they were as jittery-excited, convinced they had the perfect partner, indulging in romantic gestures and so on, in the early days, but they were also able to give a wry shrug when that settled into an altogether more familiar, accepting modus vivendi and recognise that the long haul was about two people as companions, sparring partners, good mates, ultimately, as people to be gift-wrapped in eternal romanticism.

Natalie Low, a clinical psychologist at Harvard, has been married half a century and counsels families as they live with the reality of marriage. She sees the culture of perfectionism, with couples imposing pressures on themselves, as the seeds of destruction. Couples desperately trying to nurture relationships along with raising perfect children, maintaining careers and without the help usually of extended families or communities.

A lot that I have written so far has referred to marriage but, of course, the suffering of children is the same whether their parents are married or not. Thus Sandra Davis, at the law firm Mishcon de Reya points out that while the number of children who will face family breakdown has increased from 40 per cent to 48 percent over the past decade, divorce only accounts for one in five family break-ups for children under the age of 14, the others are cohabitees. So the numbers are far greater than when divorce alone is our measure of children affected by a broken home.

Bargaining Tools

When we break up home and family we should try to be aware of the 'effect adult freedoms have upon a small child' as Pat Righelato expressed it in her introduction to the Wordsworth Classics edition of Henry James's *What Maisie Knew*, a searing portrait of a small girl caught up in her parents' 1800s divorce. Yet surely, these days, with all the knowledge we have of what divorce means for our young, you would assume anyone who cares for their children would do everything imaginable to minimise the suffering of their young. Not so. A survey of 4,000 families done by law firm Mishcon de Reya had one in five spouses admitting that a primary objective during divorce proceedings was making the experience as unpleasant as possible for a former partner. Two thirds admitted using children as 'bargaining tools'.

It is not difficult to imagine how far from a sanctuary home life must have been for those children. And haven't you, as I have, been horrified at seeing cases that bring to mind another passage from *What Maisie Knew* where the courts deal with a custody battle. 'The little girl (was) disposed of in a manner worthy of the judgement seat of Soloman. She was divided in two and the portions tossed impartially to the disputants. They would take her in rotation for six months at a time... What was clear to any spectator was that the only link binding her to either parent was this lamentable fact of her being a ready vessel for bitterness, a deep little porcelain cup in which biting acids could be mixed... her parents had looked to her to feed their love of battle.'

Perhaps the best chance of children's feelings having place in our minds when we separate, is for us to understand just what our adult freedoms feel like to them. The divorce court is not, of course, the beginning or necessarily the worst of it.

One Plus One has produced compelling work showing how painful and damaging the time building up to a couple's decision to separate, and the time between decision-making and the actual separation, can be. As director Penny Mansfield points out – and she echoes some of the most authoritative findings – one of the most upsetting things for children is conflict in the home between the only people children have there, supposedly to look after their welfare. So unless we make a concerted effort not to let rip our angry, distressed, impossible, resentful feelings in front of children – and that is never harder than when your life is turning upside down – then conflict is what children will get at home.

Georgia, 27, the daughter of Jenny who spoke earlier about the reason her marriage ended in divorce, remembers the years of 'drama and rows' in her home. 'I would be put in another room but even when I couldn't hear my parents screaming at each other I knew it was going on. Then I would hear Dad storming out. He didn't ever stay and try to chill with my mother and I felt he led the way things were.

'He and I got on very badly for a long time because I would get upset and ask why he behaved as he did. But he just asked why I didn't ask my mother the same thing.' She pauses 'I suppose I should have done so, but somewhere inside I knew that if they split up I'd probably stay with my mother, and she talked to me sometimes about how unhappy she was. I just remember thinking anything would be better than the rows which left them both so unhappy and that perhaps there would be space for my life then.

'When they did separate it took a long time. Dad started by being around the house less and less and then he would only come at weekends, then even that not often, so there was no definitive cut off point. During this time I blacked out a lot perhaps to escape from it all. I stopped trying at school and went right down. I couldn't talk to my parents about how I felt – if I tried it just turned into them slagging the other off. I did talk to friends because most of them had divorced parents. But of course that wasn't comforting either and I had no idea what a decent marriage would look like.'

Getting a home of her own, last year – her mother helped her buy a flat – has been a comfort to Georgia. 'It helps me heal some of the sense of disarray I lived with and I work hard at having good emotions there. If a friend is going through a bad time in a relationship I always see them away from my place. I want my home to be a sanctuary.'

A Sense of Homelessness

My niece Tegan was three when my brother and her mother separated and very quickly her mother moved to a house about half an hour from her father's home, taking the children with her. The mother immediately began divorce proceedings.

Tegan, now in her mid-twenties says, 'I don't remember much about the actual split. I've grown up knowing Mum in her townhouse and Dad in our country house. The difficult thing was they were on very bad terms and it used to upset me a lot when they were forever having arguments on the phone. I wanted to be a peacemaker, so my times in both their homes were fraught. My mother slagged off my father a lot, and I hated that but inevitably as my sister and I lived with her it coloured how we saw Dad. It's only now I can see that he was actually a very good father to us, and their feelings about each other should have been kept to themselves.'

For Tegan it is very sad to have no memory of being together as a family. 'I had a dream when younger of us all sitting under a tree having a picnic, and it felt so good.' Then she goes on fiercely, 'I know children of divorce are more likely to divorce themselves, but I am very very determined not to let that happen. I wouldn't want kids of mine to go through what I have.'

My parents did not split-up. Indeed, as I have written earlier I believe they had a caring marriage that both valued. Even so they had their spats. I particularly remember the sound of their raised voices in the bathroom in the mornings, my mother's shrill in her frustration at not getting my father to see her point of view. My father's voice high and matching her frustration. I would listen outside the door trying to make out what it was all about, but somehow I never could. Then I would barge into my brother's room to tell him they were rowing again.

The jittery anxiety that hung around in my young gut compounded into fully-fledged fear when I went with a friend to see a film which turned out to be about parents arguing, deciding to divorce and with the children crying pleading with them not to do so, to no effect. This convinced me the same cataclysmic situation was brewing in my home. It wasn't until my mother found me in the garden, sitting under the weeping ash, hunched up, head buried between my knees, sobbing, that I told what was bothering me. I was lucky. Mummy sat down next to me, her broad comforting arm around my shoulders and explained that she and Daddy certainly were not contemplating divorce, but that neither of them was at their best first thing in the morning, and somehow little things that seemed more important than they were, bugged them both.

It is startling to hear Lucilla, a woman, now in her 60s, who I have always seen as a model of composure and sure-footedness in life, burst out saying how she had felt homeless when her parents separated, more than 40 years ago, when I told her the subject of this book. I talk to her in the family home she has created with plump-cushioned sofas that suck you into their depths, chairs well-positioned under lights for reading, the walls are heavy with art work she and her husband have chosen, and done by one of their sons. At one end of the long room is a conservatory overlooking the verdant garden, which is the 'man cave' of Lucilla's husband. She talks of 'considering myself lucky to marry a Jewish man who prioritises home and relationships. I've learnt a huge amount from him about how incredibly important a sustaining home can be.'

Lucilla did had never thought that her parents might divorce. True, she says, there was no perceptible warmth between them but 'they did brilliantly at creating a family home in the sense of putting a roof over our heads. My father worked every evening and weekends building a family home from two cottages he had bought for £70. My mother drew plans at the weekend and we had a big garden with vegetables and chickens.

'We lived in a very empty rural area. I did not have friends around and the lack of warmth in our family life made me side with my father who was good-looking, bright and seemed glamorous to me. What I didn't realise then was that the life and colour had been drained from my mother because my father so undermined her and she was ground down.'

Yet even though Lucilla was a young adult when her parents separated, the pain of loss, the sense of displacement were great. 'I left home for university and while I was away my parents separated. It came as a total shock and after that I felt like a gypsy staying all over the place with my bag of clutter. My parents had sold the family home and had both bought little houses but there was nowhere that felt like a home for me. In fact, I felt like an orphan.'

Collaborative Divorce

Knowing what a price our young pay for our inability to make the relationships in which we have chosen to produce them, work, we might wonder whether putting our own personal happiness on the back burner for the sake of the children, would be so impossibly hard to achieve? That is the lines of Elizabeth Muirhead's thinking. She is a family lawyer and was one of the first people in the UK to train in collaborative divorce. She brought this method into her practice believing it the best way of putting children's needs first. Far better than the common adversarial model.

Parents have to choose this way or it has little chance of success she explains.

'The couple must agree they will try the collaborative approach, so by and large I'm not seeing those people who want to kill each other. The Ditch the Bitch husband going through the garbage to find proof of cheating, the wife who gets a private detective on to her husband.

'Once a couple have decided they do want to go this route, they sign a document saying they will not go to court against each other, but will come up with an agreement to be presented to the court. And the great difference between the collaborative approach and usual divorce proceedings is that the lawyers are not there to score points but they too are committed to solving the problems.' I was impressed to hear that Muirhead has anger management on tap as another way to help couples move towards collaboration. She is clear in what she says.

'Some of the best work we do as solicitors and mediators is in looking at how anger management helps people get beyond raw emotion and look at what the implications of how they separate will be.'

Doing all possible to keep the conflict out of the home so that it remains an emotionally safe place for children is important, but she does not see keeping the home intact as necessarily the best arrangement if conflict is simply going to break out again. Rather an important part of the collaborative process is to look at what kind of home arrangements will be in the children's best interests. 'It can be brutal for children to see the structure of their home ripped apart and I see a lot of unhappy house sales in divorce.'

If parents can live geographically close so that the children may move easily between them it can minimise pain, provided parents do not use their children as constant messengers delivering vitriol or gathering information to report back. When Caspar discovered his wife was having an affair with the neighbour and wanted to separate he was angry, jealous and upset but above all he did not want to lose the close and loving relationship he had with his children. He decided to stay in the family home and take in two lodgers to pay the mortgage on an apartment a street away so the children would be very close.

'I would happily have seen my wife the other side of the moon, but I knew if I or she moved say to the other side of London the boys would have all the discomfort and confusion I have heard about, of changing homes quite radically when they moved between us.

'I wasn't going to contest my wife getting residency because I have a job with long and unreliable hours. But it meant I could pick them up and bring them to me very easily, on my days for having them, or in due course they walked around the corner if I was a bit delayed. They had their local friends, I could take them to school and so on. I was a part of their normal life, which isn't how it is for kids whose fathers – usually – have them on visits and the children come to a completely alien neighbourhood. I think its been good for them, its certainly been good for me, and now their mother and I are amicable neighbours.'

Sacrifices

One of the cases Muirhead regards as a particular success, was a couple with children in a rural boarding school within commuting distance of London. They rented a house near the school, made the children day pupils, and took it in turns to stay there and do the parenting. Then there are parents who make considerable sacrifices to have a stake in bringing up their children in as normal way a way as can be managed. Jonathan

Self comes immediately to mind.

We met at a literary festival and went for a meandering walk through the Devon countryside, on one of those evenings of mellow warmth, the sun melting into evening glow. Jonathan, who voiced, at the beginning of this chapter, such a powerful loss of the spirit of home after his father had left, talked to me of the ramshackle life he had had through many years of young manhood. When Jonathan met the mother of his first son, they bought a Georgian house in Brixton and he had dreams of a conventional family life. They very quickly realised however that a too quick pregnancy had forced them into a relationship in which both were miserable. Within eighteen months they had separated.

Jonathan moved in with his father's first wife and had his son a good deal of the time. 'I was creating home life for him on the hoof and we've always had a lot of time together. I got a housing association home because I could demonstrate I had my son more than half the time. I worked for myself and squeezed work in around caring for him.'

About three years into this arrangement he met the mother of his next two children. Again pregnancy was unplanned. Jonathan sold London and bought a house in the country so that there would be a room for his first son and the new child. 'I again had a dream of creating stable family life and in due course our third son was born.

'But my partner who had come from Australia never liked England, so we bought a place in Australia with the idea we could all go there when my first boy was old enough to make the choice if he wanted to come.' But before that the mother of the second sons had left Jonathan and taken the last born boy, leaving the elder with Jonathan. He says, 'legally I could have forced my partner to come back because our youngest was born in the UK. But I had a clear vision of what a hellish home life the boys would have had if I had forced that. I figured that if she was where she wanted to be and I came and went the children had a better chance of a stable home.'

He was able to do some freelance editing for a small publishing company and had sold the advertising agency he owned. It meant there was some money available, but any career ambitions had to be abandoned as Jonathan travelled back and forth to Australia eighteen times in the first year. He says, 'I wasn't much of a priority for my parents, and I felt strongly being prioritised by me was very important for my children.' To begin with he stayed, in Australia, in a studio attached to the farmhouse he and his partner had bought but she asked him to go and he had to as the property was in her name.

'So then during my visits to Australia I stayed in a motel and the boys would stay with me. I created just as good a home for the boys in two grotty rooms with Formica furniture and uncomfortable beds as I could have done in a house. That time made me see very clearly that home is as much about what you create and do in a place as lavishness of the bricks and mortar.' I then decided that instead of coming and going for two weeks at a time, I wanted to have a more normal life with my second and third son, and although my ex-partner didn't want me around her, she was very happy for me to take the boys for a lot of time.

'I rented a house close to where they lived so they could move in with me for the three or so months that I was there at a time and go to the same school, have their friends around and so on, and in due course nip home to their mother if they felt like it.'

After two years he could afford a small 1950s house and that created a greater sense of security for the boys, giving concrete evidence that Jonathan was a permanent part of their lives. Back in the UK he spent time with his other son.

'It hasn't all been perfect for them, and my eldest boy became very angry with me for a while, being very fierce about the failings in my parenting. Even so I think I have achieved what I so wanted which was to have a loving relationship with my sons that has been built on having a proper home life with them.

'These, then, appear to be decisions made with children's wellbeing at heart. What a pity then that the courts are not always equally sensitive. Some of the stories I have heard suggest their thinking is wilfully inimical to what would be best for children, to how significant the home they know may be when everything else is falling into smithereens.

Take Mary who moved into her apartment with her daughter and Basil, the child's father – later they married – when their daughter was two.

A while after they had married, Basil began an affair but in spite of this, she says 'I was determined to keep the family together. It was stressful but I felt there are sometimes reasons these things happen and I mustn't make our daughter suffer because it upset me.'

She is quick, even now years later, to take on some blame.

'I do think he found it difficult, the amount of attention I gave our child and eventually I agreed to him moving out which was what he wanted.' Depression followed and an acrimonious divorce, but Basil paid maintenance and towards the mortgage and 'popped around sporadically to see our child'. But when Mary met a man who became her new partner Basil stopped paying maintenance or towards the mortgage.

Then came the bombshell: 'Basil, who had remarried, announced that he wanted me to sell my home, the apartment where we had lived. He knew it was important to our little girl. as her security after a pretty unpleasant time, but it made no difference. 'He went to court saying I was being obstructive and I was given an order to sell the property. The judge said we must get agents' valuations. We did this and although it was going to put us in a very tight position, my partner and I offered to buy half at the assessed price.'

At this point, she tells, Basil went to another agent who said they could get £200,000 more than the price other agents had said, which made the price prohibitive for Mary and her partner. But the court insisted if the apartment could be sold for this sum it should be and the gave Basil three months to try for a sale. Offers were made but fell through, meanwhile Mary says, her daughter was getting more and more upset at what was going on. 'She kept crying saying she didn't want to move.' Eventually Mary and her partner raised the money to buy the apartment at the high price. 'We looked at other properties but couldn't find anything that was near enough my daughter's school and friends. It worried me that my daughter was so upset at the prospect of having to leave her home. So we gambled on my partner's new business doing well enough, and bought Basil out.'

Writing this I came across the word of journalist Deborah Orr writing in the *Guardian*, which describe precisely my point in this chapter.

'If two people decide to make a family together then fail to keep that basic unit functioning so that the needs of children are met, then they have to be made aware of the consequences for their children.'

The number of divorces has gone down very slightly in the UK in the past couple of years, and perhaps this is a recognition that breaking up a home is less of a solution than it sometimes seems. Mediation and collaborative divorce are ways that children may be better protected and which make us more aware of the consequences.

All in all it would be good to think, if we pause to really

consider what a house that is not a home means for children. Then perhaps there would be less Humpty Dumpty homes that can never be put together again.

WE WANT TO BE TOGETHER

As the new millennium got underway, Sarah Berger realized that, over and over, she was getting involved in conversations with people like herself for whom the idea of a home life with communality, good neighbourliness, and where caring and sharing was built in, felt like a constructive way to go.

Sarah had been living alone in the family home after her marriage had ended some years earlier and she says, 'I never felt that living in an isolated nuclear family was a healthy or natural thing'. Her children had left home and, aged 50, she says, 'It seemed life would become the law of diminishing returns. I was very aware of how unconnected most people are, even though they live very close to each other.'

Tobias Jones who spent five years with his wife, Francesca Lenzi, staying in communities, finally establishing a communal homestead themselves, crystallizes the thought, 'While I believe passionately in the importance of family, I think the two generational nuclear family is an abnormal departure of the 20th century. The modern, narrow definition of the word has turned the family – once a castle of inclusivity – into an excuse for exclusivity.'

Which chimes with the conversations Sarah was having although too often they were wishful thinking, fanciful convivial chats, which went no further. Some did, however, and Sarah and a few others went on to join up with other people wanting to walk the walk as well as talking the talk. They set up a cohousing project, Laughton Lodge in Sussex. They were aware of the number predicting a fast collapse into chaos, but twelve years on Laughton is thriving.

Co-housing has some things in common with the 1960s commune movement – the belief that people sharing common ground, literally and metaphorically, create a healthier and happier society, than do so many of us with our boxed off homes, pressurised ways of life and lack of neighbourliness.

There have been co-housing projects since the 1960s, of course, but it is only now, as a model for 21st century living, that the idea appears to be attracting serious interest in the UK. It has already taken root more thoroughly in other parts of Europe and the US.

Laughton Lodge

Unlike many 1960s and 70s communes cohousing does not set out its stall as radical in the way of kicking out every vestige of bourgeois living style. People have their private homes, with doors that can be firmly shut on the community outside when wanted, and family life can be conducted in an entirely traditional way if they wish. One of the great virtues, as I see it, is that Laughton Lodge has no ideological belief system, or dogma to be observed.

So the people who have invested materially and emotionally in their pioneer project, have agreed they wish to live with communality, sharing fundamental aims and activities, to involve themselves in consensual decision making about running the project, while having their own privacy and autonomy.

The thing that defines each of the cohousing projects I visited is a determination to do all they can to keep the carbon footprint down, and there is much to be said for having a large group of people contributing knowledge and ideas to this end. 'We aim to live lightly on the planet' is how Sarah puts it.

William Heath, contemplating buying one of the Laughton houses, in 2012, gave a measured assessment of what he found when he visited, and also the importance of being clear about what you are doing when you sign up for such a project, and never more so than if you have been an urban soul thus far.

It's an impressive set-up. They've got lots right. There are a series of warm, well-insulated cosy light living spaces. The culture feels good. People are welcoming and open-hearted wherever you go. The day we were there children played happily and independently all over the site in several natural groups. I must have seen half a dozen musical instruments in a 90 minute visit.

Then there was the caveat.

'As my late and now bestselling friend Richard Craze put it, you'd be out of your townie mind to think this was Utopia or an easy choice. Several people echo the view that city dwellers can be unrealistic about moving to the countryside. Co-housing is not independent living, nor is it the commune style of shared housing. Decision-making with consensus is tortuous.'

It took Sarah and her group several years to get Laughton Lodge up and running, and they did so with help from the *Co-Housing Network UK*. Today it is home to some 70 like-minded stakeholders of very different generations. Some are families with children, others singles from choice, divorced or bereaved. There are ethnic minorities, gays and people of varied faiths, or none at all.

So it was that I was ushered through the front door to Sarah's brightly painted kitchen with a shelf of spices, a bowl of fruit, flowers and cards, and messages pasted up on various bits of wall space. She led me into a spacious sitting room with a lot of gleaming honey-coloured wood and large windows. Up the stairs there were two bedrooms and a study with pale walls and windows gazing towards a spreading view over green fields. Just across from here the Glyndebourne Opera Festival takes place, and If the wind blows the right way, at the right time, on summer nights, the notes of Verdi, Rossini, Puccini may be audible.

This is one of the apartments created at Laughton Lodge, an erstwhile mental institution which Sarah and her group bought by selling their individual homes, gambling on the physical restoration as well as the communal experiment coming to happy fruition. That has happened and now the place speaks of contentment, containment, tranquillity. Things that Sarah knew she wanted, as well as a sociable environment, in the place she hopes will be her home for life.

Sarah's is one of several apartments of different sizes, and there are four eco-houses in the shared 23 acres of woodland and fields. Here individual vegetable plots are carefully tended, some people own chickens; there are ponies for riding. On the day I visited one of the longest-established residents was digging, nearby his wife was standing on the patio of their home, chatting with a couple of other women while keeping an eye on a group of children from various families, playing high-spiritedly in a rough-hewn playground.

Getting the project from idealistic theory to structural

reality was laborious Sarah tells. On the one hand they had to grapple with the practicalities of finance, planning process, architecture and at the same time there was the human dimension.

'With co-housing you have your own home, but at the same time the aim is to be a community with inter-dependency' – they share washing facilities, a communal kitchen where weekly 'pot luck' meals are served and, as is usual in co-housing, there is a non-resident house which acts as a social hub. There are guest and conference rooms for rent, and activity rooms for the classes ranging from Ancient Greek to yoga, and tango lessons which the locals attend.

It doesn't surprise me to learn that harmonious interdependence took some fine-tuning and Sarah's tone is wry, 'Inevitably differences of opinion come up and conflicts about how things should be done, but the fact that you have come together because you want the benefits of being part of a group that shares and cares for each other, means you have a great vested interest in finding constructive ways to overcome problems'.

Ultimately satisfaction with cohousing is about the sum total of the people living there, and how well they can, when necessary, suspend their immediate desires for the greater good. As one co-houser put it, 'You don't have to love all your neighbours, just like them enough to make sure the project is supported.'

And the plus side, 'If you know your neighbour they won't call the police, they'll dial direct.'

Everyone I spoke with saw learning to live with others in co-operativeness as a valuable learning curve, with the benefits considerable. One described how: 'Last night I saw my neighbour having a medical problem and I drove him to the hospital. While I was here another neighbour called me and arranged to get his phone book and clothes to him. While another was helping with arrangements to get him home and make sure he was all right, when he was ready... We have our private lives but are close enough to know what is going on and help take care of each other.'

Springhill

My second visit is to Springhill in Gloucestershire. This was brought to life by David Michael, a man of flamboyant talk and prodigious energy. His village of timber clad apartments and houses linked together along ground level, with balconies on higher floors and the whole cut through with a pedestrian walkway, has the feel of a small village. Springhill, with 100 residents, is the first custom-built co-housing project in the UK.

David lived with his wife in a commune before this, and they knew they wanted a different style of communality for the years ahead. They had moved on from times when sharing everything from wheat germ shampoo to partners was *a la mode*. Rather, he declares, sitting in the carefully designed tranquillity of his large shadowy room, 'I cherish my privacy and that was not negotiable in my plan.'

A garrulous man, quick to talk about ideas and enthusiasms, David found others interested in buying into his scheme. He bought a piece of land and the outcome was 34 flats and houses as well as a large communal area for meetings, cooking, washing and, as one resident put it 'having those nice impromptu, unplanned encounters with friends.'

Such was the demand for housing at Springhill, David went on to buy a converted former Unitarian Chapel which is now 14 self-contained flats.

'You have to think about how to make it work, and I knew that balanced against the commitment of inhabitants to communality which was a must, I had to also balance the desires of a population that has grown used to having privacy, their own insulated family time and so on. A population that may want something more connected to other people, but not anything too total.'

Most particularly, he says residents buying their own places do not want to be told how they should decorate their homes, the food they should eat, how to bring up their children, how to conduct their intimate relationships.

Lodgers

Listening to all this I realise it has a ring of familiarity. It reminds me of how my own home has always operated on a communal basis but with very definite boundaries protecting privacy. Although there was no formal thinking how it happened, we have always lived with other people. It was Olly who, inadvertently laid the foundation stone for what would become a living style larger than our nuclear family life.

My father had been living, very unhappily, alone in the family home in the Home Counties, since my mother had died. His despair and loneliness filled the place like winter fog, but neither my brother nor I could face living alone with him in the family home away from work and friends and with his unhappiness tangling with our own attempts at coming to terms with our mother's death.

Yet, when we visited for weekends, it was heart-wrenching to see the paper bags from which he snacked – he was too dispirited to make himself food – littering the place, and to find him of an evening sitting hunched in the armchair next to the one my mother had always sat in, like a big, damaged bird.

It was Olly, whose own extended family, forever in and out of each others' homes and closely involved with one another-s' lives in Amsterdam, who was shocked that we didn't find a way to care for him better. Couldn't he live with us?

Not in the one room flat above the launderette, for sure, but from that thought came the idea of suggesting to Pa that he sell the family home and we get a house together in London. His delight at the idea was warming.

The house he bought and in which we were lodgers was a classic four-storey Victorian terraced home with two rooms per floor, and landings in between. It converted comfortably into a ground floor apartment with kitchen, for my father, another for Olly and me on the first floor. My brother was on the top floor. That left the basement free to be converted and my father invited a couple – friends of my brother – to live there.

In theory we were four autonomous households, but it was never like that. We all kept any eye on my father, popping in for a chat, making sure he was all right, and not, as he showed signs of early stage dementia, doing anything daft. On one occasion he decided to warm a filled rubber hot water bottle on the electric metal hotplate on his cooker and soon the smell or burning rubber filled the house.

We regularly ate together, my brother, our friends and we inviting each other and my father on an impromptu basis. Olly and I would dig and plant in the small garden with my father sitting close by in his garden chair, chatting to us, tea and biscuits on his knee.

As I arrived home from work my father would pop his head out from his sitting room door, like the cuckoo in a clock, 'wondering' if there might be a cup of tea. And up the stairs he came, making his way to settle in the big leather porter's chair in our sitting room.

We watched my father come back to life, becoming as contented as he could be without my mother. The knowledge of people and life being lived around him was all important. He dreaded loneliness as others might dread living in a busy institution.

After my father died Olly and I, as I have described earlier, moved into a large wreck of a house in North London and we had to raise money for the restoration. There was no way we could afford to live here alone and besides it would have been unreasonable to have kept empty rooms when there is a real need of places to be rented. So a great many people, including the cartoonist Mel Calman, came and went living with us at various times. Quite a few remain friends, others were disasters, and in one case, when the letting went disastrously wrong, we had a house polluted with ill-feeling for some months.

There was a delightful young American woman Lisa who came as an au pair which chiefly consisted of being the best fun elder sister to our boys, and teaching them all kind of un-*au-pair*ish tricks. She stayed a long time, and remains a valuable *ersatz* member of the family who we still see. Theo Green, a talented musician seemed to enjoy my son Cato's enthusiastic visits to listen to what he was doing, and they remain friends, Theo now helping Cato with his own burgeoning musical career.

Nor could we forget Andrew, a bachelor film producer who came to us in North London as a reclusive tenant, 24 years ago. The catalyst to his melting into sweet sociability was a group of very young ballet dancers, who moved into rooms near Andrew's for a couple of years. They would trip up and downstairs like beautiful gazelles. Andrew spruced up, became positively garrulous and a very good friend to the dancers, chauffeuring them to classes of a morning.

Now he lives with us in the present house, in a room directly opposite my sitting room door, which is almost always open. If we are having supper we generally wave to him to come and join us; he pops in for happy hour, swinging a bottle at his side, and makes regular vegetarian Sunday lunches. He also has absolute discretion about not invading uninvited. He lectures us on how to be more environmentally sound and so we have no electric clothes drier and our washing gets tangled drying on the roof but our consciences are clear. Our re-cycling system has been overhauled and we grow our own salad leaves. Andrew patted us on the back when we got secondary glazing a couple of years back.

This ad hoc caring and sharing is not of course under-pinned with a thought through philosophy for co-operative living, it has happened on the hoof. Olly and I have owned the properties and those who share are lodgers, so there is not the built in equality of co-housing. If we suddenly have a mind to we can get rid of everyone.

That is unlikely to happen because we seem to have found a way to benefit from the closeness of other people we like, and we would find it very limiting to live *a deux* now. I have also seen how valuable it is for the children to grow up knowing a diverse bunch of adults and forming their own relationships with those they like.

Integration

Our impromptu community then has evolved privately so nobody takes any notice of us. But it wasn't like that for the Laughton Lodge prospective inhabitants. Sarah recalls how public objection nearly killed the scheme before they had started. At the news of the housing scheme, the local Sussex villagers organised a petition to get it stopped.

'Initially there was a lot of opposition. We were suspected of being Moonies or some kind of cult – ironic as I'd have run a mile from anything with a guru or charismatic leader… The local petition got more than 200 signatures opposing us.'

They knew they needed a strategy to break through a resistance to something the local people did not actually know about in any detail.

'We put a lot of effort into going out into the local community, talking with people, explaining that we absolutely are not a cult, but ordinary people living ordinary lives, with a desire for communality. We won people over and now we have a very good relationship with the villagers. Most of our kids go to the local school, some of our parents are governors. We have members on the parish council and we have done quite a lot to boost trade in the village shops.

'We also have people from outside coming to the festivities we organise. For instance Laughton has a number of choirs and these include people from outside. Some strong, individual friendships have formed between those at Laughton and others locally. That interface with the local community seems very right to us, a way of extending the communality.'

David Michael can well sympathise with what Laughton Lodge went through because Springhill too hit problems from 'the misunderstanding' outsiders. In 2000, he negotiated to buy two acres of land close to the centre of Stroud on a steep, south-facing slope. By the Autumn of 2000 he had attracted some ten households, all of whom agreed to pay towards the land, proportionate to the size of home they would have.

In spring 2001 they submitted a planning application widely supported by the Town Council, Chamber of Commerce and significant others. Despite this David tells, his voice rising in irritation at the memory, 'The application was turned down through the activities of a group of Conservative and Independent district councillors who, we suspect, were concerned about an influx of 'alternative types' in an otherwise conservative ward. One councillor was quoted as saying: "this is dead weird – they want to eat together!"'.

David appealed combating the arguments put forward, and by the end of 2001 had permission to build.

Co-Housing's Pioneers

The first attempt at co-housing is said to be Skraplanet in Denmark. This project grew out of a gathering between architect Jan Gudmand-Hoyer and friends looking at ways housing could offer greater support and companionship to people, in 1964. Within a year they had bought a site outside Copenhagen and developed plans for 12 terraced houses set around a common house and swimming pool. But although city planners were supportive Gudmand-Hoyer and his group came up against neighbour opposition, just as later Sarah Berger and David Michael would, and they could not proceed with their plans to build. Such was Gurdman-Hoyer's anger he wrote an article *The Missing Link Between Utopia and the Dated One-Family House* and when this was published in a national newspaper it brought in more than 100 responses from interested families.

Around the same time Bodil Graae, too, was considering a model other than the traditional two-generational family as particularly valuable for children. In 1967 she published an article *Children Should Have One Hundred Parents*, and from this came a group of fifty families interested in creating 'a housing collective specifically designed with the value of collective concern for children in mind.

Bodil Graae had no dogmatic philosophy and her group set up the first known modern cohousing community in the world, an inspirational prototype for an intentional community composed of private homes supplemented by shared facilities. The community is planned, owned and managed by the residents

In the years since, co-housing has found an enthusiastic, if not enormous, following in Europe – Italy, Holland, Germany have an ever-growing number of projects – and in America there are over a thousand and counting. In Britain it has been slower to catch on but it seems to me co-housing is an idea coming into its time. I am struck, within my own circle, how many people are tossing around the idea of a shared home. So the likes of Sarah Berger and David Michael are less and less likely to be regarded as eccentric.

The co-housing proposals David Michael and Sarah Berger were involved with, following the excesses of the commune movement, probably came up against the fears and prejudices of the uninformed. What author Tobias Jones has talked about, having learned how trying to live in a counter-cultural way may be regarded.

'There are colossal misunderstandings and prejudices about communalism. Almost all media depictions focus on the weird and wacky cults. Books show community as something bizarre, dysfunctional or oppressive. So anyone trying to create a community has to battle against the idea that we are all nudists constantly ingesting hallucinogens, shagging one another...'

It is a view that Iro Staebler, a handsome man in his 60s, who now lives in a terraced house in North London with his vibrant wife Jane and, for the time being, his daughter Nina by a first marriage, remembers well. It was the 1960s when he lived in a commune in his native Berlin but he thinks the experience, far from making him a non-conformist, who would be dysfunctional in 'normal' society, in fact gave him an understanding of the value of communality and co-operation, and of the way good friendship becomes more important than material possessions.

We sit at a polished wooden table, in his home, his face half obscured by a vase of heavy-headed flowers, sipping companionably from the mugs of tea Iro has made. He takes himself back to his commune experience.

'I was studying medicine and a group of us were very involved in left-wing politics. There were six of us initially, male and female, and they included my girl-friend. We decided we wanted to live together and found a flat in an Art Deco building with six bedrooms. After we had moved in, we began to see ourselves as a commune. We felt strongly that we should not have possessions. We had a kitty although there was rarely any money in it, and the housework was done by rota.'

There was a holiday on an island near Denmark and the commune members stayed with one of the group's parents for six weeks.

'We slept in the same room. Then when we returned to Berlin we decided that sleeping in separate rooms was too bourgeois so we put all our mattresses into the largest room, and then in the room that had been mine before, a high bed was built. Its function was for making love. You booked an appointment to use it.'

But as the economic situation hit a downturn, the owner of the building decided to sell. For the group, Iro recollects, there was a powerful sense they must remain together as a political force.

'We were all sons and daughters of German soldiers who had been part of the war. My father grew up in Hitler's youth. As students and intellectuals we really felt we must question the values of orthodox society, and that included all its structures, among which was the idea that if you are monogamous and sleep just with the same woman, you belong to the establishment. I was keen on the idea of it being politically correct to sleep with all. But others started moving out to single rooms. I think sexual jealousy came into it.

'It was when the house sold that things fell apart. We moved into another flat but the energy had changed. People were getting into drugs. My girl friend was beguiled by the women's movement and met someone involved with the a group which had links to Baader Meinhof. She went to Italy and didn't come back.

'I became aware of dark clouds and a realization that what I had believed in had not provided answers. Now, looking back from a distance, I think that this experiment in questioning structures has stayed with me. That seems important in this day and age.'

These days he puts much creative energy into his work as an acupuncturist and giving treatments based on Chinese medicine, and he would not want to live in a commune again.

'But I think everyone would benefit from understanding that living this way is a serious experiment in creating a better way for society, not just an excuse for mass depravity. What we were doing was living in an anti-home way, challenging the comfortable complacency of the bourgeois way.'

At this he smiles, indicating the carefully decorated interior, the variety of artefacts to be seen in his present home. 'I can see this might be labelled bourgeois, but it makes sense as the sum total of much that Jane and I have chosen together. These days having a home that does not have to be re-negotiated, or to fulfil other people's ideals, is what I want.'

As Iro defends the integrity of the commune life he led, so Dr Bill Metcalf, in his book *Shared Visions, Shared Lives*, taking a retrospective look from the 1990s has it that: 'a commune is an idealised form of family, being a new sort of "primary group". Commune members have emotional bonds to the whole group and the commune is experienced with emotions.'

Gilly Lacey is another who invokes her commune years as an important education in living where home life requires you to tease out workable human values and a *modus operandi*. What a contrast she laughs with today's concern for privacy and homes that make a statement about our individualism, our desire not to belong to the group.

In the commune of which she was a founder member, in the King's Cross area of London in the late 1960s, it was an act of faith to live on as little as possible and to be creative in demonstrating alternatives to the conventional materialist way of life. She spent more than 20 years living in 'hippy or political collectives.' adding, 'At the heart of our thinking was to live among like-minded people and to demonstrate a way of living that said look at the implications for the good of people and our earth with the consumerist culture that was already building up, and think how we might do it differently.'

It is significant Gill says that, 'we, and many of the people questioning established orthodoxy around what home should be, were the first ones in our families to be educated in a way that encouraged you to challenge the status quo. Yet we have seen more and more people being educated but becoming self-interested, not using their developed minds to consider that we can't just live in a way that assumes there are endless resources, there will be limitless wealth.'

Gilly's commune evolved by chance rather than prior design.

'We had a large flat in Montague Square, Kings Cross and people kept coming in, taking rooms. We were all involved with each other and there were other places we knew where people were also creating communal situations. Our landlords stopped collecting rent because they didn't want us as sitting tenants if they chose to sell, so we saved the unpaid rent and bought a cottage in the country with a couple of acres and orchards, on a hill.

'There was just one small bedroom so we all slept there. We laid out the mattresses on the floor and people made love. We saw ourselves as overcoming traditional hang-ups and we were not supposed to be jealous. Some of us slept with quite a lot of people and I was one.

'I have tried to explain to my current partner that when I slept with people it was out of real feeling for them. I wasn't pissed and having a one night-stand. There was a good deal of conflict in fact and whatever we said philosophically, there was jealousy but we felt we mustn't let ourselves give in to it.'

Whatever society outside thought about such behaviour, Gilly is clear that this was part of a way of living intended to see if, like the new monogamists, they could rid home of the need for sexual exclusivity, yet keep a well functioning structure together.

'It was not an easy experiment. I found it terrible, absolutely terrible when my partner Ralph slept with someone else. But we were urged to get these feelings out by fighting and we encouraged each other. I beat Ralph up on several occasions and also the people he slept with. But because we wanted this home life we had initiated to help us grow, we called in a psychiatrist who held group sessions with us and we learned to discuss how we felt about all sorts of things. The other side was that we were very close and we really cared for and about each other. We all did things for the community taking it in turns to cook, I used to make clothes and I remember making things like shirts and patchwork waistcoats for everyone.'

The very real human gain Gilly describes is touching.

'We would sit around after supper and smoke joints and listen to music and chat, and that felt warm and very homely. We really felt good because we had created this way of life that didn't rely on having money, but on sharing activities, politics and being very fond of each other.'

A measure of how fibrous the bonds formed then were, is that 35 years on several of the erstwhile communarders are still in contact. So, although they haven't all continued to live communally they have taken something valuable from the time.

An Ethos of Sharing

Academic Lucy Sargisson studied the commune movement, during 2000 spending time with two New Zealand communities – Riverside and Centre point. These she particularly focused on in her paper: *Friends Have All Things in Common: Utopian Property Relations* (The British Journal of Politics and International Relations, 2010)

What she Sargisson observed, is commune living in the new millennium, with what it has taken from the 1960s era knitted together with contemporary perspectives, but with an ethos of sharing rather than private possession: 'Giving up the right to individual possessions formed part of larger goals'.

The desire by adults to take this radical experiment with their lives to far limits was the goal at Centre point, a place that left Sargisson with distinctly ambivalent feelings.

Those living there, she explains, sought ever more ways of 'dissolving the self from the other, from the normally 'private' – removing doors from bathrooms and lavatories, making childbirth and masturbation public activities. They slept side by side on mattresses in long wooden buildings, and people would move from bed to bed so as not to become possessive about sleeping spaces.

'The fundamental goal was to be close to one another and experience intimacy and nurturing. And by all accounts adult life was intense, emotional and absorbing.'

She pauses to consider what this means, 'The self-nurtured in these groups is very different from the individualist self' in that they do not feel the need to have things for their own profit and use, but are content for them to be common property. They have replaced private property with what might accurately be called common wealth, Sargisson suggests.

Yet when boundaries disappear as Sargisson describes, you see how the ideal of common wealth can too easily be construed as anything belonging to anyone with no holds barred..

When children are involved it can never be all right for the boundaries that protect them to be rationalized away. It is too easy in the name of countering society's rigid conventions, for those deep into commune thinking to assume rights over children that are not legitimate. Too easy for adults to behave inappropriately around the young in their hugely influential home environment.

Sargisson saw children running 'feral' and largely unsupervised at Centre point.

'The wrong people came in and there was no vetting procedure. Corruption took over. People were there for personal gain not the greater good'. Centre point was closed down after accusations of child abuse, and she concludes, 'Parents of the children were so busy doing for themselves they didn't notice.'

Commune Kids

When Swedish film director Lukas Moodysson made his savagely witty film *Together* set in one of Stockholm's emergent 1970s communes, it was neglect of children by parents who were physically there but emotionally entirely self-absorbed, that was one of the film's most powerful messages.

Few of these extreme communes still exist. Among those still going are communes with a religious or spiritual ideal at heart and this does appear to give the business of living harmoniously and for the common good, a particular robustness. Inspired by one, the Pilsdon Community in Dorset, based on the 'radical monasticism of the early Christian church', Tobias Jones and Francesca Lenzi, along with their three children, have created Windsor Hill Wood – 'not a community or a commune, just an 'extended household' with a few extra places laid at the table' – where they offer a place to reflect on life. This is the delicate way Jones described it.

During the five years the Joneses spent visiting and living with a variety of communities, one thing they learned was that blue skies thinking and determined optimism are not enough to sustain a community.

Before buying their traditional working woodland where they aim for a sustainable lifestyle as well as offering refuge to people with issues from personal crisis, addiction, bereavement and homelessness to just feeling 'dismayed by modern life', Jones and his wife knew, 'all about the brutal realities of communal living.'

He and his wife have written about how they set out to create a 21st century communal shelter because it is what he wants his family to experience as home.

'We've never felt like we're nobly helping out the needy, because those guests help us as much as we help them. We'll find someone else has done the cooking or the shopping or the washing up. Someone else has lit the fire or laid the table. The house and the woods have been full of music and chat. For all the difficulties of communal living, we would really struggle to go back to the ghetto of the nuclear family.'

So far, the children have probably been the main beneficiaries of this place, Jones thinks. 'Someone teaches them elementary knife skills or how to play the mouth organ. Someone makes them laugh by eating bizarre food combinations. They learn strange songs and new words in new languages. A woman from a kibbutz makes them think by listing all the things she can't do on a Sabbath.'

Community in an Urban Home

Listening to this I feel a sharp longing to step back in time and bring my children up with the pace and rhythm of rural life, of nature as it has been lived through generations, and of learning to see the value in all kinds of people who do not necessarily conform to the standards set by a typical urban society myopically focused on career, status and financial success.

And yet that nostalgia fades as lodger, Andrew, steps into the kitchen announcing that my eldest son has asked him to make vegetable pie and cauliflower cheese for supper, and can we have a communal supper? We can, and so off he trots to the farmer's market, a bag-for-life over one arm, in search of ingredients.

Our little community in the home does fairly well rubbing along together, bickering about who should buy the washing up liquid and can we bulk buy Ecover? Enjoying the bunches of daffodils that fill a big vase in the kitchen when they are in season and finding that for all our proximity – rooms leading on to the same hall and no expansive garden to spread ourselves around – we have a warming brew of humanity.

True we live in the centre of the metropolis, our wildlife is a family of blue-tits and magpies, nesting and being circled by crows determined to get the eggs. Squirrels galore leap on to our roof. Not quite the living richness Jones has on his doorstep, and our sounds are people chattering on the streets, big red buses heaving past, church bells sounding almost in our ears from the church tower that is practically beside us.

Yet the greatest virtue of urban life is that we live in a society that successfully embodies so many different races, colours, creeds, all mixing on the streets, in shops and bars, accepting and acknowledging each other. This has been my children's education.

I see, however, much in what happens within our four walls that echoes the Joneses' experience. We have not, it's true, made a specific effort to open our doors to those in crisis and spiritual need, but one way and another over Olly's and my 40 years together, quite a number have found their way and their issues have slowly unfolded.

I am remembering Angela Wheeler, who I first encountered when she was standing on the doorstep of our first North London home. She looked was lovely looking, beautifully dressed and had the air of having been spirited in from some catwalk or other. She was the possessor of all I wanted – long slender limbs, finely cut features, a cascade of thick, chestnut hair. And there she stood, an expectant smile on her face, a huge bouquet of flowers in her arms. I couldn't possibly like her.

A friend had contacted me earlier with a quick phone call asking if we might have space in our house for a friend of hers for a few nights. Angela, who had just divorced from her husband, and was in London with nowhere to go.

I had said yes, slightly reluctantly as my life with two young children, a home still in need of much work, a partner who seemed to want a fair share of attention and already a couple of people living in rooms, seemed full to capacity already. But, poor soul, we could at least offer a little TLC (tender loving care) for a couple of nights I thought piously.

It wasn't quite like that. Sure Angie, as she became known, was in need of support and comfort, but she very quickly gave as much as she got. She was lovely with our boys, helpful in an uncomplicated way with the housework, and sweetly grateful for the room we said she could have for a couple of weeks.

We discovered common ground, as two women interested in the dynamics of how relationships do and don't work. She and Olly established rapport gradually as she learned to take the mickey out of his gruff talk. Our political beliefs hit the skids in discussion regularly with plenty of growling moments, but much where we were empathetic and there was bags of affectionate hugging too.

So it was that this temporary arrangement morphed into a permanent one. We let Angie have the room for a moderate rent and payment in kind – helping with the house and the children who adored her. She picked them up from school, invented laughter-inducing games, made delicious high-teas and succeeded in setting happily abided by rules were we had failed. Her own son who was at boarding school lived with us during his free time, and he and Cato remain good friends.

This was all many years back and Angie moved on to make a successful new life for herself, but the tie between us remained strong and affectionate. We have visited each others' homes, spent Christmases and holidays together, held hands during each others' personal traumas, and our sons now adult have maintained their own enduring relationships with her.

Pooling Human Capital

Last year a group of North London residents, who formed the North London Sustainable Housing Partnership wanting to make a communal urban home. They approached the Hanover housing association which has been involved in helping set up various co-housing schemes, to ask for help in downsizing from their large family homes. Their site is a former mental hospital which is to be converted into 200 homes.

Architect Ruth Schamrothm, 52, will move with her husband and two sons and she believes now is the time. She told the *Hampstead and Highgate Express* newspaper why.

'A lot of people said they can imagine moving to co-housing in ten years time, but this is an opportunity that makes sense. It means in 20 years time when other people are selling up their homes we will be able to stay in ours.'

There is a conspicuous contrast in the careful planning going into co-housing, the fact that housing associations are becoming involved that means they are qualitatively different to the ad hoc, defiantly anti-authoritarian communes.

Capital may have become a tainted word with the fury that has been expressed at the excesses of capitalism in past years. Yet social and human capital are, in fact, important components of the attempts to create successful community. The definition of social capital given by Samuel Bowles and Herbert Gintis, American economists and social theorists make this point.

'Trust, concern for ones associates, a willingness to live by the norms of ones community with altruism high on the agenda' are, they explain the capital we give socially and very different it is to the entirely self-regarding *homo economicus*.

On a small domestic scale, I see how pooling human capital – the knowledge, education, talents, abilities we have – also has its role in creating successful community. Let's take a simple example.

My younger son, Cato, knows how to sort out my computer problems; my Japanese daughter in law can tell me where to buy quality sushi rice and how to cook it so it doesn't emerge as sludge. Andrew introduced me to Freecycle, the website for giving and getting goods with no money involved.

But when we use our human capital individually and competitively, it is more likely to be counter-productive than valuable in a communal sense.

Human and social capital focuses attention on what groups 'DO rather than what people OWN'. Bowles and Gintis insist that this has value we may not immediately recognize.

'Communities are part of good governance because they address certain problems that cannot be handled either by individuals acting alone or by markets and governments... an effective community monitors the behaviour of is members, rendering them accountable for their actions.' It is not hard to see how important this is as a basis for home life.

The desire for communal living is, on the one hand, quite clearly about finding a way to fulfil a personal goal. Yet one thinks here of John Donne's observation about no man being an island, and how the belief that we can and should be little me-islands has been in many ways counter-intuitive to a healthy happy society. That view is being graphically stated by the protesters camping outside St Paul's Cathedral in London, as I write. This is an uprising of mainly young people who see how far askew our society's values have gone. They want something done to curtail the possibility of those who make extreme money brokering the best financial deals they can for themselves and adding to the alienating inequality in our Western societies.

So these young people formed a community, albeit temporary, living in the most modest way in tents with little in the way of creature comforts for some long, cold months, united as community in their determination to be noticed and heard.

Andrew Simms and Joe Smith, authors of the uplifting *Do Good Lives Have To Cost The Earth?* (Constable) use as an example much higher levels of social trust in Norway compared with the U.S., a society tied to the individualistic, money-equates-with-success idea.　　'People who have *belief systems* that lead them to more altruistic behaviour and that put value on 'doing good' in the wider world are also generally happier.'

The philosopher A.C Grayling asks us to look at the amount of let down there is for people who cling to lifestyles where consuming, partying, putting themselves on show is what they believe in, only to find that, somehow, the fun, the pleasure, the gaiety do not seem to sustain.

'The disappointment it invites in personal experience, and in terms of the fact that it requires what has come to haunt the world: excessive consumption and production, waste, and relentless economic growth at the expense of the environment and human health'.

Community Support

By contrast building a community puts energy into forging connections that will be durable enough to withstand difficulties, doing what is possible to create a warm human environment. This lessens the need to search desperately for a lotus-eating life outside.

There is less stress on families when children have their own sub-community of friends on the premises and where the entire community 'keeps an eye' on what is going on I was told many times over. It often happens that, say, a couple of parents with suitable skills construct play structures, others create toys, puppets or set up art and acting sessions, Laughton has its own radio station.

Sarah Berger raises eyebrows considering the moral panic of which she hears tell, that children are spending so much time in front of screens, networking with virtual friends, experiencing play through interactive cyber games. 'Our children may do these things from time to time, but usually they are having too much fun creating their own games and adventures.'

The other gain for children, voiced often was that if parents split up there is a supportive group of caring adults to offer support to the children as well as the very possibly distraught parents.

As writers Gilly Smith and Jed Novick living for four years

at Laughton did, taking in a badly upset child and offering a bit of informal parenting until things are sorted out.

Gilly, who has two daughters with Jed, is thoughtful.

'Children living here of course suffer over separation as any child does, and sometimes parents can manage to stay in the project and live separately which means the kids do not lose a parent. The community does what it can to support this kind of arrangement and to at least enable one parent to stay so the children's whole lifestyles don't fall apart.'

Sarah Berger along with David Michael agreed that relationships – marriages – are seemingly protected by a communal lifestyle.

'When there is a problem it can take a lot of pressure off if one or both the partners can find someone close by who they know is part of their 'family' and a friend, and just let off steam, have a chat through the issues. You could call it informal relationship counselling.' Percentage-wise, divorces in both communities has been far lower than the national average.

Diana Leafe Christian, author of *Finding Community* makes reference to a downside, 'It can be hard having to consistently pay attention to the potential effects of your actions on fellow community members, and to be continuously vulnerable to the effect of their actions on you'.

Gilly and Jed smile knowingly. They joined Laughton with enormous enthusiasm and Jed tells, 'We put a table out on our deck as soon as we arrived saying, in effect 'we're open for business'. A lot of people passed by on their way here and there and would wander over, so we made friends incredibly quickly.' He laughs, 'I was naïve. I hadn't realised that if you do that people assume you are happy to be visited any time. I had a few spats explaining it wasn't okay to just pop in any time.'

They became very involved and active within the community, loved the sociability and sense that they were helping to build a way of life that was far more sustainable in terms of human bonding than what they had known outside. Their children joined the others in going to the local school.

Then after four years with their daughters growing up, they wanted a larger place to live than they had at Laughton, but they didn't want to lose their community. They found somewhere just a few minutes drive away. Even so they hit a disagreeable aspect of living in a community that views itself as having commitment to the mutual project.

Interweaving each others' words, the two explain that when they moved in there were people who believed there was a tacit agreement that people were there for life, and would support each other in old age.

Gilly points out that wasn't reasonable or realistic.

'As with us people had reasons for wanting to move on, perhaps for practical reasons or to experience something different, and I think that is accepted now, but when we decided to go there were people who made it plain they saw it as an act of betrayal. They felt we were undermining the community.'

They have, however, managed to overcome that and Gilly tells with very evident pleasure how good it is to live close by and maintain links, to attend events, have their Laughton friends over to their place, and for their children to still go over and see friends. So they still have an extended home.

The Dangers of Loneliness

A year ago four national charities launched the Campaign to End Loneliness, which seems to me a grim indictment of how lacking in neighbourliness we have become as a society. There is particular concern for the elderly for whom it is described as 'the hidden killer' but they are not by any means the only ones in danger of loneliness.

There are some three million people of younger ages living alone, according to the Office of National Statistics. These days one in three households has just one member, although some certainly choose to live alone and do so very contentedly. There has been a sharp rise in the number of lone parent families who are vulnerable to the stress of coping alone.

While eating alone is ever more what happens. Half the meals eaten in the UK are eaten alone, and in just 20 years the number soared from four billion to 12 billion.

I listened to people who had been through the travails of setting up cohousing as a way of regaining the warmth and involvement of home life. There were inevitable disagreements, questions about whether this was really what they wanted, would they find themselves longing for more traditional home life? Yet once they were actually living the dream, it was very clear how little loneliness featured.

Not least because loneliness is an internal state and it can feed itself if there is nothing to break it, as Emily, a busy lawyer, described with heart-touching honesty. It kicked off one evening when she had no one to visit, nobody to return home to and the prospect of an empty weekend. 'As an adult spending increasing amounts of time alone, the loneliness grew more acute. An affliction I came to describe as 'conversationalitis' started dominating my time – a constant line of chatter which wound its way through my mind.'

It helped Emily to be diagnosed as lonely, to be able to trace back some of the reasons for her state but it didn't alter the fact that, 'We live in a world where our connections with people can be fleeting and shallow. Technology is meant to have made us able to connect with others more easily, yet we are lonelier than in previous decades.'

Sociologists at Duke University in another study that could easily apply here, have found that Americans' circle of close confidantes has shrunk dramatically in the past two decades, and the number of people confessing they have nobody with whom to discuss important matters has more than doubled. Robert L. Wilson, Professor of Sociology at Duke University and an author of the study says, 'This change indicates something that is not good for society. Ties with a close network of people create a safety net. These ties also lead to civic engagement and local political action.'

In all this it becomes clear how the sociability of co-housing can help, but how also the demands of living as an inter-connected community with mutual responsibilities, can shape and give purpose to life.

One of the most depressing bits of conventional wisdom around older people, is that they become less and less participants in a vibrant society as it is assumed that with age independence becomes dependence and learned helplessness. But that is absolutely not how it need be says Maria Brenton, a senior citizen herself – one whose enormous energy and utter conviction that her age makes her more not less competent to be a mover and shaker, has been running the 'Older Women's Cohousing Group in Britain'. Over two years her energies have gone into helping a cohort of women aged 50 – 80 who have found a site and wish to create a place to live together.

When Breton, who is an academic, first expressed interest in how women age in other societies, she was given £18,000 from the Rowntree Foundation to see how cohousing works for elders in the US, Holland and Denmark. Here, she discovered, they talk of the 'young old', in itself a mind-altering label, and they are considered very capable of playing their part in working with private and public developers to form what have been called 'old-fashioned neighbourhoods created with ingenuity.'

Men, too, have similar needs and suffer loneliness just as

women do, but Maria reasons that she chose to focus on women, as they are the most likely to be on their own – half of all 75 year-olds live alone, and of these three quarters are women – as well as 'the most likely group to be materially worse off than men'. But the opportunities for elders co-housing is frequently open to men as well as women around Europe, where, Brenton points out, they are way ahead of us in seeing that cohousing can be a very positive way of living for older people. A way that encourages a can-do, rather than not-at-my-age way of thinking.

Co-Housing for Seniors

The Danish government has supported the development of over 100 senior cohousing communities since mid 1980s, both privately owned and rented. In Holland where cohousing is well established for all generations, there are around 200 groups for elders who prefer to live among their own genera-tion. These communities start at age 55 and Maria tells with a delighted hoot how 'by far the queen bee mover and shaker in one community I visited was in her 80s.

'In such countries cohousing is encouraged at every level by government, because they see that it keeps people healthier and happier and so they make less demands on the social budget.' She was less enthusiastic about the groups she found around the US – The Crone's Nest, Old Roads in the Wilderness and others she describes as 'too wacky – they were back to the land and struggling. Not replicable here.'

On the other hand the model in Holland where they have some 200 groups of senior co-housing could very easily be replicated and perhaps especially important when people have led individual lives for much of their time, was the emphasis put on spending time getting to know each other and involving themselves in activities together, before signing up.

Getting the UK scheme off the ground has taken a long time, Brenton observes tartly.

'This is basically because our society is hostile and we have approached so many housing associations because they are the only way we could get a grant. I went to one which said they weren't interested in our co-housing idea because their elderly people were perfectly happy in their sheltered accommodation.'

She found an altogether less blinkered approach when she met Bruce Moore of the Hanover housing group.

'He said 'we'll find you a site'. It was the first time we had had anyone with clout wanting to help, and they found us a good site in North London. It is an old school of less than an acre, just off Friern Barnet high street, the bus route and six minutes to the shopping centre.'

That was not the end of a battle which involved dealing with the Adult Social Care department of the local council.

'You might have expected they would be pleased we were doing something to help with their housing needs and very likely mean less mental health problems for them, less demands by lonely people on their resources.'

In the area there were 75 per cent of older people in accommodation too big for them. So we suggested trying to recruit them for co-housing if we could get it funded as social housing, but the local authority remained very unenthusiastic.'

Finally, however, they got the council's approval and funding and have since been working with the architects. They hope to be in early 2013. Brenton would like to see the Dutch model here.

'They get development grants to build projects with a special need. For example there was a group of elder people designing their place with specialist facilities to cope with health problems and impairments. They all had someone close who had had some kind of medical problem, perhaps as serious as a stroke, And if they become seriously ill, are going to die, say, they know they are among supportive friends who care for them.'

Consider what a wonderful antidote this is to a barmily wasteful use of resources in the name of elder care, snorts Charles Durrett, who, with his wife Kathryn McCamant, introduced the concept of cohousing to the U.S.

'Last year Americans drove five billion miles caring for seniors in their homes – families and friends, and services like Meals on Wheels. In our small, semi-rural county in the Sierra foothills, Telecare made 60,000 trips in lumbering, polluting van buses usually carrying only one senior at a time. Schlepping a couple of thousand seniors over hill and dale to doctor's appointments to pick up medicine or to see friends. In our cohousing community of 21 seniors, I have never seen a single Telecare bus in the driveway. It happens organically by caring neighbours 'Can I catch a ride with you?', 'Are you headed to the drug store?'

I think of my neighbour in her late 80s, desperately trying to manage in her own home. She has a carer but that is all, so she is not costing a lot, but she is lonely and emotionally fragile spending most of her time alone.

Several of us, her immediate neighbours, visit regularly, but that doesn't make for a life that feels safely and cheerily contained. Yet she detests the idea of being in a residential home, having to live by imposed rules and routine with absolutely no say in what happens.

I sit in her living room and we discuss the many things that still interest her and I can't help thinking that senior cohousing with like-minded people could make such a difference to her fearful state of mind.

Getting free of money worries is no small benefit for elder people. Deborah Althus studying senior US citizens living in communal housing reported the relief for them of finding it a way of living that meant for 69 per cent their financial situation was eased with the sharing of property taxes, property insurance and maintenance and repair costs and bulk buying of food.

What if cohousing is a choice you would like to make but you cannot afford to buy into it, as most people have done so far? This is something about which the cohousing movement is very conscious, and considerable efforts have been made to get housing associations and local authorities to help raise the money needed to build homes for tenants to rent.

The Threshold Centre in Dorset, an erstwhile Saxon farm where Michael Geddings welcomed me with beetroot soup freshly made from the organic garden. He had succeeded in getting funding to adapt the building through a collaboration with a housing association. They have all generations living there and shortly before I visited their first social tenant, Tina Smale, had moved in. She had lived in a variety of housing association homes before, but, 'I kept moving on, never really fitting in. If you are a tenant you have no say over who you have to live among. My partner Kerry and I rented privately once, but we simply couldn't afford it. I knew about co-housing but because we don't have money we assumed it wasn't an option. Then we heard that Threshold had a vacancy and approached them because we had been told they could take a housing association tenant.'

Alan Heeks a co-founder of Threshold, sees how cohousing is absolutely in tune with the idea that we need to re-think the way we live, and base what home is on less egocentric and more human caring values.

We have been through many permutations of home over

past centuries, but a hallmark of the post-war years has been the shrinking down of numbers living together so that a culture has evolved where separateness is seen as an achievement.

Now that our isolating, individually consuming, possessions exhibiting, lifestyle is undergoing something of a seismic shock with the banking crisis, the global debt and Eurozone crises, you hear the desire to at least make home more a nurturing and more environmentally sustainable place gaining ground.

Colin Tudge, biologist and polemicist is clear, 'if people cooperate then the result, truly, can be win-win… we do achieve the greatest happiness of the greatest number when we all pull together.'

10

BUILDING DREAMS

A boisterous wind shoves and pushes against us, like some overgrown mischievous kid. Olly and I are trekking over the Pembrokeshire terrain, across rutted fields of cloying mud after a recent rainstorm, up stone-chucking hills, through clusters of sessile oak, and then the smaller rowan and hazel trees. A sparrow hawk perched on a branch gives a pained look from manic golden eyes, before flying off. Honeysuckle and ivy are entwined in the bushes; there is no knowing if the path will lead to the home that Jasmine and Simon Dale have built for themselves.

Then there it is. An extraordinary structure of curved wooden beams, stone, mud and straw dug into the hillside. Arched windows with knobbly frames fashioned out of branches create the kind of windows children draw in pictures of a gingerbread house. To one side is a large greenhouse full with vegetable plants propagating nicely.

The Dale's creation, their home built according to fiercely held ideals, has been described by whimsical observers as a Hobbit home, suggesting Simon and Jasmine and their two children would emerge as quaint unworldly figures. In fact the pair who come to the entrance of what they call their Woodland Home, are an attractive, robust pair, well rooted in the 21st century world.

They met at Durham University where Simon, shaggy haired and mud-splattered, as is his way these days, was reading physics. Jasmine, with a steady gaze and an unsentimental telling of the toil involved in their building, was studying politics and international development. They might well have pursued successful careers in their subjects, but the business of how they wanted to live and the centrality of what home represents for them, became the more important.

Both in their 30s, they are of a generation that has been introduced young to the notion that the way we live has a moral and political dimension, and concern for the planet, the future home of their young, preoccupied them a good deal. There was a certain amount of experimenting with geodesic domes, a short-lived time in a commune where their child was not welcomed, Jasmine tells 'I emerged ravaged.' And time spent in temporary homes, a tin hut, a railway carriage, by this time with their second child. Still their dream of having a home that would be a lifestyle as well as a roof over their heads preoccupied the pair.

They felt it imperative to help the world understand the degree of risk to the planet if we keep on living with the same level of consumption, Simon explains.

'Our society is almost entirely dependent on the availability of increasing amounts of fossil fuel energy. This has brought us to the point at which our supplies are dwindling and our planet is in ecological catastrophe. We have no viable alternative energy source and no choice but to reduce our energy consumption. The sooner this change can be begun, the more comfortable it will be. We knew that living this way would feel very wrong to us, it would be damaging to our integrity.'

Simon had decided he wanted to live in the woodland of Wales but, searching, found there was nowhere you could buy – and particularly with the small amount of money they had – to put up a home. At which point there came 'our bit of serendipity'.

Eco-Village

The Dales heard that a new planning policy had been introduced in Pembrokeshire, permitting people to build on farm land, something that had been prohibited up until now. But Wales with a decline of 68.1 per cent in its fall in agricultural production compared with 7 per cent across the rest of the UK, could clearly not support the level of farming it had traditionally lived by. So some land was being made available for homes but with the stipulation that it must be used according to the government's One Wales: One Planet initiative which has it that within the lifetime of a generation Wales should use only its fair share of the earth's resources. They insist on buildings being very low impact and owners living in the countryside are expected to grow a reasonable proportion of their own food and to be self-supporting, not living on benefits.

Clearly this was their moment. Simon advertised for other people interested in building a village of eco-homes, and nine families with similar aspirations to theirs responded. Together they bought 76 acres of land – Jasmine and Simon's portion cost £35,000.

Buying the land and getting planning permission was one thing, then there was the daunting task of creating the house of their dreams. Simon's father-in-law along with a bunch of volunteers inspired by what was being done, worked through the rain-lashed. They collected the stone and mud churned up by a mechanical digger at the site and these were used for foundations and retaining walls. They cut and carved indoor frames retaining walls and for a spiders' web of beams on the ceiling of the round structure. The material was spare oak gathered in the surrounding woods. Straw bales were laid for the floor, on the walls and the roof for 'super insulation'. Lime plaster which breathes easily and is low energy to manufacture compared with cement covered the walls. Reclaimed larch was laid for floors and the roof is plastic sheet, mud and turf. Solar panels provide energy for lighting, music and computing, gravity brings water from a nearby spring and there is a compost toilet.

The house took four months to build, cost £8,000 in materials and paid-for labour. So the final two-bedroom structure came in under £50,000.

Such is his delight in the achievement, and his wish to inspire others, Simon put up a website describing and showing with photos just what was entailed. Jasmine has added her own wry observations on coping with camping on a building site with a baby and a toddler and without electricity or a bathroom for three months.

'Having no easy way to wash isn't the best inducement to having a cuddle, and yes, of course things got scratchy at times when we'd been up most of the night painting walls. But those things are unimportant. Having a home built according to our ethical beliefs and following our dreams keeps our souls alive.'

Simon nods, 'Creating this home together has absolutely strengthened our relationship and we feel proud to say our house reflects who we are.'

Clare Cooper Marcus is an English architecture professor now retired from the University of California in Berkeley.

During her academic years she was drawn to what the philosopher C.J. Jung had to say about the home as a symbol of self. So Simon's words would likely chime with her own findings of a profound emotional relationship between humans and their dwellings; the sum of interviews conducted with some 100 people from a great range of backgrounds and circumstances. These became the stuff of her book *House As A Mirror of Self.*

'Carl Jung's work opened a door into another level of my own consciousness which has prompted me to consider the house from a wholly different viewpoint.' A viewpoint from which we can judge how home, at best, aligns us with, rather than separating us from, our fellows.

It is not hard to see how passionate convictions, germinated young, shaped the home the Dales created, and in turn fed them back the profound sense of an ethical underlay in their lives. In discussing home so far I have been concerned with what home as a concept as well as a set of walls and a roof means to us, why and how it matters.

I have included here people whose ideas, efforts and dedication to purpose have impressed and interested me, and as such this chapter is anecdotal, a personal view. There are surely many wonderful ideological creations, architects and designers of impeccable concern with the environment or how a home may nurture us, but including them all is for another book.

House of Straw

Coming from the Dales' house with its three bedrooms roughly hewn within the circular space, the compact central kitchen where life is lived much of the time, to the Wookey's immaculate farmhouse in Wiltshire, is a study in contrasts. Yet for all that the two families shared, in their schemes, concern for the environment as a non-negotiable aspect of the homes created.

Nigel Wookey is a man of considerable charm, a farmer of many years who turned to organic farming and then decided, with his wife Linda, to construct a home carefully thought out to embody heart-felt values for their years of retirement.

'I had given up chemical farming which is rather brutal for my taste. I read Rachel Carson's *Silent Spring* when I was young, and recognising what the chemicals we use to farm were doing to the environment made a deep impression.'

The Wookeys were tenants on the farm and living in the farmhouse owned by the family trust, but a cottage on the estate fell into disrepair, yew tree roots upheaving parts of it, masonry falling, walls crumbling.

'Linda and I had in mind that we should be looking at a way to live sustainably as a logical follow on from the organic farming so we bought the cottage and pulled it down so we could start from scratch building a house that would be much better for the environment than an old property renovated.'

He had watched Grand Designs and particularly recalled places built using straw. He explains, 'We grow straw – spelt wheat – so it made sense to think about using that. I started asking local architects about creating a home with straw and thatch. I wanted to keep concrete and cement to a minimum. The architect I found was very enthusiastic but had no experience of such a project. However he pretty much did the design on the back of a fag packet with me explaining what I wanted and then he impressed me by going off to do a straw building course in Dorset. We sourced second-hand bricks, lime mortar and render.'

It would certainly have been a point of conflict with Linda, he muses, if they had not been agreed on the fundamental philosophy of the house being built, even when it meant extra cost – and they are not rich he stresses.

Nigel says, 'I was determined not to have a floor slab of concrete. We used sheep's wool in the walls for insulation and recycled plastic bottles in the ceilings. We found strawboard for stud walls. I didn't want any oil so we have a cooker that runs on logs. We have a wood burning stove in the front room and an air source heat pump under the floor.'

There is more: the photovoltaic panels on shed roof, a bore hole for water and their own septic tank. The garage has been built from mud. The spelt wheat, already bailed up for the main building, was then used as thatch.

The photographs he now displays, proudly, show an infinitely tempting cream-painted cottage with airy, light filled rooms and stylish furnishings.

'We didn't scrimp on the comforts' Nigel says. 'The house must have a considerably lower footprint than a conventional house, but that doesn't mean it has to be a hair-shirt approach.'

He and Linda are close to retirement and this will be their home, but until then they rent it out to try to recoup some of what it has cost.

It is the Wookeys gift to themselves, the best way they could think to spend savings from hard-working years. Then, slightly uncomfortable I suspect, in case he sounds sentimental, Nigel remarks, 'We have enjoyed the process of bringing our dream house to reality. Yes, I can say it is a home with heart.'

You can visualise Cooper Marcus giving a hearty thumbs-up, for one of the more melancholy observations, in her writings, is, 'the contemporary house-buyer... is not only far-removed from the skills and traditions of house-building, but must rely on a gamut of professional "others".'

I am taken back, by this observation, to the wreck of a house Olly and took on as our own first home. We needed that gamut of professionals all right – none of us was an architect, quantity surveyor, bricklayer, plumber, electrician, cabinetmaker. But what we, or more precisely Olly as our mutual representative, were was involved. Olly with his many practical skills joined in alongside the professional workers, and achieved a very amiable working relationship with the project manager. He also gathered wood from skips, including old railway sleepers which became a bed; doors, skirting boards, and many other discarded re-usables.

We did this to save money but also because it made the house very personal, very much a place we had helped to fashion. Nor could we afford to do more than the basics to begin with so we went on year after year doing up a bit more, feeling the house was suggesting what it would like done, and finding new inspiration in re-cycled materials and bargain basements.

Had we had the money, had I not left my full-time job but remained on a good salary, perhaps we would have simply handed over the whole business of doing up this house to the professionals and moved into a perfectly finished product.

I am glad that was not possible because living with our home, being an on-site, daily part of its process of change, understanding what mattered to us – a secondhand Aga which became the cosy hub of our draughty house – the sense of triumph in finding the perfect secondhand item; discovering a tiny tile shop in a dishevelled area of London, where the owner had chosen his stock – all hand-made – with such enthusiasm; creating a kitchen from cabinets found deposited on the street.

I can't claim we were driven by any clearly defined ideology, but that practical, physical involvement with our evolving house did mean it became a home that seemed aligned to who we are and how we wanted to live

An Autonomous House

Brenda and Robert Vale – architects, writers, researchers, and experts in the field of sustainable housing – were early pioneers in making real their housing dreams.

The Vales are both now professors at Victoria University of Wellington in New Zealand supervising post-graduates and doing research into state of the art sustainability. Brenda spoke to me from there, taking me back to the beginning when she and Robert were both architectural students in the 1970s living in the UK.

Her final thesis was for a single autonomous house – a house that does not rely on infra-structure support services such as the electric power grid, gas grid, municipal water and sewage treatment systems with the aim of cutting environmental impact and cost as low as possible – and Robert's the following year was for a self-build autonomous house for a commune in Wales.

They saved enough money to buy a piece of land for themselves and borrowed money from the bank to build their own autonomous house. They then wrote a book, *The Autonomous House*, a personalized technical guide to developing environmentally friendly solutions for buildings.

Their own circumstances became particularly home based when Robert was made redundant and Brenda was at home with three small children. They moved to Sheffield and set out to put their ideas into mainstream building with their own architectural practice. Their most radical creation completed in 1998 was the Hockerton Housing project in Nottinghamshire, one of the first zero energy residential systems in the UK. The five single storey terraced dwellings are six meters deep, earth sheltered at the back blending into a field but at the front are south facing conservatories running the width of the buildings which have passive solar heating, two wind turbines and a photovoltaic system providing all the energy to run the homes. They are amongst the most energy efficient, purpose built dwellings in Europe.

So as professionals they have pursued their ideological dream, as well as creating their own first home according to these principles. What, I wonder, has this determination to build their dreams, meant for their relationship?

Brenda's reply is thoughtful and amused.

'We've worked together for over 40 years. Yes, we disagree and argue, but that is often the way to move a problem forward. We still share an office at work…

'Living in a house you have designed is a great thing and we enjoyed living in our first house and in other houses we have converted. However, it taught us that how you live in a house is much more important than the design. Reducing our impact on the world comes from our behaviour and the choices we make rather than the building. We live at present in a 70-year-old Arts and Crafts style NZ house and our energy consumption meets the low energy German passive house standards without any change to the house, just because of how we live.'

'Consensus Design'

So for sure the French historian of religion Mircea Eliade who views the creation of a home as a matter of gravity would approve.

'Building… a house represents a serious decision, for the very existence of man is involved; he must in short, create his own world and assume the responsibility of maintaining and renewing it.'

That thinking resonates with what the architect Christopher Day conveyed to Olly and me the day we visited him. I had wanted to interview him after reading *Places of the Soul* a book in which he tells how his ideology embraces a deep ecological concern, but that this must be married with an emphasis on soul nurture. He writes passionately, evocatively, of the way our surroundings affect us physically and spiritually and the book *A New Life For Cities* that he was completing in early 2012, he describes as 'a practical guide to soul-nourishing sustainability.'

'Too often' Day insists 'sustainability is thought to be solely technical. Yet whether a home nurtures us and sustains the soul may contribute to stress and general malaise or balance and strengthen us.'

When I emailed asking if I might interview him, Day's courteous reply came immediately, 'I would be happy to be interviewed BUT I have a speech disability (ALS an effect of motor neurone disease) so can't answer the phone. The best way is face to face, but I live in Cardiff so this isn't so easy'.

Cardiff was not a deterrent, and so it was that Olly and I were led into the garden of the small house Day and his wife have in Cardiff, although his 'real' home he explains is a building he created in the deep countryside of Wales.

Day's wife wheeled him out and there he was greeting us from his wheelchair with a welcoming gesture. If the prospect of interviewing someone with such a fine brain but who could not speak had been daunting, Day did not allow it to be a constraint. He had a large pad of paper and pencils at the ready and I had scarcely got my questions out before his face lit with understanding and he was writing like an adrenaline-fuelled spider, narrow spiky letters across a page and an illustration if it seemed appropriate. When we were talking about the need for human involvement in the way we live in our homes, he drew a heart.

He gave us a condensed version of the thought expressed in *Places Of The Soul*, 'I am always astonished when I speak to people who have hired an architect to design them a house, a task which is then duly completed without a single visit to the site. I also see plans for houses which have no relationship at

all to the site, the views, the sun, the seasons or even the inhabitants...' And if our homes are just another commodity, the
best we can afford, a convenience, an investment in the hope
of profit but not of ourselves, then it becomes one more thing
that we do not value at a deep or emotional level.

The writing on the pages becomes faster as he spells out the
notion of 'consensus design', the title of another of his books,
the way a future dweller shall be involved in the creation of
their home. It begins with visiting and contemplating the site:
what is physically there, trying to get a sense of its spirit.

He then asks his clients to work with clay models to form
the buildings, considering how they will be built and with what
materials – protecting the environment has always been high
on his agenda. Only after this will he begin drawing. His ideological commitment to ensuring that a home has spirit is spelt
out, 'through the intricate inter-relationships of the human
beings who will live in, use, and help to build that place, we can
realise the healthy, healing and sensitive growth we seek.'

It may be difficult to imagine this gentle man losing his
cool, but on paper there is a flood of opprobrium when he
contemplates what too much of the modern architecture has
become.

'Architectural fashion is guided by what is individualistically
new... a tendency intensified by the focus of architectural
magazines on buildings as dramatic objects... sterile spaces
which depend upon deception – cosmetic surface, mood-
manipulative lighting, for instance – or upon contents to make
them habitable.'

Don't we understand that, surrounded by harsh hardness,
the aesthetic sensitivities, and with them moral discernments,
are blunted? There will, I don't doubt, be plenty who disagree
with this condemnation of a futuristic architectural style that
reflects today's technological age, but Day believes fervently in

the harm it does to our sensitivities to be 'surrounded... by lifeless man-made matter.'

Future-Proofing

Taus Larsen is an architect, who also has ecological concerns high on his agenda, and indeed has been inspired by Day's work. But he is early in his career and at age 34 he is still developing his ideas on "future-proofing", as a guiding principle.

By this he means: 'adapting to a post fossil fuel society, to resource scarcity by creating different ways of making places that might not seem habitable, an option'. For his generation it is essential to bear in mind that the future planet they and their children inhabit will be hugely affected by how seriously looking after the environment and off-setting climate change is taken.

You sense that Christopher Day would be encouraged by Taus and the home he designed with his Zedfactory colleagues. It is a pair of zero carbon two storey houseboats moored near Vauxhall Bridge in London. The curved body sits atop two hand-built steel hulls. There are big windows and terraces looking out over the luminous mud and soaring city buildings, with a billowing sky the ever-present backdrop. Seagulls cavort overhead; a heron perches nearby and in summer ducks take cheeky delight in inhabiting the decks.

For the inside wood has been well used and in the one-bedroom apartment Taus has on ground – or rather water – level, he sits next to a wood log burner. He could attach a back boiler, but for now hot water comes from a communal cylinder attached to a wood pellet boiler which feeds individual cylinders in each apartment.

When I ask how the two boats, which are linked around a pontoon, have been made carbon-zero, enthusiasm brings

Taus' answers in a helter-skelter rush.

'The starting point was the hulls. We found a boatyard on an island in Hampton Court, the only people in the UK who can build hulls the size we wanted. They were brought to the mooring and the rest was built after.'

It was a lengthy process, 'Two years to build the waterproof shell with floors and wall insulation done for us, and we took it on from there using pulverized fly ash from power stations as a substitute for cement to ballast the boat. There are photo-voltaic panels feeding the boats electricity and we are installing solar thermal panels to generate hot water.'

The boats house seven people in three apartments, but for the Zedfactory this is not an end product. They see the boats as a prototype for affordable carbon zero housing that could be situated along the Thames or in other rivers, creating 'floating streets'.

'In terms of inner city living it is do-able and affordable' Taus insists. 'And if people can feel as good as I do living this way then that is absolutely a bonus. It quite simply feels right to have a home with a value system that is precious to me.'

A Home for the Soul

It is not the lingua franca of our times to talk of home as inti-mately linked to our emotional lives. But for Lindsay Halton, an architect who was for some time the Welsh representative of the Ecological Design Association, and also an advisor to the *Green Building Digest*, his design won the Channel Four Grand Designs Eco Home of the year award in 2008, the meaning of home for the soul is integral.

His ideological belief in the significance of home as a place for the soul came through an interest in athletics which led him to study physical and then spiritual health and he left 'a good career in architecture to focus on a more holistic approach to what home means.'

So over 15 years Halton began to go into homes, invited by people to help them understand how the home which is theoretically a safe place, could be made to feel more so.

'Through discussing Feng Shui with people I found myself learning more about them. I began to intuit things about my clients and it led on to my unearthing buried feelings, desires, dissatisfactions which could then be addressed.'

This work which Halton describes took over, for a while, from architecture, and he wrote his book *The Secret Of The Home* (O Books) with the idea that people could delve into it and find ways to help them come to terms with difficult issues in their lives and homes.

He gives an example of how he works: 'A woman asked me to visit her home and I knew intuitively to go to the room on the right which had a particular meaning. I noticed immediately two pictures on facing walls and I sensed that I was following a trail. There was this picture of a little girl behind glass which was broken. When I asked about it, the woman told me it was she as a little girl and that she hadn't been happy with the way she looked. The picture on the opposite wall was a painting of a woman's back but it had a strength and conviction to the posture, you could see the woman was very much in her body.

'As I talked about this the woman told me how she had not been happy in her own body and this is how she would like to have been. From there we got to talking about her life and what things there were about how she was living in the home that we could think about. She had come to me because she knew of my Homesouls work.'

Halton says, 'In the biggest sense home is where our whole life story resides. Our houses may have been built by others, but it is we who furnish and live in them. Consequently, they mirror our hopes, problems and self-imposed obstacles. Read insightfully they can lead us towards healing deeply concealed problems.'

He likens architecture when it is simply the process of 'designing a machine to live in' without knowing the clients well, as like medical doctors who take just a few minutes to talk, look and listen before they diagnose and prescribe.

'If we want a more perceptive view we have to go elsewhere, to find an alternative – a complementary medicine. Perhaps Homesouls is a complementary medicine for the life of a house, or simply an inspiration to pause for a little longer at the beginning, to look and to listen more deeply.'

'I see Homesouls work as a way to make the most of your life – a psychology of home through which we can explore the deeper connections between the life we have and the places we live in. I set out to help people see how home is a reflection of what is happening in their lives, and to work with the home to build a better life.'

Twin Oaks

An ideology that brings together environmental concerns, spirituality and the desire to live without reliance on a highly technological life style, has of course been a fundamental of many communities set up with great enthusiasm but which have not survived. In the U.S. Twin Oaks is a striking exception. It is often picked out as a particularly interesting example of a model that has evolved and modernized, surviving over decades.

This point is very visible around a table in the garden where a group of people, sat with their computers which are connected to wireless internet, are their taking on the aspects of technological development that are valuable to them. Yet the essential first principles put in place when Twin Oaks was founded in the American state of Virginia in 1967, still shape the way this lifestyle is lived.

They are a virtually self-supporting community with home-based work, and they are self-sufficient in energy and food. They have individual living quarters, but private space is minimal, the essence of this community is to be united in running the place and living as a democratic, egalitarian community committed to keeping their lifestyle viable.

The sun was high and achingly hot the day I went to visit the 450 acres site which some 100 people, from newborn to 75 years, call home. Beds of crops stretched away into the distance tended by people in big straw hats, stopping periodically to wipe their brows, rub down sweaty arms, stretch out backs. Everybody takes a turn working the land.

The main building which leads on to a cluster of other buildings and off to woodland where separate homes have been built, was comfortingly cool and full of the sounds of people preparing the communal lunch, in the kitchen.

Here I was greeted by Valerie who has been nearly 20 years at Twin Oaks. She is a narrowly built woman, clear-faced and full of a zesty delight in the lifestyle she has chosen, although she is quick to say that of course even a place like this, imbued with so many of her own values, is not without stresses, strains and conflicts.

'Of course we have our own problems and issues, but the difference is that at Twin Oaks we want to sort those out and live as a harmonious community, it seems to me that, so often people outside simply cut off from others when they have a problem. But it is our involvement with each other that makes this place feel like a real home.'

She came across Twin Oaks when, age 24, she was travelling and happened upon it. She spent three weeks on the visitor programme that is run so that people interested can spend time understanding how Twin Oaks functions. At the end of that time, 'I realised I had found a place to make my home that most closely matched my own internal value system. By that I mean people choosing to support themselves outside of mainstream values.

'Also feminism was very important to me so the absolute commitment to equality was significant to me and it made me feel protected as a woman'. She adds, 'A feeling not unconnected to having grown up in a home where there was domestic violence.'

One aspect of the philosophy that Valerie holds particularly dear, is that it costs nothing to become a member of the community. 'It means we really do have a mixed population. People who do not have the kind of resources you often need to join co-housing schemes are as welcome to join as those from more prosperous backgrounds. This matters a great deal if you believe, as Valerie does, that our society is badly atomised and fragile because of inequality, and that the difference between the kind of housing people of low-income must so often accept, and the richness of life at Twin Oaks, is life transforming.

The founders were, however, peculiarly fortunate in that the property, a former tobacco farm, was donated by a supportive benefactor to a group of eight people. But a rapid turnover of members meant a struggle to make the project viable. Kat Kinkade, one of the earliest members of Twin Oaks credits its survival to having avoided the problems of 'laziness, freeloading and excessive lack of structure' that upended many communities.

Residents own, and are responsible for running the place collectively and although there is no charge for making your home at Twin Oaks people are vetted by the existing community to check their genuine dedication before being invited to join. Everyone works a 42-hour week doing a variety of jobs from agriculture and income-generating work to domestic tasks, and for this they get housing, food, clothes, healthcare. The income sharing philosophy means that everybody gets the same small amount of personal money.

They take no state benefits and pay for healthcare and the needs of elderly residents through the community's income-generating work making hammocks, tofu and indexing books for publishers.

Living costs are low because enough food is grown and cultivated by residents. Vegetables from the three-acre garden are enough to be frozen for winter. There is a dairy barn with cows for milk, cheese, butter and bulls for beef, killed in their own abattoir. Chickens supply eggs and some are eaten. They grow wheat and make bread in their bakery. Valerie considers that: 'being able to feed, getting pleasure from making meals and sharing them when we feel like it, is a very big part of creating homeliness.'

People with private means or money outside may not use it while they live at Twin Oaks.

Valerie is clear, 'That would unbalance the ecology of the place. Imagine one person being able to buy expensive clothes and furnishings, bring in all kinds of gadgets and so on that others could not have. Then Twin Oaks would become a microcosm of the unequal society outside.'

She leads me through an arbor of creepers and roses intertwined and into a flower garden vivid with tall feathery red flowers, delphiniums, poppies and a carpet of star-like blue flowers. People plant what they wish, contributing to this communal area with its seats and open spaces.

These days Valerie does not spend much time contemplating how Twin Oaks meets her ideological desires. She simply lives it. When asked the question, however, she is clear.

'The ideological heart to our home here is that it offers a way of life that is more connected to the experience of being human than the usual way outside. We have midwives here so babies can be born at home among people who are like family. We offer home-schooling for the children, although some do go outside. We don't spend time and energy going to a workplace so we have that time to spend as community. And if you die at Twin Oaks, you are buried here not on the land of some institution.'

She pauses: 'That's the point if you live the 'real' life in the outside world so much of the time life is outside of your control and having that control, that sense of creating the life that feels right with people we cherish, is very important to me.'

Then I am shown the 48 photovoltaic panels they have installed, providing 10,000 kilowatts hours of energy which more than meets their needs. Will this be home forever? Valerie contemplates the question for some moments.

'I can't answer that. People do leave and to say forever is a big thing. But I can't imagine signing up for a life that diminished home as the central theme to how I live. I look at the world outside where people give up their time, their energy, their hearts, to trying to find a way of life that makes them feel safe and happy, yet in the doing they have so little left for themselves. So few opportunities for trying to do less damage to the environment, for understanding the value of a life that feels safe and peaceful as we have here.'

'Free Spirits'

Feeling safe and cherished if you are learning disabled or have some disability which means you live in a residential home, is not necessarily how it is, as we know from grisly reports demonstrating how very far from homely and nurturing these places can be.

Creating a vibrant and life-supporting home life lies at the heart of the Camphill Village Trust philosophy, with its eleven communities around the UK offering a home to those with special needs from young children to the elderly.

Camphill, founded in 1939 by the Austrian paediatrician Karl Koning, its underlying principles inspired by the anthro-posophist Rudolph Steiner, is described as a 'life-sharing community'. Here the able live full-time among those with disabilities, treating them so far as possible as equals, in family homes and where their own children may live too. Konig believed that every human has something special to offer and that the able gain from the disabled, as well as vice versa.

The success of Camphill communities which take people from young children to the elderly, has always relied on the committed ideology of those who choose to live at the mostly rural, farming-based centres. These house-parents, support workers, teachers and others do not earn a salary but have their basic living taken care of by the Trust, including medical, education, training and basic expenses. Those who make the choice to work at Camphill come because it is a chosen way of life rather than a conventional job.

Judy Bailey, who describes herself as a support worker, and lives with her husband in a house with adults who have a range of disabilities including three with Down's Syndrome, came more twenty years ago.

She credits her childhood, during which she went on the back of her psychiatrist father's bike to visit his patients in locked wards, with their often eccentric behaviour, mental health problems and limited capabilities, as having led her to Camphill.

'My father helped me see that these people had been picked out by society as too strange for the 'normal' world, but who in fact had something to offer. That they were free spirits.'

So when Judy who lives at The Grange community, a bio-dynamic farm in The Forest of Dean, Gloucestershire, first came across the Camphill philosophy she realized, 'I found my own values'.

Fairly soon after arriving she met her husband Ian, second-ed from another Camphill, and they set up as a team at The Grange. Judy contemplates how difficult it would be if you had a partner who did not understand the way a living style must be shaped around the needs of the residents.

'If you live with people with learning disabilities you have to have self discipline. You can't just lose yourself in alcohol or go to bed late night after night. The people rely on you entire-ly and they need your attention and energy almost all the time. I am aware there are people who would think us a strange couple choosing such restrictions but we are very fulfilled by the people who live with us. Of course it's stressful at times.'

She sees what the Rowntree report observed as interde-pendence rather than independence. 'Through sharing house-work, cooking, cultural activities, working on the land along with the residents, we get to see what the residents have to offer as well as what they need to be given to make their lives good.'

A well-built lad, beaming with delight as he squats beside a goat, is being taught by Marghareta Herman how to milk the goat, gently massaging her teats. As milk comes the lad gives a hoot of delight and Marghareta praises him before turning around to greet me.

Marghareta has had a similar trajectory to Judy, in that she moved to the Grange as a co-worker and met her husband David who was already working there, running the farm.

Looking back on these years before she had her now grown up children, she thinks people planning to have their own family life completely intertwined with those of residents living with them, need to understand what it means. She offers her own experience.

'To begin with it was difficult to establish my relationship with David when the residents were in rooms so close. At the breakfast table I would hear them talking about my quarrels with my husband.'

They decided to move out when they wanted to start a family, although they continued to work at The Grange during the days. 'But that was not the answer either' Marghareta says. 'I was working full time as a music therapist five days a week and by the time I had journeyed home from The Grange I had little or no time for my own kids. Also David and I missed the lifestyle at Camphill, being a total part of the community.

'So we moved back and I was able to do my job and be at home with the children when they were home from school. As the residents were mostly out working either on the farm or in one of the workshops where they make things to sell, that was a good way.

Yet there have been times when, she realizes she has put residents' needs in front of those of her own children which she now thinks unfair as they had not made this lifestyle choice.

'There was a good deal of guilt involved when the children were young. In some ways it is easier to give attention to residents than to your own children because their needs are so obvious, whereas I just assumed my children would accept less knowing they were unconditionally loved.'

She saw the other side clearly the occasion when her daughter was nine and there were four residents living in the family house.

'One resident was retired from the community work schedule and was around the house a great deal. One day my daughter arrived home saying she was very hungry and could she have an egg. The retired resident came in and I automatically offered him an egg too. My daughter exploded. She said, 'Mum this is my egg time and I don't want to share it. That made me realise that there had to be a time for the residents and separate time for my children, and that it was not unreasonable for me to insist on that.'

Yet for all the difficult times, Marghareta says very firmly that the experience of growing up this way has been beneficial and enjoyable for her children'. She looks out across the undulating countryside, richly green after days of rain, over to where the farm, with animals, is based.

'When they were little our children enjoyed playing with the residents. They would do things like sit on the tractors together and pretend to be driving them. The fact their friends were learning disabled really didn't matter. Then as they grew up our children went off to school, and their separate ways, but they were friends still with our extended family of residents. I think it has been hugely valuable for them to see disability as just a part of life not something that forces you to be an outsider.' In fact, Marghareta tells, her daughter comes back and takes over the house when she goes on holiday.

One of Camphill's most vocal champions is journalist and Alexander Technique teacher Anita Bennett, now co-chair of RESCARE, an organization for families of the learning disabled. When her daughter Isabel, 24, was born with Downs Syndrome, Anita was advised by her family doctor to look at what Camphill might have to offer as she grew up. Anita, a single parent – Isabel's father had deserted – looked into this and agreed the approach was what she wanted for her daughter.

'When Isabel was nine she got a place at the Ringwood

Camphill Sheiling residential school. She had become increasingly unhappy in a mainstream primary where children rejected her because of her learning disability, and she had no friends and only me at home.'

At Ringwood Isabel was immediately embraced by a young family with little children. She began to see them as her own extended family, and has very happy memories of the time there.

'For families who care passionately about continuity of care, about quality of cultural life and long for the work ethic to also be inculcated into our loved ones with special needs Camphill is hard to beat.

'The learning disabled can never create a self-supporting family of their own so the life-sharing co-worker family gives them a sense of love and belonging that at times I envy.'

I have visited several Camphill communities, and known Anita through the years in which she has battled the authorities and opposed the forceful campaigning convinced that learning disabled people are much better living in the mainstream.

'I felt that as mother I knew best the kind of community that would help my daughter flourish.'

ABC

People who have lived for generations in closely bonded local communities which are now falling into dereliction and dying, can equally easily become outcasts, their grief not recognized. Which makes the ardent determination of people like Joanie Speers and Roger Mears to save and re-invigorate such communities so important.

In 1979 Roger Mears, an architect specialising in historic domestic architecture, and his wife Joanie Speers, bought a derelict house and watermill in Carmarthenshire. During the time they were restoring and living in their watermill and its buildings, they saw how this western end of the Brecon Beacons was at risk of vanishing.

Says Joanie: 'There are a great many derelict vernacular buildings slowly falling into disrepair and taking with them the history, heritage, culture and stories of their communities.'

They watched as the situation got progressively worse until finally, Joanie decided to see if they could come up with a solution that would save the communities from being so depleted because there was no affordable housing for local people.

'It became very clear to us that local people could not afford to buy on the open market and the strict planning regulations in the national park made it difficult to carry out work on very derelict buildings.'

In June 2008, Roger and Joanie set up Adfer Ban a Chwm, a building preservation trust with the aim of restoring the derelict stone buildings as part of the environment's heritage and, when appropriate, turning them into affordable homes for local families. Otherwise turning them into some other community use.

ABC's purpose is to help support the local community and to encourage appreciation of the contribution that vernacular architecture has made over time – encapsulating the skills and history of generations of hill farmers, how they lived their lives and created a community around themselves.

ABC was the catalyst for a housing needs survey run in the area. Explains Joanie: 'This demonstrated the need for affordable housing. They organised a seminar on redundant rural buildings with the Prince's Regeneration Trust at Llwynywermod, Prince Charles's home in Myddfai, and have held two public meetings in the area. They have formed a partnership with a Carmarthenshire housing association and have received a small grant from the Architectural Heritage Fund to help them identify and apply for funds.

They were encouraged by the Heritage Lottery Fund to apply, and in the process of drawing up the proposal Joanie and Roger identified 25 organisations keen to be involved. They succeeded in getting provisional agreement for funding from the Brecon Beacons National Park. Meanwhile they were negotiating to buy the house they wanted to renovate first as a prototype. It was then they learned they had not got the HLF funding.

It was with a weary determination to get back to fighting that Joanie explained how history coloured the outside view of what they were trying to do.

They encountered a problem inherited from the boom time when 'incomers' were buying holiday homes in Wales. They were buying 'hope value' – the hope that planning regulations would change, so enabling them to modernise or replace with new the derelict cottages and so make a fortune on the open market.

But, Joanie points out: 'The chances of planning policy moving in this direction is very unlikely and so what this means in reality is that those buildings will eventually fall down and will never be rebuilt.

'The other challenge is the cost but the renovation we want to do would last generations and could therefore provide generations of housing.'

So what Joanie says makes sense, 'If we can restore the vernacular buildings it will regenerate the community and it will mean people can appreciate the heritage, the history, the culture that is embodied in these old buildings.'

ABC would have the building work done by local people so reviving local building skills. They would train apprentices and use local materials.

They are determined too that the buildings they restore will not be available as profit-making capital assets. They will be sold to their housing association partner who will always retain a percentage of the equity so they can never be resold on the open market for personal gain. The money paid by the housing association to purchase these finished buildings will be used to fund subsequent ABC projects.

'Post-Carbon Cities'

Paul Chatterton is a young man of zealous determination whose childhood on a housing estate, and latter years living in Leeds, has made him very clear about the importance of an egalitarian society powered by social justice. One of the greatest areas of social injustice is in housing, he says emphatically.

If you have money you have choices about where and how you live, and whether your home feels the way you want it to. You probably have some power over decisions made about what happens to the building, and money enables us to decorate our homes as we wish.

If, on the other hand, you are without money then none of the above apply. You take what you are given, no matter how unsatisfactory or unsuitable. If you are on housing benefit and renting then you are powerless. The National Housing Federation warned last year that more than 750,000 people in the South-East of the country alone are at risk of losing their homes because of the government's change to housing benefits and they foresee an increasing number of homeless on our streets.

What does it mean to be the person who, every two minutes faces the prospect of losing their home, at a time when, Shelter points out, the Government is planning to pass laws reducing the limited protection council tenants have so far had, not least by scrapping the rules that mean your council has to find you a stable or secure place to live if you lose your home?

How just is it that those areas with the highest unemployment tend to be hardest hit by eviction rates?

How will the government's announcement in November last year, that two million council houses will be sold to tenants – if they can afford them even with the 50 percent discount offered?

Chatterton, a PhD lecturer in geography at Leeds University, talks of creating, as social housing, 'post-carbon cities' where buildings are as close to carbon neutral as possible, where a structure is set up to foster communality and collective concern among neighbours, and everyone has an equal say in what happens to their neighbourhood. His most radical plan is that the housing should fixed at an affordable price in perpetuity, so that it can never be sold at an open market price.

Chatterton has drawn together an ever growing group of like-minded people who were fed up, they told a local newspaper, with, 'The lack of community spirit in their neighbourhoods, a shortage of environmentally-friendly housing stock, and the sheer cost of buying a property in 21st century Britain.' The group of 22 adults, some with children, representing a future 14 households, came together five years ago to thrash out the embryonic thoughts they had. They co-founded LILAC – Low-Impact Living Affordable Community.

This group with its eclectic gathering of people – teachers, doctors, musicians, health workers, bouncers, carers, and retired community workers – formed the first Mutual Home Ownership Society in the UK and purchased land in the Bramley area of Leeds, from the council. Chatterton explains.

'The council saw the value in what we are doing because our aim is to create a replicable model that could be used nationwide, not just a lifeboat for ourselves.'

Grants came from the Department for Energy and Climate

Change and the Homes and Communities Agency, both with an interest in seeing the LILAC idea made real. The New Economics Foundation and CDS – the largest co-operative housing service agency in England – set up to promote, develop and service housing co-operatives, controlled by the people who live in them, helped with the initial thinking. They came up with a model of shared equity for leaseholders.

So, Chatterton says, the houses are owned by the co-operative and residents lease them for 35 per cent of their net household income There are none of the deposits which make it so impossible for many people to have ownership of their homes. In effect they buy shares in the co-op with each payment so that they have equity to sell if they want to move on, but it must be sold for the equivalent of what was paid, allowing for inflation, but not according to market forces value. 'This way we can be sure the homes remain affordable forever' explains Chatterton 'and that is critical if we want to present a way of housing people that involves genuine social justice.

Once plans had been drawn up, planning permission obtained and other technical problems ironed out, building began. Mindful of the fact that conventionally built homes produce around 50 tonnes of Co2 during construction, while a home built using straw bale as insulation actually stores Co2, Chatterton and his group have had the frames of the buildings made from straw and timber and they are guaranteed water and fire-proof. By locking in Co2 the walls are made carbon-negative. To minimise the huge carbon footprint made on the planet by the making and moving of new construction materials, LILAC have committed to using locally sourced, natural building materials.

All being well in October 2012 they will move into what Chatterton enthusiastically calls, 'the UK's first ever affordable ecological community-housing project'.

For this chapter I have chosen a variety of homes and home projects that have come into being and continue to exist because those responsible for their being are fuelled by ideology. There is a conviction among these people they must play an active role in making sure there are appropriate homes available for those who need them, and that all possible should be done to animate the soul of our homes.

At the same time, a value system embedded in each of the home-creation schemes I have considered links the importance of treating human beings with dignity and caring, with concern for the environment, doing all possible to protect and care for it.

What I have found is cheering and life-enhancing, and hopefully a growing fight-back antidote to the melancholy observation made by Peter Carolin, former Professor of Architecture at Cambridge University.

'When it comes to housing we've generally lost our sensitivity and awareness of the psychological issues. This is because our houses and flats have become more commodities than homes. We've lost the ability to be shelter makers.'

Not so with these ideologues, who are building shelter with purpose. They, if anyone, bring the meaning of home to the built environment, heeding the words of Winston Churchill, 'We shape our environment and our environment shapes us.'

11

FRIENDSHIP FAMILIES

It is 5.45 in the evening, a purple winter sky hangs behind the window panes. The stove just loaded up with oak logs is full of acrobatic flames. My son Zek and his wife Kimiko have just come into our sitting room, their eleven month-old daughter, Isana, squirming in her father's arms. She greets us with a high-five hand gesture and a grin, anticipating the nursery rhymes I will put on the CD player and the fun she has when Olly tosses her up and down, higher and higher. Or when her uncle Cato zooms her around the room, pretending she is a bee, so that she hoots with laughter.

This end of the day interlude with our first grandchild has become an almost daily ritual, a time when our home is so tangibly the place for the very particular joy there is in being extended family.

A year ago, when Kimiko was pregnant, she mentioned that she would like to live near family when she had her baby. In

Japan, where she comes from children expect to be close to family if at all possible. And tradition has it that the grandparents make space for their own children who, in due course, may take care of them. This tradition is perhaps less universal in Tokyo and transient urban communities, but in the kind of rural prefecture Kimiko comes from families assume they will live in a multi-generational way. It meant that Kimiko, as a child, was cared for first by her great grandmother while her own mother and grandmother worked, then after the death of the great grandmother, by her grandmother.

Being on her own in the London flat where she and my son were living, with him out at work all day, seemed, to Kimiko, a bleak way to be a mother and so it was that she made plain she would like to be us.

But what of my son, who had left home emphatically, in his '20s, making very plain that as a single young man with his own way of doing things, living with his mother and father was not what he wanted? Yet there he was, asking on behalf of them both, how we would feel if they moved into the first-floor of our house.

It took Olly and me by surprise, and we had to do some quick thinking around how to re-configure our own living arrangements, but it seemed more than worth the adjustment to having less free-range space to have our extended family in the same building. But with definite separateness and privacy. My First Born is not the only one who feels the need of boundaries.

Our family re-shaping took place as I was interviewing people in preparation for this chapter on what I call friendship families. That is people, whether blood relatives or not, who have created a home together. Groupings where friendship as much as blood ties is the essential glue to the relationship.

Multi-generational families who have chosen to live in the

same house or in intimate proximity because that closeness feels right, is one style of friendship family, but by no means the only one, nor necessarily better than the other arrangements I describe.

There are good reasons why the friendship family is a growing phenomenon in the 21st century. A response to a range of issues from the demographics of the ageing baby bulge, and greater longevity, which can be a pleasure if you are living in a way that feels fruitful and companionable, but hellish if you are one of the too-many older people who suffers from loneliness and a sense of being one of society's discards. On top of that women are likely to outlive their male partners and may be left, unhappily, with a home echoing with emptiness.

Add to these the divorce rate which climbed ever higher last century so that today close to half of all marriages come to grief, and we see this happening increasingly in late middle age when you might hope people can enjoy growing older together, contemplating their lives' stories.

Of course at this point it needs saying that for some living alone is the preferred state, and Eric Klinenberg author of a new book *Going Solo: The Extraordinary Rise And Surprising Appeal of Living Alone* (Penguin Press), sees a highly significant shift in what people want at home, in those choosing to live alone.

'Great numbers of people – at all ages, in all places, of every political persuasion – have begun settling down as singletons.'

For all that, there are evidently, a great many people who do want companionship, and social connectedness at home, and for them the friendship family seems to offer an enticing 21st century choice.

So what is a friendship family? I define it as people making the decision to live together with a commitment that goes beyond the casual home-share. A closeness which, in today's atomized, mobile society, represents the kind of kinship among neighbours and friends that, like an edifice being chipped away at, has gotten ever smaller. Michael Young and Peter Wilmott in their seminal study *Family and Kinship in East London*, written in the mid-1900s, noted the pre-figuring of a culture that has done much to pitch people against each other rather than creating bonds.

'In a life now house-centred instead of kinship-centred, competition for status takes the form of a struggle for material acquisition.'

In the absence of small groups which join one family to another, in the absence of strong personal associations which extend from one household to another, people think that they are judged and judge others, by the material standards which are the outward and visible mark of respectability.'

Nothing wrong with respectability of course, provided it doesn't get in the way of enabling friendships, trust and confidence. I used to listen in wonderment to gurus of the 1960s and 1970s arguing that the highest human state was to be able to be entirely alone and to need nobody. If there's one thing we do need as the species inhabiting this complex, chaotic world of ours, it is to be closer to not more closed off from, each other.

This then is the point of my chapter on friendship families, and I think it worth cocking an ear towards the late Muhammad Ali who said, 'Friendship… is not something you learn in school. But if you haven't learned the meaning of friendship, you really haven't learned anything.'

I have chosen here a selection of different types and examples of friendship families because I find them touching, inspirational and worth hearing. It is anecdotal, not comprehensive. When talking about the way older people may live I have not discussed residential care or the horror stories of nursing homes. That has been well covered in the media, and in more depth than I could manage here. There may well be other permutations of friendship family I have not embraced.

Single Parents Living Together

Lucy is a single parent, coping alone, and she does not like it. 'At the end of the day when my son Marcus is exhausted and can be very trying, when I get low with the prospect of an evening ahead and no adult companionship, I think I would have been better letting Marcus's father have custody. Then I cry even thinking of being without my little boy.'

Chances are that this stress and sense of aloneness is echoed in many homes There are, 1.9 million lone parents in Britain today with three million children living with a single parent, around 10 percent of them men – this amounts to almost a quarter of all dependent children.

The statistics, whether we are talking about the endlessly reprised reports on the number of young, single women having babies on their own – in fact less than two percent of single parents are teenagers – or the fall out from divorce, most of us will have heard sagas like Lucy's where the pleasure of children within a companionable setting, is conspicuously absent. Of course not all single parents live on their own, and some do so from choice, but judging by a recent thread on the Mumsnet website a great many do not enjoy a solitary home. Voices spoke poignantly of the desire to share a home with others in the same situation.

A 40-something single, working, professional mother, with a six-year-old boy, in central London, put out her wish.

'I'd like to find another single parent to share with… And help each other out with the ups and downs of parenting. I've always thought that if you have the room for this, it could be a wonderful solution to babysitting dilemmas and loneliness.'

There followed a cascade of enthusiasm at the idea this could be possible, along with requests for any such arrangements with a vacancy to be posted, or for a word from other single parents wanting to set one up themselves.

Separated fathers revealed a similar yearning, often wanting a proper home for children they had at weekends or during the week. One wrote, 'it's exactly what I am looking for. I need to find a child friendly place to have my two and a half year old daughter a few nights a week.'

The 34-year old father of a three year old son was willing to relocate for such an arrangement, although he might have made some possible sharers think twice with his final prescriptive line, 'I don't smoke and neither should you; it's bad for your health.'

The post from a 50-year-old single mother asking if anyone wanted to share a large detached Devon farmhouse with her and her 10-year-old daughter and another younger woman, brought great response. She wrote, 'It's a real home for another mum or dad plus child(ren).

Abi Horsfall did not find such offers but took the initiative herself. She is the single parent of Billie, 8, whom she has brought up since birth and she wrote a heart-touching article for the Guardian about the difficulty of trying to rent a home in London if you have a child. She tells how she answered home-share after home-share advertisement to be told children were not wanted. She did not earn enough in her new job to rent more than a cramped one room in a less than desirable area, on her own.

It is a prime example of how having several people would make it possible to rent a whole apartment, so that you would not be asking childless tenants to cope with the needs, and pleasures, of having a child in their midst.

'I came to the conclusion there that there must be another woman out there with the same dilemma and wouldn't it make sense to pool resources?' Abi wrote.

She saw a posting on the Gumtree website from the single mother of a daughter, mirroring her requirements. Abi made contact and they met, but it was not until they had met several times and felt they knew each other well enough to get through any difficulties they might encounter, that they took the step of renting together.

The article Abi wrote is a paean to the pleasure the arrangement has brought. The daughters have adapted well while the women soon became support systems for each other, helping out with children, enabling each to have a social life. They can lean on each other when the going is tough and, when the children are in bed, share a companionable adult time.

The arrangement may not last if one finds a new relationship, or has to move away for work, for example. Abi acknowledges this, but there is no reason why it cannot be repeated with somebody else.

Not all these friendship families, based on mutual need will work out, and if parents' children do not get on it can make the arrangement unworkable. Yet it is certainly an idea worth pursuing as an antidote to the loneliness, the exhaustion and the resentment so many lone parents may feel when doing 24/7 caring. A larger family, with several parents and children could feel more like a real-life, vibrant family.

This kind of home life might also help children if their parents get involved in a new relationship. The mother of a teenage daughter who has had sole care since she asked the father to leave their flat were because he was becoming more and more disagreeable to be with, thinks this an important point to consider.

'I have met a few men in the years since we separated, with

whom I anticipated worthwhile relationships. I was always careful about going on discreet dates, not having them around the house or introducing them to my daughter until it seemed clear this would be a long term relationship.

'Even so the relationships didn't last forever and in the cases where the men had become friends with my daughter, we had been on holidays together, or they had stayed a lot, it was hard. I was suffering and it was painful for my daughter too. She had my unhappiness to bear and sometimes quite a lot of anger, as well as missing the men herself.'

On such occasions this mother was very aware that she needed to protect her daughter as best she could from her own feelings, but also from feeling bemused and puzzled at being abandoned by men who had in some cases treated her like a daughter. She can see now that having another family or so around could have been a help to them both.

Georgie Hanby a single mother, living in Australia, moved in to share a house with another single parent family having struggled to make ends meet after her marriage ended. 'I was living in a small flat, working full time and caring for my 4-year old son. It was extremely tough going, financially and emotionally.'

She happened to be talking with a friend in a similar situation and it struck her she could achieve 'a safe, warm and happy family environment for my son' if they pooled resources and moved in together. And so they did, finding they could afford a big house with a decent backyard. They juggled school runs, work commitments and housework. Then there was the adult friendship gain as Georgie spells it out, 'Best of all, when the kids had been read their bedtime stories and were safely asleep, the other mother and I got to enjoy a wine together, talk, unwind and share our ideas on parenting.' The children grew close almost regarding each other as siblings.

'Mom-Matching'

The women talk of it as serendipity that they were agreed on trying this living situation, and it struck another friend, Lauren Doolan, that there must be a lot of parents who would appreciate help in setting up such an arrangement. She founded Share Parents, an online service, with a business partner specifically to help put single parent families under one roof. They documented applicants wanting to share under profession, interests, age of children and so on, so short-circuiting a lot of the work a lone parent might have to do to find a suitable housemate.

The desire to help organise a civilised and safe home environment is particularly strong for Doolan when she comes across women who may be trapped in abusive relationships, where there is domestic violence, or where they have been abandoned by partners in very painful situations, and who feel helpless, hopeless, and broken. Explains Doolan, 'For these mothers we offer a form where they can connect with each other and reach out for friendship and comfort as much as anything.'

Carmel Sullivan, a professional artist born in Ireland and now living in America, feels strongly about the importance of community support for families. The idea for CoAbode the agency she has set up as an online 'mom-matching' service, came from her own experience after her divorce when she was on her own most of the time with her son Cooper, then seven. She had had an emotionally and economically secure existence so fat.

'Life after the divorce was tough – very tough. I felt such a sense of doom and gloom… It was the loneliness and not understanding my place in the world anymore. For the first time in my adult life I felt powerless.'

As she began talking to other mothers like herself, it stuck Carmel that there needed to be a reliable way they could be helped to connect, with a view to sharing a home. There was an ideological slant to her thinking, 'It doesn't really matter how a parent or parents define their family, the most important thing is that the environment they create for their child is loving and nurturing, which is not always easy for a lone parent. I also believe in the notion 'it takes a village to raise a child'. I see Co-Abode as a means for single mothers to create their own village...'

Co-Abode grew from a personal quest. Carmel looked for a house big enough for two families and when she found it she advertised for a single mother to share. 'She interviewed 18 single mothers and found a good match, but she realised that if there were that many one parent families in her small area wanting this arrangement, something needed to be done. 'I researched and found that there were 13 million single mothers in the United States and no forum where they could find each other to house share. It struck me, why shouldn't I take the initiative...'

Today Co-Abode has some 20,000 members, many of whom are sharing homes all over America. So the need for this kind of friendship family is very clear.

Not only are we talking about companionship – although I can imagine only too well how dispirited and depressed I could have become trying to manage with young children on my own – but also the fact that poverty and hardship are so often a problem for lone parents. Sharing can be a valuable way to share resources and cut costs.

Britain has the highest number of single parent families in Europe, so there is clearly a place for a CoAbode style of service which seems precisely to pick up John Lennon's famous line 'I get along with a little help from my friends'.

The closest I could find was the friendship groups, described on the website of Gingerbread, the organization for one-parent families. These are run by single parents and make it possible for people in similar situations to contact one another and come together to share experiences, make friends and support each other.

Friends as the New Family

The weakening of blood ties among family members, the lessening intimacy in a society where mobility has people living far from each other can be sad. Generations are less tolerant of each others' shortcomings, parents downsize when children go so that so there is only space for offspring to make guest-like visits.

The situation has, however, led to an appreciation of how important friends can be.

Californian researchers questioning under 45-year-olds heard over and over that friends are considered as important as family these days. Another study had 67 per cent of people describing their best friend as having the status of a family member, while one in three rely on friends in a health crisis. These are the findings of psychologist Dr Larry Lachman, author *of The Fabric of Unity*, and those polled said things like, 'Friends are people that you choose, family are people you are stuck with.' A depressing reflection on the atrophying of family ties.

Presumably this has something to do with the fact that younger people have taken up the idea of the framily as an extension of the transitory home-share set-ups many of us had in our youthful years. Framilies go deeper and are seen as a group of friends putting down a root, with the idea of a lasting situation, together. But it is more than that, in the view of Dr Lachman, 'They (framilies) replace the social support and companionship that, in the past living with multi generations of extended family, or in rural close knit communities did.' Whether this will prove enduringly so, remains to be seen, but the concept has become fashionable enough for an unmemorable eponymous film to be made, and for framily to gain a listing in the Macmillan Dictionary as a buzz word describing 'a new social group underpinned by the principle that good friends we can pick for ourselves when we do not feel we get what we want from our biological families.' Yet implicit in the word framily is that it takes the best of what family can be.

The work of Matthew Brashears, an assistant professor at Cornell University, suggests caution in seeing the framily as something built on the same solid foundations as the bonds that form in caring – if sometimes challenging – families. He questioned 2,000 adults about closeness to friends and found that after initial enthusiasms and declarations of eternal friendship, people today tend to have few real-life close friends. The average number Brashears found was 2.03 close friends while the cyber world, where we do not deal with the demands of real-life friendship, provided 130 online friends per interviewee.

Yet how often have you heard older people lamenting the loss of friends and wishing they had more time for the most precious. We may be too busy, preoccupied with work, children, an adventurous life, to bother too much about investing in making and nurturing intimate friends while young, but in later years the companionship of friends can be a crucial support structure.

Maryse Anand, 68, sees the Cudlees eco-village which she is in the process of setting up for a small group of ageing people, on the 124 acre farm she owns in Scotland, as just such a support structure.

'My life has been thrilling, terrifying, exciting, emotionally draining and now the thing I crave is friendship and companionship that I can give and receive, for the rest of my life.'

Then she is off telling of a life in which her husband died young of a stroke, leaving her with two young children and a stack of debts. Two weeks later her son had a serious accident and her daughter a breakdown.

'I worked very hard, devoted myself to caring for the children and getting rid of the debts. Then when the children were independent I bought a castle in Scotland and lived like a hermit for 12 years. I had the company of many ghosts.'

In time, however, she felt she needed adult companionship and moved to a small town where she set up a spiritual study centre leading to weekends when people gathered for animated conversations about 'every kind of human emotion and anxiety. Those conversations which might take all day, bonded us closely'.

She bought the farm armed with dreams of how her village could be started, but everything came to a standstill when a neighbour who had had cattle on her land for 10 years refused to move them even when they ate all the trees she planted.

'It took two years before a judge ruled that the cattle must be removed. Then we could really get moving. My idea for the village drew a lot of volunteers from around the world wanting to help make it work. It made me very aware of what a yearning there is to live in homes where engaging with like-minded people is what can be done. These included a Japanese nun and a monk who are still with me.

'At present we live in old garrisons and I still need finance, but we have the plans and everything is to be ecologically sound. We are setting up a woodland burial site and the idea is that when someone buries a loved one they can plant a tree on the grave. The wonderful thing is the whole of the community outside is interested in what is happening.'

Maryse believes that living like this, in harmony with friends whose fundamental values are similar and who are invested in creating their home together as a place to end life, is a protection against the need for the people here to go into residential care when they become old and infirm.

'Old age, unless you get a serious illness, is simply the body winding down. If you have a friendship family where people help the frailer members, spend time with them, and make sure they get the opportunity to be part of the community so far as possible, they are likely to do well far longer than in a residential home. I have seen too much of people deteriorating very quickly because they cannot live a normal life. Cudlees is certainly where I intend to end my days.'

Friendship Family for Life

Sigrid Niemer is in her 60s now and is very happy that the youthful dream she pursued of getting together with a group of people to share a life built around cultural interests, in the Schoenberg district of Germany, is indeed a friendship family for life. She moved from her own family home in the 1970s when her goals were very different to those of her biological family.

'It was a time of great questioning in Germany. I didn't want to pursue the conventional marriage and career path of my parents. I wanted to study arts and education, and I became involved with the women's movement, but also with a lot of men who had similar interests to mine.'

The group squatted a vast building complex and decorative erstwhile cinema, that had been the former UFA-Film Copy Center. After some battles with the authorities they got a contract to remain until 2047.

Together the friends – now a well established performing

arts group – and residents involved with the ecological development of the place, which now has 30 residents and around
160 co-workers, set up ufaFabrik fur Kultur, Sport und
Handwerk in 1976.

There were youthful tussles over common purpose and
establishing how a group of fiercely individualistic young
people would co-habit. But they established a framework for
making the accommodation work and they created a circus
troupe of 30 people from which has grown their hugely inventive repertoire of artistic activities.

They relied for their livelihood on a café and bakery and
flats they renovated and let for an income. The neighbours
reported to the authorities that they were running a business
and should pay taxes. But Sigrid and others countered this,
arguing that they were a family, creating a new kind of
economy and that there should be special laws for such situations. The authorities did not agree but gave UfaFabrik subsi-
dies for their work.

When I visited the enclosure of buildings, gardens and
newly installed photovoltaic panels from which the sun blazed
metallically in the steamy afternoon, I learned that these days
there are roughly half and half men and women – couples,
parents with children, singles. Sigrid has a son, who grew up at
the UfaFabrik and is now 26 years old. She and the father separated but he remained at the UfaFabrik in order to see his
child, as did other parents who separated. Even so she was
effectively a lone parent when looking after the boy she recollects.

'While he was small I lived here closely with a woman also
on her own with a child, and I think our supportive friendship
enabled me to be a far better mother than I would have been
otherwise. I was able to go on performing in the circus because
we made a childcare schedule giving us both time for our cul-

tural work. She has since married and her husband of five years has joined the community, but only with the agreement of her UfaFabrik friendship family.

If somebody leaves, Sigrid explains, a replacement will be chosen after a brief 'trial' stay and the decision will be on the basis of friendship. They have a second generation, 'Some of the children go on living here, others move away. We don't expect people to commit for life, but some of us feel it is reassuring that we can be here if we wish.'

She smiles recalling, 'We had a guy who lived to 94 having come here in his '70s. He left, briefly, after meeting a group of older people and decided to join them. Three weeks later he called up and asked us to take him back. He couldn't bear it because, he said: "there are only old people".'

In earlier times the mood was for sharing everything possible, but Sigrid sees how ageing with friendship supporting them, has altered things. 'Slowly we changed, recognising that we are getting older. We want more privacy, and recognition of what our needs are as we approach real old age. We have started discussing the issue of ageing seriously and you can see some parts of our buildings are being renewed so they will be as we need them for the next years. We have organized in-house carers who can deal with illness. We've had a few people die here and we have managed to take care of them.'

In the buzzy, bohemian Kreuzberg quarter of Berlin, a group of women are gathered. They include Edith Storch, a gently forceful woman who believed buying a gigantic erstwhile chocolate factory – the Schokofabrik – which had been squatted and restored 30 years ago by a group of determined women, would be a good venture.

In earlier times half had been established as a hugely popular women's centre with much on offer, including a furniture, woodwork and interior design studio, and the

Schokowerkstatt where woodwork classes are given to women living in the vicinity. There are fitness classes, a refuge for women who have been victims of violence and a Hamam traditional Turkish bath with massage, attracting women of all ethnic backgrounds, including those from Kreuzberg's largely Turkish neighbourhood. There is a kindergarten for women with children who live locally.

When I visited I was offered a pretty studio apartment in the echoing halls of the Shokofabrik to rent for a couple of nights. It is an extraordinary building and the group of women have renovated the half not in use creating apartments. Pam Ferguson, a close friend of the group, and a frequent visitor, describes how they converted their flats themselves with beautiful wood, cabinet and tile work. These have been sold or rented to women. Men may only stay there on invitation.

I meet Edith, Ulli Schlun and Rosi Klein, all entrepreneurs, who have been key members of the women's community for many years. They describe themselves, when we talk together and I ask their ages, with great hoots of laughter, as middle-aged.

The striking thing is what a solid friendship holds this group of women together, and indeed has got them through the kind of emotional upheavals that would have split many people asunder. They have chosen to live in a tight cluster of homes, and to be frequent visitors to each other. Ulli used to be a life-partner with Rosi, and although she is with Edith now – and there was some pain in that re-arrangement – she is also now Rosi's business partner in the Schokowerkstatt. Edith and Ulli have a *pied-a-terre* in the Shockofabrik above the flat where Rosi lives with her daughter, Jamina. They also have a home they converted in the country outside Berlin. Carien Wijnen, Edith's former partner, a medical doctor and a choir teacher, lives close by.

Edith talks openly of what she went through when the relationship with Carien ended, and how affection and caring overcame distress.

'I had been with Carien a long time and the separation was very hard. She fell in love with someone else. We had been living with four other women, but it was too painful for me to stay. The pain went on a long time.'

Sometime later she met Ulli who, at the time, was studying with a natural healer which brought her close to Edith who runs a shiatsu practice. But Edith did not find it easy at first that Ulli and Rosi remained close running their woodwork design studio.

'Time has soothed, however,' Edith says, 'Rosi and I are good friends now and I can take pleasure in the fact that Ulli is close to Rosi's daughter. With our apartment in the Shockofabrik they can see each other easily. In fact the daughter includes me, calling us her big family.'

The women pause before answering when I ask how much they see themselves this way, as a friendship family. Rosi answers: 'many of us in the apartments are friends and we are good neighbours to each other. We live our own lives and have the odd summer party on the roof, but I feel that there is a sense among most of the women in the building, that we are more than just tenants – we belong together and you could ask anyone if you needed help, or even companionship.' Edith adds, 'There is a connection that we all understand and regard as something special, something that means we know we are there for each other.'

A Female Thing

A piece of research from Harvard Medical School found that women who had a close friend and confidante were more likely to survive the loss of their spouse without 'permanent loss of vitality. Those without friends were not always so lucky.'

There is also a mountain of research demonstrating how friendship and companionship can be protective of health. Take the review of 148 studies done by Julianne Holt-Lunstad at Brigham Young University, Utah. She found over and over that a circle of close friends and strong family can boost a person's health more than exercise, losing weight or quitting cigarettes.

One study found people had a 50 per cent better survival rate if they belonged to a wide social group of friends, neighbours, relatives or others

'Sociable people seem to feel less stressed, take better care of themselves and have less risky lifestyles than those more isolated' Holt-Lunstad concluded. The studies she followed tracked social inter-actions and the health of more than 300,000 people over an average of seven and a half years. When someone is connected to a group and feels responsibility to other people, that sense of purpose and meaning translates into taking better care of themselves.'

It is hardly surprising that women are more inclined to seek out a friend with whom to share a home. From a young age girls tend to have a same sex friend as their close confidante, and they learn how rewarding, at best, a truly trustworthy, dear woman friend can be. This experience may be why, increasingly, women in the maturing years are choosing to set up homes intended for the long haul, with female friends.

Louise and Mandy are one such pair of platonic friends. They had a bleak vision of ageing with visions of illness, incapacity and, ultimately too much aloneness. Occasionally they joked about how they would sit side by side in rocking chairs, in an old folks' home. The prospect was sufficiently dismal that it spurred them to action.

Louise, a divorcee, and Mandy who is single found a house they could buy together and got an architect to convert it into two interlinked but separate ground floor apartments. Their pleasure in the arrangement which gives as much privacy as they wish, but also easy neighbourliness. Is very evident.

An article in the New York Times explored what is seen as a growing trend in America for the 'friends-helping-friends' arrangement for the ageing years. 'Women, single, widowed or divorced are considerably more likely than men to see the value in this kind of emotional and sharing lifestyle' says Jane Gross, author of the article.

In her view, 'Women of the baby boom generation, many of whom have managed businesses or owned real estate, are accustomed to controlling their own lives'. They commonly have close female friendships. Many have watched the slow death of their parents, dependent on children or caregivers, and they don't want it to be that way.

Living with the Elderly

This resonates for me. As I have descibed, my father lived with me and Olly and my brother for several years before he died, and much as we loved him he became increasingly infirm and needy. When we were away for a weekend or holiday he pined and we felt guilty.

The fact there were three of us to share the responsibility, and friends living in our basement, meant we were able to meet his needs between us, giving him the companionship he craved, and making sure he didn't harm himself.

Shortly before my father died it became clear that dementia was setting in. He became increasingly forgetful of routine things, disorganized in his behaviour and one night we got a call from the police saying they had this man who had been using a credit card to try to get money from a machine. When we went to collect him, we found my father dressed in his most threadbare and grubby clothes, an old Pan-Am bag slung across his chest. It was understandable the police did not take much notice when he told them he was a forensic psychiatrist and author of several books and with a Harley Street practice of his own.

I am glad we were able to keep my father with us until the end, but I do not want to impose how it would have been had my father lived, deteriorating all the time, on my children. Neither Olly nor I want them to feel they must provide a home for us, if we are ageing problematically. We loathe the idea of being a burden complicating their lives. I would rather they saw us with lives supported by companionship and a role of reciprocal caring with friends in a set-up with access to health care.

That is unless they actively choose a carefully thought out intergenerational home with us in our later years.

In one Manhattan high-rise complex there are so many elderly residents moved in that a link up with social services is in place. In her New York Times article Gross notes the thing observed among elders in co-housing, that supportive friendship makes it far easier to laugh at troubles or to cope better with scary things like a fall, than they would do if they were living in isolation.

Sociologists, meanwhile, are saying the friendship family has a logic that will make it one of the obvious, rather than obscure, choices for people who do not need nursing care, in the future. This was the thinking of the woman building contractor in her early 50s who has built a house for herself and three friends in the countryside. An exercise room and outdoor hot tub are much used.

Although it is far more unusual you do find older men and women friends making a home together. For instance Lina and

Greg, who met through political connections and became close, have done this.

'When a flat in my housing association house came up, Greg was able to re-locate and take it. So he lives above me now which is companionable – we read the papers and have coffee together, go for walks and he fixes my technology, I cook for him sometimes. Neither of us wants more.'

Yet recently Lina has discovered that there is more.

'Greg is a decade older than I am and he has various ailments which may well get worse. I realise I will take on looking after him as best I can, but obviously that will alter the way we can be together. When I broke a bone a year ago, he shopped and cleaned for me, and I think saw that it was a moment when, tacitly, we were accepting that we are like family to each other and will do what we can to care for each other.

'People say to me "you are younger, you will probably also live more years than Greg, isn't it a bit of a burden on the years you could be enjoying when you are not even related?" And I tell them "sure it's a bore, and no I don't relish the prospect of possibly being tied to an invalid, but that's what friends are for", and never more so than in today's selfish world.

'I am not religious or in any way a martyr, I don't believe there are any rewards for decent behaviour on this earth, but I do think we can make friendship more than just fair weather stuff.'

Circuitous Paths

It is hard to imagine that Woody Allen and his ex would be able to exchange so much as a civilized word or choose to be in the same room, let alone a friendship family, after his savage quip.

'The only time my wife and I had a simultaneous orgasm was when the judge signed the divorce papers.'

Nor is divorce set up to be a process leaving the door open for a couple's future affection. As author and playwright Jean Kerr observed, 'A lawyer is never entirely comfortable with a friendly divorce, anymore than a good mortician wants to finish his job and then have the patient sit up on the table.'

Yet we live long lives these days, and although some wounds go too deep to be overcome and some partings are so acrimonious the partners would happily never see the other again, there are an increasing number of erstwhile couples who unearth surprising friendship in later life.

Kristen Houghton writing on Familylobby.com talks of 'a growing trend in the 2000s where couples with no children or grown children, live separate lives but choose to live in the same house. Like room-mates they share expenses, shopping and chores. Unlike room-mates they own property together, have joint assets and bank accounts in common. To all intents and purposes their physical marriages are over but their financial affairs are still married. They stay together for practical reasons. A legal divorce would cost money, property would have to be sold, assets divided.'

That agreed, ways can be found to be amicable and even friendly neighbours in the same house.

Then there are couples whose relationships have broken down in earlier years and they have gone their separate ways. They may have re-married, have seen their children leave the nest, and through it all retained some kind of contact with their former partner. By circuitous paths very often, they realise that, with the mellowing of time and the issues that caused such trouble out the way, they quite like and appreciate each other. They wouldn't mind companionship once again, and so their family is reconstituted on the basis of friendship. Sexual intimacy may or may not follow.

When Beatrice Lejours and her husband returned from

holiday together to their chalet style home in the mountains above Lake Lausanne in Switzerland. She gave Jean Pierre an affectionate hug and went through her door to the top of the house. He smiled 'au revoir' at her before going through his separate entrance leading to the ground floor.

Beatrice and Jean Pierre married when she was 21 and she remembers her panic the day before the wedding, 'I didn't want to marry but it would have caused horror, huge condemnation if I hadn't done it.'

A particular problem, Beatrice says, is that Jean Pierre had not wanted children and she did very much. When she was 24 she told him she would leave if they couldn't have children.

'He agreed this would happen when he finished his university thesis. And we did. Once the children came he loved them and cared for them as much as I did.'

Even so the marriage remained difficult as it had been from the beginning and the couples' two daughters were aware that their parents did not get on, as they grew up.

Neither Beatrice nor Jean Pierre was satisfied with the relationship, and both had long-lasting affairs, but ultimately these did not survive. Both acknowledged that they did not see the marriage as something to which they were tied.

So they did not have to pretend the marriage was a fulfilling one, but they went on living in the same house. Although there were tensions at times they had 15 'positive years' faithful to each other.

However, Beatrice had always intended to leave when her youngest daughter finished university, and it was at this time she met another man who became a lover. Her husband discovered and was very upset. They discussed separating and selling the house.

'That was a wake-up call' Beatrice admits 'I realized what a huge change of life it would be. How I would lose all the things

I recognized as meaning home.' Even so she did leave, feeling a lot of guilt, and missing her home very much.

'For my husband it was a catastrophe. He tried to get me to stay. He offered me inducements and even said I could have my lover to visit at the weekends.'

Instead, Beatrice asked her husband if she could return home with her lover living upstairs with her.

It is difficult to imagine many people agreeing to such an arrangement, but Jean Pierre was, by now, over feeling jealousy and wanted his wife's company in the home. He and her lover worked on separating the house into two apartments with private entrances.

Beatrice acknowledges, 'in theory it was all very civilized, but I knew I was hurting my husband because it was humiliating, and it made me very guilty. Even now I feel horrible when I remember how painful that time must have been for Jean Pierre, but I saw our marriage as over at the time and was hardhearted believing he must get on with his own life.'

He had, seemingly, accepted the arrangement, but once she and her lover were living together Jean Pierre wanted to demonstrate his own independence. He divorced Beatrice.

Four years on Beatrice discovered that her lover had been 'cheating' on her with several women, and she says, knowing she cannot expect sympathy, 'I realized I had given my life to this man who wasn't worth it, while hurting a man who had been so decent to me. I went into a dark depression for two years and when my lover wanted to come back I told him every time he phoned that it was over.'

Once she was alone Jean Pierre became friendly, if distant, but slowly they began talking more, having an occasional coffee together which turned into meals. Beatrice says: 'We realised that we got on well, a lot of the things we had liked about each other in the early years were there again, but we agreed we were both happy to have separate parts of the house. We have been like this for some years and we help each other out a lot, visit each other, and we have family get togethers with our daughters. Jean Pierre and I enjoy going on holiday as a couple of friends and I think we agree we are now happy to make the rest of our lives together this way.'

Barbara and Julia met in their 20s and shared a home in London for 17 years, as a couple. But then Barbara, the younger of the two, wanted to experience more of life as a free person. She knew Julia was upset so was struck by her generosity.

'She behaved with enormous dignity and grace and it was possible to keep a friendship, albeit slightly strained. Also, we shared a dog and had joint 'custody' which obliged us to meet regularly, even when our lives went in very different directions.

Through the next 13 years Barbara had several tempestuous relationships but as she went into her 50s and built up a freelance alternative health clinic she felt she had neither time nor energy for more relationships. She bought a caravan on an estuary in the home counties and spent weekends, then whole weeks, there.

One weekend she invited Julia to stay. She gives a high-wattage grin recalling how, 'here we were in our 60s discovering each other all over again, and talking about what we had each done with our separate time.

'It turned out that Julia had also been thinking of a place out of London. So after a few more equally successful visits we decided to take a very deep breath and try to find somewhere together.'

Neither wanted to be on their own for the years ahead, and both felt friendship was what they most wanted. By now Barbara was sure she was not interested in pursuing relationships that would threaten their friendship. It did not take them long to find a small house near where Julia had her base. You can't miss Barbara's delight at how it is working out.

'Julia and I realise we have a much deeper sense of happiness and contentment through our shared venture than we had before, or in other relationships we got into. Getting a home together at this mature stage in our lives, has opened us both up, we are not guarded. We both trust absolutely that neither of us will walk out on the other. It is a very nourishing situation. We are capable of saying if something emotional needs dealing with.'

Sex is not part of what they have, but love there certainly is Barbara says very emphatically. She and Julia have talked of marriage for 'practical inheritance reasons' and 'because life is too short not to acknowledge the depth of our caring for each other.'

I am sitting on a bench overlooking the Hudson River, boats moving crisply past, birds circling overhead. With me is Lisa del Rosso whom I call my *'ersatz'* daughter, such is her place in my heart. For some years when my children were little and I needed home based help, she lived with us in North London. She might not have ticked all the boxes the upmarket nanny agencies insist on, but she was the 'nanny' that my boys adored the most. She played wild, noisy games with them, threatening to pull down their trousers so they shrieked with delight and fear; she taught them appalling American slang, piggy-backed them home from primary school; made additive-laden coloured cakes with them, and joined wholeheartedly in giggling her guts out at some lewd film on the TV, her arms warmly around their squirmy bodies.

Lisa also exposed the boys to her distinctly adult brand of glamour – long curled black hair, lavishly red-painted lips, skin tight clothes. My younger son, Cato, has never got over it – to this day his loves are of similar style.

When Lisa left us, still in her 20s, returning in due course to her native U.S., we kept in touch and I followed her picaresque existence through to her late '30s when she married Mark Lawitz, 38. As so many had, he found her flamboyant, hugely animated, ambitious personality, her quick-fire gabby way of conversation, as irresistible as my kids and Olly and I had.

I see so little of her these days, so it was a delight to meet up while I was visiting New York. She agreed to tell me how she and Mark have carved their own idiosyncratic friendship family.

Mark is thoughtful, shyly lacking confidence in his capabilities. This is particularly true of writing which he would do but always avoid finishing. He is a successful maitre d' at a smart restaurant in New York's Manhattan where they live. Lisa has a burgeoning scriptwriting career, and Mark delights in the zest and talent with which she produces work. Theirs, she tells, was an attraction of opposites.

They were delighted to find an 'almost big' apartment in the Upper West Side, a liberal, artsy, Jewish, and left-leaning neighbourhood. Lisa describes herself as someone who 'invests a lot of myself in my home' and being in a community that fits her style is very important.

She set about decorating the place with Mediterranean and Indian colours, golden yellows, brick red, a flash of bright turquoise.

'Putting my very personal stamp on a place matters a lot to me, and Mark was happy for me to do it, as he was a man who had long lived in white rooms with cardboard boxes dotting the periphery. Even if I had money I would no way call in an interior designer to tell me how to decorate, insisting on grey walls here, fuchsia there, or more beige than a person should tolerate. I was creating a very personal nest for us.'

Four and a half years later they divorced. Looking back at

this time Lisa grimaces as she analyses how the marriage unraveled. She was happy when Mark announced he was doing a degree in English. He wanted the Bachelor's Degree so he could prove to himself that he could write and finish something. His therapist at the time suggested it to him.

Weekend after weekend Lisa, understandingly, took herself off for solitary walks on gleaming afternoons, because Mark told her he must do homework. Then she would get home to find he had done nothing and was feeling despondent with himself.

'At this point it seemed intolerable, a sign that our life would be a perpetual cycle of him failing to accept himself as he was, as not having to write – and I was quite happy with that – then failing to meet the demands he put on himself' Lisa explains.

They had 'screaming fights, and the thing that drains life out of a home for me, is fighting. Home closes in on me, it is not big enough for two warring people.'

Eventually Mark told her Lisa he had quit the degree course. She would have accepted that if he had done so, and that was that. But it was clear the sense of failure was compounded.

She wanted to separate but had no money to rent elsewhere, and so Mark agreed to sleep on the sofa in the sitting room and they co-existed in a state of sadness.

'It was horrible. Our home was no longer a place of intimacy and joy. It had become a divisive home' Lisa tells.

She had 'a zillion affairs which achieved nothing'. They staggered on for some time longer. Mark went back to his degree and got his BA and having achieved this he decided he would not go further with his studies or do anything with the degree. The decision was a relief for Lisa who hoped he would now be content.

'Truthfully, if he had told me he was going to pursue a master's after that whole arduous task, you would have interviewed me from JAIL, because I would have killed him. Even so he tormented himself because he did nothing with the degree. He did not change jobs, although he was qualified to do something other than wait tables, which he said did not fulfil him. Ironic really because he was a very good maitre' d and highly regarded by his boss. On the other hand, he wasn't writing, either. He was still stuck somewhere, and the degree seemed to make no difference to his sense of hopelessness.'

Lisa pauses and her face, almost always full of bright animation, is overshadowed with sadness. 'I felt hopeless. This funny, generous man I still cared about could not find self-acceptance'.

She instigated a divorce which devastated Mark but still they went on living at the apartment, partly for financial reasons, but partly because of a lethargy that had filled their lives.

'Then a curious thing happened' says Lisa with her bright smile 'once the divorce was through I found I was no longer angry with Mark and wanted to build on this. Then there was a space in my head to see that I needed to grow up and appreciate Mark's value, but he needed help too.'

She persuaded him to go again to a therapist, as she was doing, and slowly he began to accept that he was content doing his job well and having Lisa happy. He took more free time so they could do things together.

As this happened Lisa realised she 'forgave Mark for not accepting himself, and what he put me through, and he forgave me for the affairs I had told him about. The result is now we are brutally honest with each other, keep the lines of communication open, and try not to harbour any grudges. That's huge, for both of us and it means our friendship is really supportive.'

Marge's husband is dead, and she is very glad, she reflects, that she did not allow all the upheaval during their years as a couple and when they were divorced, to prevent her making a home with him at the end.

'My husband and I had a conventional marriage with three children and perhaps it would simply have gone on that way. But I fell in love with a younger man, it knocked me off my perch, it became like an obsession. It was an unreasonable passion which covered my eyes to all that I had and could lose.'

Her husband found out and Marge told him he couldn't stop her. Now tells what harm it did.

'He was never confident sexually or emotionally for all his outward swagger and his competence as a very good photographer. I think he would have forgiven me if I had stopped the affair but I didn't.'

She is a handsome woman, exotically dressed and with thick grey hair elegantly swept up, and it is easy to imagine that, even now that she is in later life, younger men would find her desirable.

'The thing I feel so bad about is that my middle son realised, I think, but he would never talk about it. Even now that he is an adult he is impatient with me. The irony is that a couple of years later I introduced him to a young woman, the age of our daughter, who was also doing photography. They got on very well and they began an affair. Then he gave me a letter to read in which this young woman said she wanted to marry him.'

In fact, Marge goes on, he was uncertain if he wanted this but she decided she should divorce him so that he could choose from a position of freedom.

'I couldn't make him happy, and he couldn't make me happy. The young woman was living abroad and, having persuaded my husband to marry, she was coming to England and had nowhere to stay. He told her she could move into our home. I said OK but I'm not moving out. It was clearly going to be tricky.'

In fact the marriage lasted just six months, Marge recollects.

'She left him. He wasn't very nice to her and he was scared because his work was dying out, he had no money. They kept in touch, he went to see her sometimes, they even slept together occasionally. But she was very angry that he wouldn't sell our house so that she would have some money.'

She and her ex-husband stayed together in the house as acquaintances with a friendship. The way they were with each other had changed a great deal since the marriage days.

'When I was married to him my husband was high-handed and dominating but now I wasn't submissive any longer, I had developed a successful career and independence. I remember him saying me one day "I have no dominion over you".'

Then the estranged young wife died unexpectedly. It was then that the family accountant stepped in and warned them, Nella tells, that she and her ex-husband would have to move out of the house or re-marry because, if one died the other would have large death duties to pay.

'That was the biggest low. I was obsessed with my house as my one stable point. The thing that had remained a constant pleasure through everything.

'Nor did he want to sell. So we re-married and slowly we found something positive again, we became good partners in calm waters, true friends. We lived in the same space taking care of each other.'

It was two months before the 50th anniversary of their first marriage, that her husband died of a heart attack. She realised then how much she missed him, how empty and strange the home felt without him. 'I think the house had a deep meaning for him, too. It was so much the centre of family life with our children and for all that went wrong that was constant for the two of us. My husband always said if anything goes wrong the children must know they can come here.

'I can see how easily I could have broken the home in those early days and how very, very glad I am that somehow the home held me and my husband and gave us a second chance to be good together in it.'

Multigenerational Households

If you want a high-profile cheerleader for the inter-generational family just turn to Dame Judy Dench, one of the UK's pre-eminent mature actors. She has spoken zestily about how, for many years, she and her husband lived happily with his parents and her mother.

Less well known, but enduringly committed to their friendship family, are Zoe Redhead, daughter of the controversial educationalist A.S. Neill, and now head of Summerhill, the school he founded. She and her husband Tony Redhead have lived and worked in Suffolk, with their four children and now grandchildren, for many years.

As we sit together in their farmhouse home, the conversation is a spirited assessment of their inter-generational closeness. Their son Henry, recently married, thinks it strange that I should ask if they regard each other as friends.

'We're the very best of friends. We choose to be with each other a great deal of the time because we have the best times – we're great at chatting, we laugh a lot, we can be emotional, we are interested in each other. You don't have that with so many people.'

Later the only daughter, Amy, who is married with her own children and lives very close, and who has joined her father working on his farm said, without prompting, 'We are all great friends. We have tussles at times but they have never been serious and we always turn to each other if there is a problem.'

She says this in a voice of soft inflexion, while we sit around the lamp-lit stable where she is delivering a lamb from the vastly distended belly of its mother, pulling the back legs free then wiping down the tiny, shivering creature before putting it at the ewe's side.

Zoe Redhead, in her 60s, became very aware of just how important it was to have her family close when she contracted a very serious cancer a few years ago. She required major surgery and was homebound for a good while afterwards, shaken by just how feeble she felt.

'During my weeks in hospital the family were there every day and when I got home they all looked after me, visiting, doing everything that was needed. It was a fantastic feeling and made me determined to get better because I damned well wasn't leaving these wonderful people.'

Henry adds, 'In a situation like that it shakes the family and it reinforced how important it was to us, how much we love and trust each other.' Neill, less seemingly comfortable with this degree of seriousness says, 'But we joked about it too. It was an obstacle and we got on with it.' Tony whose fear was written greyly into his face at the time, quips now, 'we just said to Zoe sign this…' Then he adds seriously, 'The young made a big difference to me at that time. You realise the importance of having a family who are closest friends, and you feel sorry for people who don't have that.'

As valuable as anything was the fact that William, the eldest child, stepped in to run Summerhill. He recognised that if Zoe was to have peace of mind he, with the most experience of how the school functioned, needed to take charge. Zoe is damp-eyed as she recalls the conversation when she thanked him and he said simply 'you left the suitcases in the hall. Somebody had to pick them up.' The 'other kids gave him all the support they could'.

The members of this family have, in fact, spent very little

time apart. The Redhead children had their school years at Summerhill, and although William and Henry went away for a while when they had finished GCSEs, to study their chosen subjects, both returned before long, William to teach wood-work and Henry to give music lessons and set up a recording studio. These two now live at Summerhill, down the road, while Amy lives on the family farm with her husband and two children who are at school at Summerhill. Neill went straight from school to work with his father on the farm, and lives at home.

It delights Zoe that the grandchildren are being given the same childhood experience she had, 'the gift my father gave me of letting me have real freedom, the chance to take responsi-bility for my life and to be my own person. She adds, looking at those around the table with an uncharacteristic sentimental-ity, 'it is wonderful having the grandkids at school. I get such pleasure from seeing them getting on with their lives, and knowing all we have done together in helping Summerhill survive for other kids, as well as ours, since my dad Neill died.'

The 1960s was the era when the younger generation often moved heaven and earth to get out of the family home and into a place – no matter how grotty – that represented their own home. I was one of them.

Aged 19 I spent the biggest part of the £8 a week I was earning in my first journalism job on a tiny room with an unre-liable gas fire, dust erupting from the curtains every time I went near them, and an ex-Bluebell girl as a landlady. What lunacy. I had a comfortable, welcoming home offered to me by my parents for no more than a contribution to bills, where nobody was putting constraints on me, just half an hour from central London. But, hey, so long as I was at home I was my parent's kid.

For us baby boomers, cutting loose from the kind of

knitted-together, kinship families of the years past was a badge of honour.

That was then, and now is now as American psychologist Susan Newman said, emphatically, in a *New York Times* article.

'Not since the Great Depression have so many young adults turned to their immediate relatives as an economic lifeline. In the 1960s, for example, independence was the strived-for virtue; returning home, 'unthinkable.' If children didn't grow up, find jobs and live independently, parents were seen as enablers, the children as failures.'

By which measure the severe economic decline we have seen in Europe and America in the past years, has created a whole raft of over-indulgent parents and failure kids. For Boomerang Children, as they are known – children who have left home but are returning – are vastly on the increase.

Nor is it just children who are returning home. Elder members of families are re-joining their young – 'baby boomerangers' they have been tagged – because living on their own has become unviable and the alternatives either too bleak or too pricey.

It can also be a way the 'sandwich generation', as those who have dependent children one side and elderly parents in need of care and TLC the other are labelled, may keep financially afloat.

A recent study published in the American journal *Transitions to Adulthood What's Going on with Young People Today? The Long and Twisting Path to Adulthood* concluded that the economic down-turn has caused an entire generation to delay adulthood. In 1969, only about 10 percent of men in their early thirties had wages that were below poverty level. By 2004, the share had more than doubled. Overall, the share of young adults in 2005 living in poverty was higher than the national average, and with unemployment of the young reaching record heights in the

UK, and climbing even higher in Europe and the US, that percentage is likely to keep growing.

Children living with parents has given rise to what Abbey
Mortgages refers to as the Kidult syndrome. That is grown
children living with parents and even grandparents. In 2009
they found that numbers of 30-plus living with parents had
risen to 1.6 million from 500,000 the preceding year. A further
300,000 people aged 35 to 54 are in this position because
cannot afford place of their own.

If the situation is less choice than necessity there is no guar-
antee it will be a friendship family.

It is a solution that brings a good deal of sneering in the
media, and with strident articles inveighing against our infan-
tilised young people, parents neurotically clinging to their full
nest, how the young will ever learn independence. I find myself
being positively shifty at times about the fact that our youngest,
now 32, who has been away for years, has expressed the desire
for a room in the house for the half months he works in
London, while living with his girl-friend in Seville the other
half.

Yet in many countries, notably those around the
Mediterranean, it is entirely normal for adult children to be
part of their biological families while it being understood they
have a good degree of independence – work, lovers, networking, social life – away from home. There may well be situations
when, in an ideal world, the young person would move out or
the parents open the front door decisively, but I have seen over
and over among the Mediterranean families I know how this is
a chosen situation that suits everyone. It is about pleasure and
friendship, even if there are some full-blooded rows from time
to time.

Here, on the other hand, we seem too often to have an
almost punitive approach to the idea that living with our family

could be beneficial, and not a *faut de mieux* option.

'Isn't it time for a change of this value system?', demands US radio journalist Gregory Warner. To stress the point he describes a Russian 28-year-old investment banker friend, Eugene, who lives in Connecticut with his parents, and with their agreement puts the money saved on rent towards co-ownership of a restaurant. It is an arrangement the whole family agrees is absolute sense in today's tough economic climate, and why wouldn't parents want to offer this aid to building their son's future?

'Eugene spends evenings eating his Mom's cooking and happily discussing with his parents his latest capitalist schemes. His parents, no slouches themselves, are astonished by what their son has managed to achieve in this country.'

The point Warner makes is that these parents love having Eugene around, just as his own Russian mother-in-law very willingly gives a great deal of time to his daughter. She may be a high powered businesswoman, but she declares that an old woman's time and knee should be for a grandchild.

So, suggests Warner, we need to instate new more expansive and embracing family values for the new century. Values where generations assume that living close provides the strength and comfort of blood bonds in a world that can often be challenging or difficult.

After all, forcing young adults into poverty is as wasteful of human wellbeing and aspirations as it gets. However, my focus here is to look at how we may find something positive that could emerge from the enforced closeness. Isn't it perhaps possible that out of the present crisis we will return to an understanding of human values that has been well trampled underfoot in the past decades, with their urgent quest for expensive individualism and privacy? And what there is to be gained by finding a way to live alongside our extended families?

Sharing the costs of a single home between a range of family members may be the difference between having to move, or dropping a standard of living in order, as one husband who has welcomed his widowed mother in law to stay, describes as, 'constructively filling a room we really don't use, and having someone to mind the kids when necessary after school, cook us a meal when we are exhausted and look after the cat when we are away. Oh and who is good company in her own right!'

A survey by the Mental Health Foundation, London, found that one in three people would like to move closer to their families, while another survey had one in six adults saying they regard their parents as friends. So Newman may be right to be optimistic about an enforced family closeness being resurrected. The 'stigmatized view' of children at home being a failure has faded fast during the recession, she says, and 'family of origin has become a lifeboat for roughly one in five 25- to 34-year-olds (in the US) who move in with parents to wait out the economic storm. Sure, there are potential complications and emotional minefields left over from the parenting years, but once the kinks are sorted out, the benefits for young and old are clear.'

Which is encouraging as Sharon Graham Niederhaus, co-author with John L. Graham of *Together Again: A Creative Guide to Successful Multigenerational Living* talking of the United States, declares, 'Multigenerational living is ahead for all of us. Baby boomers will be living with their kids as they begin to experience the infirmities of old age. By 2020 they'll need help with their disabilities, and the most sensible helpers will be members of the extended family living close by. The practice now of living together as adults across generations will be a big help.

'Boomerang kids and baby boomers are learning about the

balancing act between proximity and privacy that will be required in modern families for the remainder of this century. Extended family members are already creatively designing a new future in these tough times. Indeed, now is the time to get ready for the coming changes in the American family.'

This could be said of the adult 'child' who has returned to a home where reciprocal need is a bond.

'My sons and I live with my folks and it's a blessing for us all that we do. They help me, of course, because financially I am not living with wolves at the door as I might well be otherwise, and I help them by taking care of them. I am my mother's caregiver (she is paralyzed from a stroke) and my father at 83 depends on my sons and I more and more everyday. It is a joy and a gift that love and duty are both present in our lives.

'That being said there is a balance that must be kept of respect – a hierarchy that must be understood and nurtured by all – and most of all an environment where we are able to be frail and human and know that those around us will allow us our weak moments and then shove us back in the mix. We're all in it together and when we aren't anymore we'll be sorry it is over!'

Around one million households in Britain has adults aged 35-64, many with children and one or both parents living at home. They are labelled 3G (three generation) families, according to research by retirement housing and finance specialist Economic Lifestyle.

The 'Changing Times Study' by Ancestry.co.uk found in early 2012, that the number of households with three or more generations of the same family has reached levels last seen in the Victorian era. One in ten parents have their grow-up children living with them.

The writer Kate Mosse, her husband Greg, their teenage son and 20s daughter, her mother in law Rosie, 80, her parents

Barbara, 79, and Richard, 86, live together. They are three generations spanning eight decades.

Kate talked about how it happened.

'Of course in other countries and cultures multi-generational households have always been seen as sensible and desirable. But in Britain for all the capital made out of the grey vote, old age is not valued. And when friends learn how the household is structured, it's depressing how many react with raised eyebrows, assuming it can't be fun.'

As young parents she and her husband moved from London to Sussex.

The asked Rosie to join them as a way of sorting out her rather complicated living arrangements and because she had been much involved with their lives.

Ten years later they found themselves discussing bringing Kate's parents into an extended home. They bought a former nurse's hostel in need of renovation. Her parents would have the self-contained ground floor annexe with their own front door.

'The garden looks fabulous because we have three keen gardeners on site. My husband grows most of our fruit and veg, helped by Rosie.'

The scheme was 18-months old when Kate described how it was going.

'It has worked pretty well, despite my father's deteriorating health. Not for us the silence of the empty nest. Would I recommend it? Absolutely, but with the caveat that you must enjoy one another's company.'

The Skipton Building Society in 2010 predicted that the number of 3G 'extended financial families' will triple in Britain over the next 20 years. The financial benefits are cited as self-evident: fewer properties and cars to run, bills and expenses shared, very possibly childcare and granny-care on tap.

Plus virtue. The eco-friendly aspect. Teaming up as family cuts out the need for carbon-footprinting travel. Peter Head from the London Sustainable Development Commission has pointed out how effectively we may reduce the carbon footprint by having elderly parents move in. Childcare, having people around to help, eating communally and heating or cooling only one house instead of two or three, is much more efficient in extended than single households.

There are, of course, families that cannot and should not live together. Families where relationships are too volatile, abusive or cruel and where it would be insanity to have them under one roof.

An article in the *American Psychology Today* magazine pointed out that families aiming to make a go of living in extended form need to spend time working out how the practical arrangements will work, everyone's responsibilities and duties, the financial arrangements, how privacy can be maintained, what is wanted and expected from the arrangement so that everyone feels at home.

The same is no less true when it is elder family members moving into the home of their young, or their relatives. And while there are clear potential benefits for elder people becoming part of 3G families instead of going into retirement housing and homes, Judith Healy and Stella Yarrow at the Policy Studies Institute found that parents going to live with children were often beset with anxiety about 'being a burden'. This is more of an issue if they live as a family within the same house, yet all interviewed were clear they paid their way, contributing pension money to the household budget, paying a share of bills and helping with childcare and chores when appropriate.

Although most of the adult children found the caring required manageable, all agreed it was stressful, and often respite help or other support would have minimised the risk of the 3G family becoming too strained or failing.

Lucy Darwall-Smith shared a home with her daughter and her mother, until her mother died. She knows how much the support she got from a private carer coming in to help her mother as she became very frail, mattered. It enabled her to be out at work and to know if her mother suddenly needed to be taken to the doctor or to the hospital, it would be organized.

'If my mother had not able to cover that cost we would have relied on the local council and I know from friends how overstretched they are. I don't think it would have enabled me to manage as I did, and enjoy doing so.'

Lucy's mother, Anne Eade, sold her cottage to help Lucy and her husband Philip Darwall-Smith buy their family home in Sussex.

Anne, who was widowed, had been finding it increasingly hard to keep up her home and garden and she saw too little of her grandchild. It was possible to have a granny flat converted at the top.

Doing this can be costly, and the family realized they must work out who would pay for what from the beginning of contemplating sharing a home.

Lucy thinks back with a gentle smile, 'We had a no-holds-barred discussion about how it would work, what ground rules we needed to safeguard privacy and so that nobody felt exploited. For example Mummy paid one-third of all house and utility bills. As she grew older and needed care she paid for that with money put aside.

'She was a wonderful gardener and loved being able to contribute by managing a portion of our garden. She referred to herself as 'the Department of Parks and Gardens'. She used to come to lunch frequently when I had friends – otherwise she mostly ate upstairs – because they found her such good company. But she was very discreet about not being around too much. In fact I think she valued her alone time too.

'She was also a great friend to my daughter Daisy, who visited her a lot, spent evenings with her if I was out, and told her things she didn't want to share with me! They were the greatest mates.'

But as Anne became increasingly infirm, Lucy, by now divorced, admits it became harder.

'She needed quite a lot of attention from me when I was home. I had to help her to the toilet, bath her and I took her a lot of meals, but she was mentally all there and very rewarding as a person. I was absolutely determined she would not go into a home although I suppose if she had become senile and I couldn't cope I would have had to consider it then. Overwhelmingly my memories are of Mummy as a spirited, loving protector, with a gloriously droll sense of humour. And it makes me very happy to remember her saying the years we were living together were the best in her life.'

When Chris Lovell's wife Arlene died, very suddenly, in 2008, grief stopped him in his tracks. He had been a success-ful model-maker for commercials and films, and had worked with such people as Nick Roeg, Tony and Ridley Scott. Yet now he felt he could not go on.

He had intended to return to painting – his early passion – and portraits he did of Arlene cover the walls in his home. Yet at this time he had no enthusiasm for trying to paint again. He slips into the vernacular of his native South Africa, 'Everything was a *dwaal* (nightmare).'

Chris's daughter Annelies, 42, and her writer-director husband Dominic Lees, 46, knew something must be done. Annelies remembers, 'we were aware how very unhappy Dad was, and we lived quite a way from him, so it meant a lot of driving when we wanted to see him. We decided the solution was to be together. So Dominic phoned the local primary school near what had been the family home for me, in Surrey, and got a place for our son Theo. We moved in with Dad.'

This was always intended as a temporary arrangement. Annelies and Dominic had intended to buy their own family home. Now they searched instead for a house that would allow Chris to be with them as well, but have his autonomy and a good studio to work in. Says Annelies, 'With us around he was coping with Mum's death much better.'

They saw several houses with so-called 'granny flats'. Annelies grimaces recalling these, 'There was a place with a kind of dungeon apartment in the basement, with no light, and another house had a kind of electricity substation in the garden.'

The house they eventually found had one-seventh of an acre of land and, 'by an extraordinary stroke of luck', Annelies tells 'there was planning permission to build a small separate house on this land, which would still leave a sizeable garden. It seemed the answer.'

Chris was enthusiastic but they realised they must resolve the issue of who would pay for the house to be built, and who would own it. Chris was happy to sell his family home, buy the land and pay for the cost of building the house, and with the guidance of a solicitor they drew up separate deeds so that he would be able to sell and move if he wanted.

When Chris was in a state of such misery he could barely cope with himself, let alone think about what losing the family home might mean, Annelies and Dominic took careful photographs of the family home so that, if he wished, Chris would be able to re-create something of his home with Arlene.

Chris worked with the architect designing the home and making sure there was space for the important pieces of furniture – a huge dresser in the kitchen, and the family dining table

– from his life with Arlene. He designed a double-height sitting room where his pictures, sculptures and models fill the walls and shelf spaces. He says, 'It was important to make the place mine in a new way, but I needed familiar objects to remind me who I am and that I really can recognize it as home.'

It is four years now that the extended family has lived together and one of the things Annelies values particularly is the way her relationship with her father has become 'much more real. Before I was the daughter and very close to my mother. I always loved Dad but now I know him far more as a friend, and as someone I want to care for, as his family.'

The pattern of life is well established. Chris is cheery describing what the arrangement means, 'I have a house of my own to groove around in. I have independence. I can also be a help to Theo, my grandson, keeping an eye on him for the young if they want to go out. We get on very well together. I find it wonderful now he is growing up and he wanders over to show me things he is doing at school.' He smiles almost shyly gesturing towards Annelies, 'And it is terrific having these guys next door. I get invited over for the odd off-cut and they pop in for tea or a meal.'

That, Annelies parries, is an understatement. 'He makes the best barbecues and we come over very happily. Our friends who loved Mum and Dad always want to go and visit him. Often we'll wonder where they are, and there is Dad opening the wine and chatting away with them. They have completely forgotten it is us they are visiting!'

She and Dominic are clear they will do everything they can to make sure Chris's ageing years are as he wants them. 'It is a good feeling, and not just one to do with family duty, that he has family close enough that doesn't have to worry if, say, he has a health problem.'

She has, however, wondered how it would be if Chris

moved a woman in with him. 'If he was with someone we didn't like I suppose that would be a bit difficult, but it wouldn't make me move or not want to see Dad. And if he were blissfully happy with someone it would make us happy too.'

Meanwhile for Chris the very particular joy is that he has begun painting again. He says with an expansive gesture, 'They have given me the gift of being able to do what I love, once more, and I am excited about time ahead.'

Today much is being made of the value – emotional and financial – that grandparents can provide if they are living in an extended family, helping with children and childcare, gardens, housework, as has been seen in the stories above, and how this can be one of the very real gains of the situation. Young and Wilmott explain this: 'If they have children and grandchildren around them (the grandparent generation) can not only be of some value to youth, they can also enjoy the reward of being appreciated.'

At the same time reciprocity is called on for their needs as we saw happening with Lucy and her mother.

'In their declining years they can call on their descendants to complete the circle of care by easing the strain of infirmity, illness and bereavement. In a three generation family the old as well as the young both receive and give services… In most of the families duty and affection seem to coexist and reinforce each other, duty fostering affection as much as much as affection fosters duty.'

We have become very accustomed to the idea that moving around the country and abroad, even though it separates us very thoroughly from our blood relatives, is a dynamic thing to do, well worth the price for job promotion. Or else families are forced to migrate to get work or to be able to afford homes.

Yet this may carry a higher price than we or the present government, that threatens to blithely uproot people who cannot afford to stay in their homes and neighbourhoods, realise.

Here again Wilmott and Young have an observation. They demonstrated in their interviews that when young couples move away it 'interposes a barrier of distance which impedes the reciprocal flow of services between the generations… It seems that when the balance of a three generation family is disturbed, the task of caring for dependants at both ends of life, always one of the great and indispensable functions of any society becomes unmanageable.'

That experience of closeness to parents, as a child, has also informed the way Tina Riley, with her husband Paul, are instigating their four-generation family all together. Tina, an only child, had a particularly close relationship with her parents Milos and Mimi. They had fled to England from Czechoslovakia in 1953 and when Tina and her husband married they lived close by in London. Her father, who worked for the Foreign Office, was retired when the couple decided to move to Devon. Milos and Mimi were delighted at the suggestion they should come too. They sold their house and paid to have the small, dilapidated stone house attached to Tina and Paul's house restored for themselves. They also gave the couple money to help them setting up residential art courses and a gallery. Paul is still the lead tutor, and the art gallery which Tina has been responsible for is now handed over to daughter Lara, along with the Coombe Farm Studios business

'Having my parents so close meant our three children really got to know them. Mimi, who refers to herself as 'the Background Noise', helped with the art students, took an interest in the gallery and helped in many other ways.'

For Milos, 14 years older than Mimi, 90, and who died in 1989, the arrangement 'gave him great peace of mind' Tina reflects.

The Riley sons Mark and Anthony have been involved with

the family art business, and have for a time lived at home. But now daughter Lara, her husband Martin and one-year-old daughter Sasha, are not only moving in, but taking over the family home as their own, while the Rileys will move out to a wood and glass house just along the lane of the main house, which they have designed and are involved in building themselves.

Paul and Tina raised the money to build their house and Lara and Martin are selling their house to invest into the business.

All have agreed it is a sensible arrangement, not least because for Lara to live on the premises while running the business means she can spend the maximum time with Sasha. However they are equally aware it is not altogether easy for the parents who have lived in the large house throughout their married life, to vacate and know that once Lara and family are in, they will have to knock before going in, and understand it is no longer their territory.

Paul, however, is convinced it makes sense and that they are part of 'a phenomenon occurring for today's young. As a family if you can find a way to rally resources it may give them a time and financial space to get themselves set up in today's difficult world. But I can see it may go wrong if parents think they are simply there to support their kids for ever, even though they are grown up. That's why it matters that Lara and Martin put some of their own money in, and that they are working and earning their own keep, while benefiting of course from the arrangement which means they aren't tied up in mortgages or working for exploitative wages.'

Lara knows they all have to feel their way and also have an agreement on how they unravel the arrangement if it doesn't work out, in time, but she says, 'I would rather put faith in my family and what they have built up than an organization that is anonymous. I've done the packing my bags and leaving home stuff earlier on, and I came back to Devon because I love it, and I've come back to Coombe because it's a wonderful lifestyle as well as work.'

Then there is Mimi, just turned 90 and still living there as she has for so long. Lara has a very close relationship with her, and wants Sasha to get to know her great-grandmother well. Tina relishes the idea of no longer working full time and being able to help out with childcare, just as Mimi helped her out with Mark, Anthony and Lara. She is also keen to spend more time with Mimi, 'We love travelling to Prague, where she lived, and I plan more trips doing that and going to European cities. I am very close to her. She calls herself the "Background Noise", but she's still a powerful life force around the place and wonderfully glamorous. Through the years she's been a valuable sounding board when things have been difficult in the family, as it seems to me is inevitable in a long marriage. And I hope I can do the same, if necessary for Lara, Mark and Antony. Having a close family and having them close seems to me something worthwhile enough to go through the inevitable tough bits of a family on top of each other.'

My own multi-generational family under one roof is too recent – less than a year – for me to be able to say this, but already we have had our moments of potential conflict, found aspects of this burgeoning new lifestyle to wonder about. But to Olly and I at least, this seems insignificant beside the immense pleasure we feel in having 'the young', as we refer to my son and his family, downstairs.

I cannot speak for them, but Kim tells me she is pleased to be living in the family home. While Zek, ever cautious with his parents, has observed several times that it is 'a good arrangement'.

A pattern is evolving. Apart from the bath-time routine

when it has become custom for us to have a spell playing with Isana in our sitting room, Olly and I often take her across the road to our local Italian deli when we go for morning coffee. It is special time with our granddaughter and we love it, introducing her to the other coffee regulars, basking in the bright shout of Piero or Christian behind the counter, to Isana, 'Ciao Bella'.

When the young have been in need of a Saturday morning break we are delighted to whisk her away for an hour or two up to Hampstead Heath, shopping, or to a local gallery. Zek suggested we go on holiday with them for a week this summer, hastily adding (in case I see it as a willing tightening of the Oedipal bonds) that it's because we will be helpful as baby minders.

We regularly have meals together, around the big table in our living area. It is a chance to spend an hour or two catching up on news, throwing ideas around, fitting in a joke, an amiable disagreement, or finding a full-blooded *contre-temps* erupting. Andrew, who has known my kids since they were knee-high to a frog, and who is getting to know Isana in his own fashion, may wander in to join us.

After these gatherings Olly and I reflect how very different the situation would be if Zek and Kimiko were living in their own flat, not far from our home, but far enough that seeing Isana would be a fully-fledged visit. A meal together would somehow require more time together, more elaborate cooking perhaps, and there would be none of the ebb and flow of companionable popping in, which is deepening our family relationship as adults.

AFTERWORD

I set out to write a book about home. It started with my own tale of how I had come to see why home mattered so much in my life, which led me to want to know more about the meaning of home for other people, in different contexts.

What I have learned along the way convinces me that a home which we give time and attention, and in turn allow to be our private refuge, is an integral part of our psychological and spiritual, as well as physical, well-being.

I have seen too how cultural values help us to value home or pull us away from it.

When I began this book Olly and I had just embarked on our separate togetherness and, as I said, in that first chapter I was not sure where it would lead. Would we pull ever farther apart and choose to abandon our cherished home, or would the space between enable us to re-find closeness?

I have woven my own experience of home past and present through the thoughts and experiences of others, seeing what a vital role home has in life's continuum. So I am blessedly glad that Olly and I have stuck with our home and allowed this place, in which I am now sitting in my roof-level office, to help us find the best rather than the worst of what we have together as family.

It's been a bumpy enough journey. We are two volatile characters, not quick to tolerate each other's irritating characteristics, what we see as failings, or failure to do the things we require of each other. I can't imagine a life in which we will not have flare-ups, and indeed days or even weeks when we might prefer not to be sharing home with the other.

But the point is, we also see that we have far too much invested in this now extended family home to lose it over foolish behaviour. We have matured a bit, and that's not just the wrinkly outward bit. We now find designating together time, say early evening when we usually sit and read, have a glass of wine, chat if we wish, or not if we don't, before trotting off to bed together, gives our relationship a good bit of breathing space. Home has assumed a greater importance as the place where the good things happen.

Dr Johnson thought that, 'to be happy at home is the ultimate of all ambition'. That may seem a restricted view at a time when much that is entertaining, stimulating, erotic, social, happens outside the home. But as I flop on the battered old leather sofa, which has been a train, a ship, a horse and heaven knows what else during the kids' growing years, which still has our dead dog's hairs buried under the cushions, and which is all set to morph into a clambering place for Isana, it strikes there is a wisdom worth hearing in what the old sage has to say.

FURTHER READING

1

The Best Kept Secret, Janet Reibstein (Bloomsbury)

2

'The Meaning of Home' in *And Our Faces, My Heart, Brief as Photos*, John Berger
    (Pantheon)
Sissinghurst an Unfinished History, Adam Nicolson (Harper Press)
Sacred Space, Edited by Barbara Bonner (Milkweed)
Authors at Home (Cassell)
Arts and Crafts Style, Isabelle Anscombe (Phaidon)
House, Julie Myerson (Harper Perennial)
Bird Cloud, Annie Proulx (Simon and Schuster)

3

The Frenzy of Renown: Fame and its History, Leo Braudy (Vintage Books)
Affluenza, Oliver James (Vermillion)
Fame, Glenn Wilson and Andrew Evans (Satin Publications)
The Spirit Level, Richard Wilkinson and Kate Pickett (Penguin)
Half A Wife: The Working Family's Guide to Getting a Life Back, Gaby Hinsliff (Chatto &
    Windus)
The English, Jeremy Paxman (Penguin)

4

Estates, Lynsey Hanley (Granta)
The Architecture of Happiness, Alain de Botton (Hamish Hamilton)
Locked In – Locked Out, Angela Neustatter(Calouste Gulbenkian)
The Hidden Injuries of Class, Richard Sennettt and Jonathan Cobb (Norton)

5

I Don't Know How She Does It, Allison Pearson (Vintage)
I Think I Love You, Allison Pearson (Vintage)
The Commercialization of Intimate Life, Arlie Russell Hochschild (University of California
    Press)
Essays on Love, Alain de Botton (Picador)
Devil's Casino, Vicky Ward (Wiley)
The Meaning of Cooking, John Claude Kaufmann (Polity Press)
The Surprising Power of Family Meals, Miriam Weinstein (Steerforth)
Emotional Terrorism, Michael Vincent Miller (Norton)
The Best Kept Secret, Janet Reibstein (Bloomsbury)

6

Understanding New Monogamies, Meg Barker and Darren Longridge (Routledge)

Getting the Sex You Want, Tammy Nelson (www.drtammynelson.com)
Adultery, Louise de Salvo (Beacon Press)
The Ethical Slut, Dossie Easton and Janet W.Hardy
The Warden, Anthony Trollope (Penguin Classics)
Adultery, Annette Lawson (Basic Books)
The Erotic Silence of the Married Woman, Dalma Heyn (Bloomsbury)

7

Sexual Arrangements, Jaet Reibstein and Martin Richards (Mandarin)
A Perfectly Good Family, Lionel Shriver (Harper)
Staying Alive, Janet Reibstein (Bloomsbury)
A Good Childhood, Richard Layard and Judy Dunn (Penguin)
The Continuum Concept, Jean Liedloff (Arkana)
Your Baby From Birth, Penelope Leach (Penguin)
Ten Mindful Minutes, Goldie Hawn (The Hawn Foundation)
Attachment and Loss, John Bowlby (Basic books)
Shattered, Rebecca Asher (Harvill Secker)
Emotional Intelligence, Daniel Goleman (Bantam)
The Heart of Parenting, John Gottman (Bloomsbury)
My Father at 100, Ron Regan (Viking)
Battle Hymn of the Tiger Mother, Amy Chua (Penguin)
Children of Fast Track Parents, Andree (Aelion Brooks)
The Drama of the Gifted Child, Alice Miller (Basic Books)

8

Rethinking Families, - Fiona Williams (Calouste Gulbenkian)
This Is Our Time, Angela Neustatter (Legends Press)
It's Not the End of the World, Judy Blume (Random House)
What Maisie Knew, Henry James (Wordsworth Classics)
Self-Abuse, Jonathan Self (John Murray)

9

Do Good Lives Have to Cost the Earth?, Edited by Andrew Simms and Joe Smith
    (Constable)
Finding Community, Diana Leafe Christian (www.dianaleafechristian.org)

10

The House as a Mirror of Self, Clare Cooper Marcus (Nicholas Hays)
The Autonomous House, Brenda and Robert Vale (NY Universe Books)
Places of the Soul, Christopher Day (Thorson)
The Secret of the Home, Lindsay Halton (O Books)

11

Going Solo, Eric Klinenberg (Penguin)

ACKNOWLEDGEMENTS

My greatest fear when compiling thanks and acknowledgements is that I will offend those I miss out unintentionally. I am hugely grateful to the many people who in different ways have given time, support, guidance, advice, their experiences, and strong cups of coffee through the process of producing *A Home for the Heart*.

Thanks, in particular, to Sam Taylor for her discreet help and support always offered at the right moments; to Pam Ferguson who was my cheerleader from across the Atlantic and led me to so many valuable interview subjects and some fun times in the doing; and thanks to Cec Darker for her very individual style of support.

I much appreciated the time, thoughtfulness, insights and intimacy that people gave when talking to me for this book. So much gratitude to Allison Pearson, Jonathan Self, Lynsey Hanley, Clare Moynihan, Sue Peart, Gill Hudson, Helena Kennedy, Clio Kennedy Hutchison, Sarah Berger, Christopher Day, Taus Larson, Paul Chatterton, Simon and Jasmine Dale, Dame Elizabeth Murdoch, Gilly Smith, Jed Novick, and to those whose names have been changed at their request. And I appreciate Kate Mosse giving permission for her experience of extended family to be used.

I have been greatly helped with expertise and professional input by Anita Bennett, Janet Reibstein, Penny Mansfield, Elizabeth Muirhead, Benita Refson, Meg Barker, Jacqui Gabb, Lucy Sargisson, Ruth Ibegbuna.

Isabelle Grey was invaluable reading my disarray chapters as they came off the computer, and making astute and ever helpful comments.

My publisher Martin provided an indecent number of cappuccinos at Islington's chicest watering spot as a way of urging me on in his beguilingly dogged fashion.

Richard and Sheila Johnson who were ever welcoming when I needed to retreat and write, at their blissfully comfortable, bohemian hotel Fingals in the heart of Devon.

Piero, Rosanna and Christian got me going on more mornings than I can count with the best of macchiatos at their Italian deli.

Very special thanks to Christine Roche for understanding just what I was getting at with her cover design and chapter sketches.

And thanks to my parents who gave me a template for what a home with a heart feels like.